Shadowed Soul

Shadowed Soul

Wandering to Find Your Inner Compass

One Woman's Worldwide Quest for Understanding and Liberating the Divine Within

by
Melissa Jennewein

Cover Illustration by Daniel Gonzalez
Editing by Michael K. Ireland
Formatting and Interior Design by PRESStinely
Published by Soul Curiosity Press LLC

ISBN Paperback: 978-1-7376886-1-7
ISBN Hardcover: 978-1-7376886-2-4
ISBN Electronic: 978-1-7376886-0-0

Library of Congress Control Number: 2021923245

This book is not intended as a substitute for the medical advice of physicians. The reader should regularly consult a physician in matters relating to his/her health and particularly with respect to any symptoms that may require diagnosis or medical attention. *The author does not take responsibility for the reader's use of any procedure or protocol that may be mentioned in this book.*

I have recreated events, locales, and conversations from my memories, diaries, and through contact with the characters in the book. In order to maintain their anonymity, in some instances, I have changed the names and some identifying characteristics of individuals represented in the story.

Printed in the United States of America.

Melissa Jennewein
www.melissajennewein.com

This Book Is Dedicated To:

My two best friends, Harley and Paul. I miss you both more than words can describe.

All the guides met along the way—many of whom are named in this story.

To Mom.
It was your love and support that kept me going through it all.
We all know I would have made a terrible doctor.
People would have died.
I guess that's why you always took me to the library and
nurtured my love for adventure through literature.
Thank you for always believing in me.

"Where to next?" she asked.

"I don't know. I only have $500.00 in cash left—enough for gas to get to Florida and a one-way ticket to Europe. And I still have credit cards to pay."

"What will you do in Europe?"

"I'm not sure. I trust it'll all work out. What else can I do?"

She smiled and raised her glass. "To the unknown," she said.

"To the unknown."

Table Of Continents

Shadowed Soul

List Of Photos

Preface

We tell stories for lots of reasons. Sometimes we write to advance knowledge; sometimes to record history. We tell stories to keep things alive—and to pass on what mattered most to us. I am sharing this story of adversity, persistence, and divine intervention to encourage empowerment, and to challenge limits, beliefs, and barriers.

This book was birthed deep in the silence of the Sahara Desert, where it's easy to listen. During a forty-day silent retreat, where we danced with our shadows and found inspiration, the words poured onto the pages.

The lessons are divided by years and over continents. At the end of each year, you are invited to pause and reflect. Questions are available to ponder as we move through our unconscious minds together. It is my sincere hope is that you leave these stories with new understanding about yourself that aids in your expansion.

The aim of the story and the reflection questions is to help you learn to trust your divine inner guidance system. One way to reach this place is through what I like to call "Shadow Dancing."

Ready? Let's dance....

Acknowledgments

This book would not have been possible without the support of my tribe of friends and family. Without your first draft feedback, and preorders, this story just wouldn't be here. You know who you are. Thank you.

To my mother, Cherri. Thank you for always having my back, even when what I was doing didn't make any real sense. You have always been my biggest supporter and guide, and I feel lucky to have such a positive role model. "Remember, if you're going dumpster diving, make sure you are looking for treasure, not trash." -Mom

To my old terrier, Chico. You have always been my "Yes" man. Except for that one time at the "How Weird Street Fair" in San Francisco. I'm still sorry for keeping you there longer than you wanted. Thank you.

To Charles Dinkel. My muse and the man with many plans. Thank you.

To Simon Kramer, thank you for your belief in me and your support while this book was underway. I am so blessed to be dancing along this path with you.

To my advisor, beta reader, and friend, Sinjun Wesson. You walked with me through so many important steps and stayed true and solid toward the aim all the way through. Thank you, my friend, for your art, encouragement, support, and enthusiasm.

To Michael K. Ireland, my writing coach and editor. Without your patience and expertise, who knows where this book might have gone? Probably nowhere fast. Thank you.

To Kristen Wise, Maira Pedierra, and the team at Presstinely. Thank you for your help in ensuring this book looks great and can be easily found.

To Megan Crawford, thank you for encouraging me to get out... and to think about my carbon footprint along the way.

To Charles Kunow, a very special thanks. You made me mad enough to push through to the end. Sometimes I hate loving you. But I appreciate you just the same.

To Larry Woods. Your quiet but continued support helped to make all of this possible. Thank you.

To Kristina Smith. My oracle, my guide, my goddess dressed in plain clothes. You have always been a guiding light. Thank you.

To the spirits guiding me and protecting me. Thank you for the abundance of assists. I am honored to be of service.

A very special thanks to Patrick Taylor, Cherri Jennewein, David Meyers, Jason Wiltsey, James Kliegl, and Nathan Slone. Your selfless generosity assisted greatly in the printing of these pages.

And to all you wonderful folks who are reading this book, thank you for allowing me share my stories with you. You're awesome. Happy travels!

–Melissa.

Year 1

The Americas

Chapter One

Until Death Do Us Part

The nervousness and anxiety hadn't subsided in weeks. My mood was black—like the bubbling tar pits down the road from me in Southern California. I was suffering; I no longer recognized who I was. I couldn't remember who I used to be.

Trembling, hands gripping the edges of the bathroom sink, I looked in the mirror. Make-up dripped from my eyes. My once-shiny copper hair was matted, lusterless. There was a shadow in my hazel eyes that haunted me. I dropped my head and stared into the sink. Bubbles of mascara-stained tears rolled toward the drain and disappeared. *Who are you? What have you become? What's happening?* I asked myself as I attempted to steady my knees.

That lost look was unfamiliar, and then and there, I knew: Something had to change, and the change needed to come from within.

It began with two life-changing events a couple of weeks apart. First, my best friend of twenty-four years, Harley, was dying from cervical cancer at the vibrant age of thirty-two. She'd fought it off twice, a couple of years earlier, but this time it had returned with a vengeance.

The second was that my once-solid six-year marriage was dissolving. I felt paralyzed, afraid, lost, and confused. I wasn't sure what to do.

Harley was feisty, and through the years, she taught me about roughness, soccer, New Orleans, Jack Daniel's, and, most importantly, what friendship meant.

Our small Florida town has beaches as bright and white as the moon and saltwater, the color of emeralds. Harley and I first met in grade school when we were ten. She was a tough girl who moved with a fierce yet friendly determination. Her brown hair was twice as thick as mine, and she wore two long braids. She had an intimidating smile. At first, I felt awkward meeting her; her strength and beauty threatened me—and she played soccer so aggressively! It was a kick to the shin during a school soccer match that brought us together. I rolled around on the grass, grasping my damaged leg as she approached.

"Sorry about that. Does it hurt?" She pulled me up from the ground.

"We're on the same team! Why did you kick me?"

"It was an accident. I was going for the ball."

The clash broke not only my skin but my fear of her, and we became fast friends. Over the following two decades, we shared plenty of laughs and a whole slew of hardships. She was one of the few friends I'd kept close through challenges and changes, and I knew I could confide in her. She knew all of my secrets—and most of my fears.

There were events in my childhood that were considered violent. Harley was present for a few of those explosions when my dad couldn't contain his anger and threw it in my direction. Once, she and I were hanging out in my bedroom, and Dad burst through the door in one of his ever-spiraling moods. As he grabbed at me, Harley jumped from the floor, pushed him aside, took me by the wrist, and pulled me out the door. We ran down the hallway and straight out of the back of the house without stopping or looking back. We kept running the entire three miles to her place. We arrived winded, drenched in sweat—but no longer afraid. Little did I know—and I wouldn't find out for years—that she had pulled me from my hell into hers.

I didn't stay much longer in my parents' house. By my sixteenth birthday, I had earned my GED, left home, enrolled in college, and entered the working world in America. I welcomed the sudden shift from child to adult. It was empowering to decide whether the space around me would be peaceful—or not. I begged my mom to co-sign on an apartment for me and took to my new space with confidence, joy, and ease. Finally, I felt free. Harley, my two brothers, and other friends would visit often, and sleepovers were common. It was a time of celebration and independence that fueled my confidence in my ability to care for myself and others.

As Harley was dying, I replayed these memories from a more innocent era. She had one last request to see the giant Redwood Forest north of San Francisco, not far from where we were. But cancer took her ability to travel, and we'd never see those Redwood trees together. That confidence in my ability to care for others was missing. I felt helpless—how could I give her what she wanted or needed?

During Harley's final weeks, I sat at her bedside and watched as cancer destroyed her body. There was nothing left of her—she had become so small. Her skin was pale, and she'd lost all her hair. She was covered with fentanyl patches but was still in so much pain. She was a ghost of my friend, no longer the girl with a wicked smile, not my girl with braids like ropes. Her spirit was the same, but her body wasn't. What could I do for her? I was powerless, defeated. I couldn't breathe. I promised myself: *I'll never feel helpless like this again.*

Harley died in 2012, surrounded by friends and family. Talula was there and called me right after Harley had taken her last breath.

"Um, Mel... She's free now," she said.

My heart dropped. I couldn't speak.

"Are you still there?" she asked.

"Yeah."

"Oh, Mel," she said. "Harley stopped taking her meds and was fully present with everyone. She wanted to feel everything. I held her hand and told her we all loved her. She tapped my hand twice as she took her last breath. It was magical."

I was happy that Talula was with her. I know in my heart that's what Harley wanted. For over two decades, Talula had been her priestess of sorts—the one who always had the right words to provide comfort, and who always knew when to remain silent. I considered her an angel in human form; a goddess with endless compassion.

"Thank you for being there. I just couldn't...," I said.

"It's OK, Melon ball. She went peacefully and was surrounded by love."

"I need to go to meditate now,"

"I understand. I love you."

"I love you, too."

Even with her words of comfort, the loss hurt me deeply. My body carried physical pains from her passing—I felt an emptiness in my chest. There were knots in my stomach. When her soul left her body, a part of mine went with it—I was fragmented without her.

I didn't know that this pain, this incredible feeling of loss, would ultimately become the catalyst for a journey around the world and into myself. I needed to find the answers to support my healing. I wanted to know what to do if I were ever faced with this kind of challenge again.

Had I known then what I know now, honestly, I probably wouldn't have changed a thing—even though the process tore me apart.

9

My marriage ending was another crushing blow to my heart. My husband, Jack, was one of the most incredible men who had ever graced my path. He was loving and kind and everyone I introduced him to liked him immediately. I met Jack at a party in Los Angeles. I was working the door at a nightclub with my friend Sara when I noticed him standing in the line. He was tall, slender, and had light brown skin and a sly smile. I sensed we were fated for one another.

"Hey Sara. See that man with the dark black hair, with a white mohawk stripe?"

"Yeah, I see him. What's up?"

"I don't know how I know this, but I think I'm going to marry him."

"What's his name?"

"I don't know yet."

We both laughed.

Jack asked me out on several dates over the following weeks. I rejected his advances because when he came near me, I got so nervous I couldn't speak. For some reason this man left me breathless and afraid. However, his persistence finally overrode my angst. One day, I said yes. He was a gentleman. Courteous, sweet, and so damn attractive. A year later, we were at a party and Sara saw us.

"Hey!" she yelled across the room. "Oh my gosh! Are those wedding rings?"

"They are! We got married last week in Las Vegas."

"I remember you said you'd marry him. I thought you were kidding! Well, congratulations, you two. You look adorable together."

Jack and I were a great couple. We never argued or fought (that I can recall), and we enjoyed many of the same things. It wasn't until the last year of our union that I noticed I was unable to appreciate him fully, and was incapable of reciprocating with the same intensity all the love he gave. Why? We'd promised "until death do us part." But it wasn't a physical death that ended our relationship—it was a kind of spiritual death.

I felt my walls cracking. *What's happening?* I needed answers.

Losing my loves had taken its toll on me in every possible way. I was living alone in the apartment I'd once shared with Jack. I'd lost weight, lost my connection with the world, lost my drive and motivation, lost parts of myself. I wanted to live. Not just live, but understand what living meant.

My frightened self stared back at me from the mirror. I bowed my head again, tried to stop the violent shaking that rocked every cell in my body. I was weak. Vulnerable. *Something has to happen, or I'll never know my soul.* My knees gave way, and I crumpled to the floor like a paper doll. *How long was I on the floor? A couple of hours? A couple of days?*

Suddenly, I heard a loud knock at the front door. Unable to move or speak, I continued to cry. I felt a hand touch my head, and a familiar voice said, "Can you drive?"

I looked up from the cold misery of the floor and saw my friend and neighbor, Stephanie, standing over me.

Without skipping a beat, she said: "I've been listening to you cry through these walls too long. Can you drive? Let me help you up." She took me by the arms, lifted me from the floor, and guided me into the living room. I collapsed onto the couch. "Can you drive?"

I looked at her through swollen eyes, confused. "Why? Where's your car?"

"My brother borrowed it," she said. "It's not far to where we're going, but we need to go soon because it's getting late."

Seeing the earnestness behind her eyes, I stood up, scanned the room for my car keys. "Okay," I said.

Stephanie became a great friend the moment we met. She and her brother moved in across the hall from Jack and me. She was a few years younger, and her seemingly endless supply of enthusiasm and excitement for life was intoxicating. Stephanie was that friend who's always finding the next great band, event, recipe, job, outfit, or adventure. I enjoyed that about her. She was energetic and bold, always doing what she wanted, without fear of what others might think. Wearing her sundresses short and her hair even shorter, she appeared to have the perfect masculine and feminine energy balance. I always sensed this was lacking in me, and I secretly hoped I'd have that kind of harmony one day.

As we walked toward my car that evening, I didn't ask where we were going—the mischievous look on her face told me I'd know soon enough. My job was to drive and follow her directions. A few turns and a few minutes later, she said, "Here. Park right here."

I pulled to the curb and parked in front of a row of businesses. Stephanie jumped from the car and went to the store opposite us. Tugging at the door as I approached, she sighed heavily and said, "Oh man, I think we missed it. It's locked."

I joined her at the single glass door and realized where she'd taken me. It was some sort of sex shop, and apparently, it was closed. I understood her intention. She wanted me to feel good and thought some pleasure might help my sad situation. I sensed it was going to take more than this. I just wasn't sure what it would be.

As a teacher and office administrator at a Fine Arts Preschool, I knew I couldn't give exceptional care to my students in this state of mind. On Monday morning, I stepped out of my souped-up Toyota Celica GTS into the school parking lot. *How did I get here?*

My breath was labored. My fingers felt numb as I punched in the gate code. The iron bars on the heavy security door buzzed and clicked. The locks were released.

Slowly, like a caterpillar might approach a flower, I walked through the lightless corridor. I hesitated at the entranceway to the office. My breath was shallow. I took the door handle in my weakened grip.

"Good morning, dear," said Nasrin, the preschool director.

I stared at the floor.

"Is everything alright, dear? I've been worried about you lately. How are you feeling?" she said, straightening a pile of papers on her desk.

"Nasrin, I need to tell you something."

"Well, come in. What is it?"

My body was frozen in time. As I shifted my awareness, I found my outstretched hand resting on the office chair. I used to dance around that chair after class in the afternoons, pumped up from teaching. I pulled the chair from the desk, and as the body frost melted away, I collapsed into it. "I can't continue in this way," I said, burying my face in trembling hands. Tears burned my cheeks.

Silently, she crossed the room and placed her hand gently on my shoulder.

"I feel this incredible sense of loss. I don't eat well. I don't sleep well. I don't remember driving here. I have to resign. I can't care for the children as I could before."

Nasrin said nothing.

The tears surged out of me. When my heart was empty, Nasrin spoke.

"You poor dear. I can see this is hard for you. Why don't you take a month or two off, then come back?

Perhaps you need time to grieve. I'll hold your teaching and office positions for you."

I'd already considered asking for more time off. The past couple of weeks away hadn't helped much. I knew intuitively I wouldn't be back in a couple of months. *What would I do? Where would I go?*

"I appreciate you, Nasrin. I love this school and all of you—especially the children."

Suddenly, I was shrouded in nostalgia. It was the children who reminded me of being playful. *Had this whole "growing up" thing ripped the curiosity and wonder right out of me?* The more we had played, the more I had remembered my lost innocence. I wanted—no, I needed—to nurture that childish wonder within me. My life depended on it.

"I just can't do it anymore, Nasrin," I said. "I've thought about this a lot. It'll be best for everyone. I can give you a month to find a replacement; I'll prepare them for a smooth transition."

Nasrin was motionless.

"This week, I'll organize my binders and computer folders." I swiveled into action with a determination that surprised me. "Whoever sits in this chair next will find everything they need easily."

A couple of weeks later, Nasrin realized I was serious. She didn't want to replace me. I was flattered but concerned—my roles included doing tasks necessary for a seamless day, and I didn't want my situation to create stress for anyone there. They had been so generous with me. For three years, Nasrin allowed me to practice what I was learning in my evening college classes during the school day. In the office, I watched her interact with the parents and learned poise and grace. During our annual school fundraisers, I learned to be shameless in asking for what I wanted or needed to accelerate my vision. She taught me to inspire community involvement in every goal with grace. She was a fantastic mentor: sassy, patient, and kind. She also never wore the same outfit twice. I still don't know how she did that.

For three days before I left, I prepared the woman who succeeded me as best I could. I said my goodbyes to Nasrin and the team of teachers. As I walked across the playground and waved to the children, my heart shattered. *Have I made the right decision?*

It was all gone. Harley, Jack, and now, the school. So much joy. Gone. Life as I knew it—as I liked it—as I expected it to be, no longer existed.

Back at home, I collapsed on the floor. *What should I do?* Like a searing hot knife, reality sliced through me. I did what I've always done when unsure about something. I called my mom.

Mom said, "Well, honey, if you're not sure of what to do, it might be best not to do anything just yet."

Immediately after hanging up, I did the exact opposite: I decided I'd see the world. Why? I needed to remind myself that life can be wonderful. If I didn't, well, I'd most certainly be dead from heartbreak within a year.

I had only $1,200 in cash and was almost $3,000 in debt—something's missing. *I need abundance in my life. These persistent feelings: lack, loss, suffering. This pity party needs to end. I must regain my power. I have to understand what's holding me back from being the best version of myself. Venturing into the unfamiliar will bring clarity, right?*

An hour later, my friend Mimi messaged me. "Hey! Want to go to Mexico with me for the Rainbow Gathering? It's an end-of-the-world celebration!"

15

"Really?" I replied. "I'm stuck in the end-of-the-world loop already...so, yes!"

I'd met Mimi in an Early Childhood Education Art class. I remember that moment clearly because a group of young women were bullying me. I wasn't welcome. They had their private little clique, and outsiders were, well, outsiders. Sad. These are future teachers—I thought all teachers were compassionate, considerate, and caring. *Maybe some training will change them?*

As I looked for a less hostile seat, I saw Mimi standing at the far end of the room, one hand to the sky, the other behind her. She was pulling one leg up and back as she balanced on the other leg.

I walked up to her and said, "Hey, you look like a friend. Are you a friend?"

"Why yes, I am a friend!" she said.

We chose a table in the corner of the room to sit at and prepared for class. Once settled, Mimi threw up her arms, exposing her hairy armpits.

I stared. She glared at me.

"What?" I said. "Are you European? Is that why you don't shave?"

She scowled. "No, I'm a feminist!"

I chuckled. I'd found a friend. Over the next couple of years, we ended up enrolling in more Early Childhood Education classes, working at the same preschool and traveling—oh yes, the traveling.

A week after accepting Mimi's invitation, I sold a few items and donated some to Goodwill. I filled two suitcases with clothes and treasures and stashed them in the trunk of my car. I stuffed my backpack with useful things for the trip and put the rest of the apartment in storage. As I still wasn't speaking to Jack, I gave my brother-in-law a key to the storage unit.

I was ready to go shopping. *What should I take on this trip? Where were we going? For how long? Flexibility brings freedom....*

First, I purchased a wonderful Lawson-brand tent-hammock. Its unique hybrid design allows the user to sleep between trees or on the ground and is water- and insect-proof. I found an MSR whisper-light camp stove at a co-op called Recreation Equipment Incorporated (REI). It burns white gas, kerosene, or unleaded auto fuel. While there, I also bought several bags of dehydrated foods and a sixty-liter backpack. *I was beginning to feel... was it... confidence?*

I returned to my car and drove to Talula's house to begin packing for my journey. Weight was a concern. The muscles in my legs were still weak from a series of knee surgeries I'd had from 2005 to 2009 after a motorcycle accident. I needed to consider every item I placed in the bag. *What else would I need?* Clothes, shoes, a towel, toiletries, bug spray, a knife, and pepper spray (just in case)? Extra rope, a first aid kit, medicines, and a headlamp with spare batteries. When I was done, I went to the grocery store with the loaded backpack and weighed it on their scale. Thirty-five pounds. I added a book, a journal, two pens, my LED glow, and flag poi. Poi are tethered weights that can be made from various materials, and playing them involves swinging the weights through a variety of geometric patterns. I think they help to quiet the mind and get you in touch with the body. And they are just plain fun to play with! *That should do it.*

With my Toyota sports car packed to capacity and feeling electrified, I hit the freeway at dawn. But as the miles rolled away, my confidence faded. Bombarded by doubt, I was losing my mojo. *What am I doing? What have I done?* Destructive thoughts swirled around in my brain. It was too late to turn back. What was done was done. Six hours later, I arrived in San Francisco. Suddenly, I "came to." *How did I get here?* Again, time was missing. *Where had I been?*

That day, my friend David called to invite me to lunch with him and his girlfriend, Cat, at a hillside café in the city.

"So, what's your plan?" David asked, picking up his sandwich.

"I don't know. Mimi invited me to Mexico for the Rainbow Gathering, and I was feeling pretty good about it, but now I'm not so sure," I said, poking at my salad. It looked delicious, but the knots in my belly refused to relax. *Yep, my confidence is gone.*

"Yeah, well, it's pretty crazy. I don't get it," he said, licking sauce from his fingertips.

"I just feel pain. In my chest, in my stomach—nothing's the same anymore. I'm scared. I feel broken and lost." I set my fork down and pushed my plate away. "I know I'm missing something, but I don't know what it is. I think I need help," I said.

"Why did you quit your job, give away all of your stuff?" David asked. "That was pretty stupid. What do you have now? Nothing. No wonder you feel like you're missing something. You gave it all away."

This isn't helping. I wasn't missing my things; I was missing a connection to my soul...

Cat sat across the table from us, enchanted by a green smoothie. Her eyes sparkled, and a radiant glow shone from within her. She smiled as her eyes met mine. Pushing a lock of hot pink hair from her face, she set down her glass and asked: "Do you have some free time tomorrow? I'd love to introduce you to someone before you go."

I felt apprehensive, but then a glimmer of curiosity snaked through my body. "Yeah," I said. "Where would you like to meet?"

"I'll text you the address. Can you be there at noon?"

"Sure. Do I need to bring anything?"

"Just a comfortable change of clothes."

Cool. My adventure had already begun.

Chapter Two

Dark Reflections and Light Manifestations

The house stood on the crest of a hill at the edge of the city, flanked by a row of eucalyptus trees. My tired Toyota struggled up the steep driveway and died before reaching the top. *That's fitting. The struggle is real—even for my car.*

I peered through my grimy windshield at the strange house. An army of little silver robotic-looking creatures climbed the yellow panels above the garage door. Waves of blue and pink paint were splashed around the corners. At some point, the garage and house had become a graffiti artist's canvas—weird, whimsical scenes crept across the building. The blazing California sun bounced off the exterior and cut through the hazy film on my window like a laser cuts through metal. For a moment, I was blinded.

"Hey! You made it!" Cat appeared and squealed with delight. She beckoned me to follow her toward a set of stairs on the side of the house. "Come on!"

How long had she been standing there?

I jerked myself from the car and grabbed my backpack. I tried to force myself into her level of excitement. Instead, I climbed the steps feeling apprehensive and anxious.

The garden was more expansive than it appeared from the driveway. I stopped at the entrance, took a deep breath, and lifted my head to the sky. Above me, a gentle breeze blew life into small square flags that zig-zagged back and forth across the patio. Their subtle dance mesmerized me.

"Those are Tibetan prayer flags," a woman's voice said. "The different colors represent the different elements. The wind carries the prayers."

I turned toward the voice. Standing in the doorway to the house was a woman with long, blond dreadlocks. She smiled. "Would you like to come in for tea?"

I entered the sacred space. It was unusual, and I felt it held a gift for me—though I wasn't sure yet what it was. Cat introduced the woman as Opal and guided me past the round dining table to a merlot-colored velvet couch. The inside of the house was just as interesting as the outside. The walls were a cheerful yellow; the antique furniture from foreign lands gave the entire room an old-world charm. Dark red, blue, and cream-colored runner carpets stretched across high-traffic areas on the bare wooden floors.

Opal and Cat went into the kitchen. I could hear them chatting. I felt my energy shift as I took in the seemingly expanding dimensions of the room. *Was it the house? The art? The company?*

When they returned, Opal carried a tray that held a Japanese-looking teapot and a couple of porcelain cups. "Do you like hibiscus tea?" she asked as she laid the tray on the table.

I nodded. She poured us both a cup and took a seat.

Cat stood silent but grinning in the curved stone archway, holding a pink smoothie that matched her pink hair. I wondered what was in it.

"My friend here tells me you've made a bold and difficult choice recently, and you're unsure about it. Is that accurate?" Opal asked.

"Spot on, I'd say."

Opal didn't respond, only lifted her tea and took a sip. She closed her eyes.

I watched her. She seemed to send out an invisible request to the spirits—or was she receiving some sort of message?

She opened her eyes. "I'd like to offer you a mini-retreat before your trip if you're interested."

"A mini-retreat? That sounds good."

"Follow me, and I'll show you the sauna and float rooms."

Placing my cup on the table, I stood and followed her out of the living room.

We moved through the modest, amber-lit room the infrared sauna was in. Opal explained that I'd shower before entering the sauna. "I'll set the timer for fifteen minutes," she said. "When you hear it go off, exit the sauna and shower again. Don't put on any lotions or creams. There's a robe for you in the bath," she said, pointing to a door next to the sauna as we crossed the room and descended a set of stairs. She lit a candle and approached a door. "In here is the float tank. It holds 800 pounds of Epsom salts in about eleven inches of water. There are new earplugs on the shelf inside. I recommend you use them."

"What happens in there?" I asked.

"Well, first, you float in the silence and darkness. The rest depends on what is meant for you. It could be like a lot of things—a rebirth, expansion, transformation—it depends on the individual and what they might need. After an hour, I'll ring these chimes to let you know it's time to return to the waking world," she said, running her fingers across metal tubes hanging from the wall. Before returning upstairs, she said, "If you'd like, you may stay here tonight as our guest. I suggest you rest after your retreat, allow whatever needs to transform the time and space to do so, before rushing back out into the world."

"That sounds good. I'd love to stay. Thank you."

After the sauna, I made my way to the tank. I hung up the robe, opened the door, and peered into the darkness beyond. I took a deep breath and then stepped inside. *I wonder what'll happen in here....*

After kneeling, I put in the earplugs, sat down, closed the door, and let myself fall on top of the water. The capsule was much larger than it looked—my hands and feet couldn't find the edges.

As if floating in space, I felt weightless. No light. No sound. I closed my eyes and just let myself drift. Then it began: the show, that is. The one that lives deep within the crevices of my unconscious. A screen flickered on in my mind, playing a smattering of long-lost, forgotten memories. Images appeared—memories that, in most circumstances, might have elicited emotion. But they didn't; it was strange. Past relationships and traumatic events from my childhood took the stage. Unmoved, unattached, I watched this film... starring myself.

Then, a single drop of water landed on my forehead. It surprised me, and my eyes snapped open. Staring into the darkness, I saw a reflection of my body hovering above me. I looked at her—at me. *How am I seeing this?* I imagined reaching out my hands and plunging my reflection under the water, holding her there gently, watching as she let bubbles roll from her lips and released her last breath. *Is this my imagination? It doesn't feel like I'm creating it....*

The peacefully drowning beauty didn't last long, though. Suddenly, she grew fangs and long nails. She scratched my arms and tried to bite me. Her fierceness shocked me. I released my hand from her chest, pulled her to me, and hugged her. Holding her face close to mine, I looked lovingly into her eyes. Then I pushed her under the water again.

She cried, begged for her life for a few seconds. Then she was back to clawing at my arms. This fighting and begging made its way through a few intense rounds before she finally disappeared from view. Immediately, I felt a sense of ease and calm. I moved my body until I could touch the sides of the capsule. I sat up and hugged my knees close to my chest. My hair felt like a piece of thick cardboard. *How long had I been in there?* A moment later, I heard the faint sound of chimes. *I guess it's been an hour. It felt like ten minutes.*

I sat for a minute before rising to my knees. Finding the door handle, I opened the chamber, and was welcomed with the scent of lavender. Soft music played upstairs. I felt euphoric. I wrapped myself in the bathrobe and moved as though someone had tranquilized me. Each step required extra coordination and effort.

After bathing and washing my hair, I put the robe on and made my way slowly to the plush velvet couch, where Opal had left some warm tea and honey for me. Lifting the cup, I inhaled the sweet scent, and closed my eyes. I recalled a scene from a movie called *Revolver*, where, toward the end, the main character gets stuck in an elevator and meets the ego part of himself. The ego fights and screams at him while he remains calm and says, simply: "I can see you. I can see you. You don't control me; I control you." *Is that what just happened in there? Did I just meet my ego-self? She seemed to want control and was willing to fight for it. This is getting weird. What do I do?* My lack of confidence had turned into curiosity. Exhausted, I fell into a dreamless, tranquil sleep.

Mimi and I met the following day, dropped my car off at Jade's house, and took a one-way flight from the San Francisco airport to Oaxaca, Mexico.

We were excited as we made our way to the baggage claim area. The bags floated past, and Mimi fidgeted nervously with the bracelet her mother had given her before the trip. Her hazel eyes showed worry, and the freckles on her face seemed to wrinkle with every passing whirl and click of the carousel.

"Don't worry, Mimi, it'll be OK. I'm sure it'll show up," I said.

We waited until an elderly couple retrieved the last two suitcases, and the carousel stopped. I looked at Mimi and noticed she wasn't OK. Her face had lost its color, her hands were trembling, and she paced back and forth.

"You could leave a contact number or the name of our hostel," I said. Before she had decided what to do, she walked out the doors of the terminal. I followed her, and as we walked toward the bus stop, she struggled with what to do about her missing backpack. Should she make a claim? Should she let it go?

Several artisans lined the street with handmade wares, and one yelled to her: "Scorpio! Your energy is Rojo! You'll find what you are looking for!"

Mimi smiled, and we boarded the bus to the hostel. Once there, she called the airport, made her claim over the phone, and left the hostel's name.

After the call, we settled in. I sensed Mimi's apprehension in asking for anything, so I unpacked my massive sixty-liter backpack. I dumped everything out on the bed.

"You can use anything you need," I said.

"Anything? Mel, I don't even have underwear!" She buried her face in her hands. Tears flowed.

I watched her panic from the other side of the room. She seemed genuinely afraid. I joined her on the bed, put my arm around her sunken shoulders. "Which underwear do you want? I have two regular panties and three thongs."

Mimi burst into laughter. I jumped up, threw the pile of underwear at her, and started rummaging for other items.

"Seems we'll need to share a toothbrush for the time being, too, yes? I heard once if you burn it with hot water before sharing it, germs die immediately."

Mimi looked up from the panties and smiled. "Is it true?"

"It must be! Come on, let's get some rest. We'll manifest your bag and be on our way soon. Don't you worry."

We woke up early and went exploring. Oaxaca is a charming city with many natural wonders nearby, and we visited the famous petrified waterfalls of Hierve el Agua. The site (about forty miles east of the city) consisted of two "frozen" waterfalls. The hike to the top took about an hour, and when we arrived, we couldn't believe our eyes. Small, twisted craters inked in red, orange, and yellow and filled with shallow turquoise water were carved into the ground.

I felt like a giant walking through a flooded Sahara as I tiptoed toward the edge of the cliff across the exposed, hardened peaks of the craters. These led us to a natural infinity pool; the water flowed over a rounded edge. The illusion was that it appeared to have no boundaries—it just extended into the horizon. We peeked over the edge to find that the water dropped off a foot before flowing to another edge and trickling down the rock face.

It was just what we needed to take our minds off the missing backpack and remind us of the beauty surrounding us—if only we'd take time to notice. We did. We took the entire day to drink in the natural beauty and loved every minute.

There was no word about Mimi's backpack when we arrived at the hostel, and her anxiety returned. Two days passed. We explored all day both days, and she worried during the night about how we'd continue. Mimi kept going back and forth between wanting to wait for and wanting to leave the backpack behind.

"It's your call, girl. You can use anything I have. I'm here to help," I told her.

After mulling it over on the third day, she said, "OK, this is my final choice. If my bag doesn't manifest by noon tomorrow, we leave it behind and forget about it. We should be at the gathering by now. The longer we wait, the harder it's going to be to get a prime camping spot. They'll already be taken."

"I have a good feeling about tomorrow," I said. "It'll all work out—your backpack will come, and we'll find the perfect camping space."

She pulled the blankets into her chest. She was still unsure if everything would unfold effortlessly.

I closed my eyes. I was not only talking to Mimi—but also to myself. I had to believe things would be exceptional. I sure wasn't. Deep down, I was shattered—smashed into tiny bits and also in need of reassurance. *Things have to work out. They just have to—I'm so tired of everything going terribly wrong.* I was still struggling to fill the gaping hole left in my chest after Harley's death and my separation from the man I loved.

Mimi was also venturing out with a broken heart. She'd recently come out queer, and her first same-sex partner—the woman who was supposed to join her on this trip—had ended their relationship a month ago. To say we were both in a delicate space was an understatement.

It was December 20, 2012. I grabbed *The Abounding River Personal Logbook: An Unfamiliar View of Being Abundance* from my backpack and was prompted to note the following phrase eight times in my journal: "I now take responsibility for being the creator of my experience. I am present to my abundance now." This affirmation resonated. Yeah, sounds great. I'd like to feel abundance now… writing the words felt good, even when they contradicted what I was feeling inside.

We woke early and prepared for our day's journey. At 9:30 a.m., there was a loud knock on our door. Mimi's eyes darted across the room with anticipation before she answered. She took a deep breath and swung the door open. Immediately, she began jumping up and down in a frantic kind of prayer dance. I looked past her: Resting in the doorway was a giant green backpack with a wide red sticker attached to it. Mimi hugged the bag and started laughing. "What's so funny?" I asked.

"Look at this sticker, Mel! It says 'Manifest Bag!'"

An old American school bus, dolled up like a Las Vegas showgirl, roared up the dusty street. It came to a screeching halt in a cloud of black smoke a few feet from where we stood. The name Gabriella glittered in gold down the length of each side, and the rest was painted in vivid hues of turquoise, dark blue, and green with chrome accents. *This must be the "chicken bus" some helpful travelers at the hostel had told us about.* It was beautiful.

A man jumped from the open swinging door and waved his arms wildly while corralling prospective customers. We watched as he collected money from the locals to get an idea of the fare. (The "gringo tax" was alive and well in Central America. If you aren't aware it exists, you might be paying higher prices than everyone else.) After we felt confident about this being the right bus and that we were paying the correct price, we handed off our backpacks to the attendant, who placed them in a rack on the roof. I held on to a smaller pack that cradled my passport, money, journal, computer, and a couple of other items. When we boarded, the term "chicken bus" made sense. The bus was packed with people, and you guessed it—with chickens. Not cages of chickens stacked neatly in the corners, but loose chickens' passengers held in their laps. Some birds squawked in protest and flapped their wings, while children as young as five held tightly to their legs. Speakers hung throughout the bus, and fast, horn-filled music (so loud it could have shattered glass) blasted through the space.

The three-person bench seats were bolted so close together; we barely had enough leg room for our five-foot-six frames. After contorting ourselves into the cramped space, we were on our way. The bus bounced along single-lane mountain roads at speeds usually reserved for Formula One race cars, while we held on to the seats, our knuckles white.

We stopped regularly—and abruptly—in tiny villages, and locals jumped on and off to sell nuts, tortillas, water, and sweets; or to transport their livestock. During one of those quick stops, a young boy entered, selling some kind of tortilla roll-up thing. He couldn't have been more than ten years old and he moved through the crowded bus like a fish in the ocean, swimming with ease through the sea of people. He found Mimi, who was eager to try his offerings. She bought two tortillas, and as quickly as the boy had appeared, he disappeared back into the street, swallowed up by a thick black curtain of exhaust smoke as the bus rumbled away.

A couple of hours later, the bus stopped again, and an ancient-looking woman boarded. She made her way over to me, flashed a toothless smile, and sat on my lap. I looked over at Mimi; she shrugged and smiled. The woman didn't say a word during the hour she rode on my lap, and while I thought it was unusual, I didn't mind. Mimi and I were busy riding our "Manifest Bag" high and still too excited to care much about comfort—until, that is, Mimi's stomach started rumbling.

"I don't know if those tortillas were good," she said. "My stomach—it really hurts."

"I have some activated charcoal in my backpack on the roof if you want to take some. I think we are almost at the gathering." I said.

"Yeah. I think I might have food poisoning. Does charcoal work?"

"I haven't taken it yet, but I read somewhere that it's great for that. You can try it when we stop."

As we rolled along, I replayed the previous days' events silently in my mind. Mimi was an inexperienced traveler, but I didn't realize just how much angst she felt. I felt it would be a disadvantage not to confront our fears consciously. I knew we had to address them right away if we were to travel together for the next few weeks. I waited for an opportunity. The bus stopped, and the older woman slowly rose from my lap. She wobbled from side to side toward the door and disappeared into the street. I turned to Mimi.

"During the past few days, while we waited for your things," I said, "I heard so many fears from you, and I can't recall one scenario having a drop of abundance or trust lining it. What are you so afraid of?"

"I don't know. I was just scared."

"Yeah, I know you were. I get scared sometimes, too. I'd like to use part of this trip to explore the practice of trust and abundance. Are you open to looking at our fears? I think it's important we both check ourselves along the way. We are protected—we must believe that."

Mimi pondered this for some time before she replied. "What do we need to do?" she asked. "I'm not sure how to change this."

I reflected on my recent situation—the deep, empty feelings had all but consumed me. Then I remembered the only book I'd packed and the one I'd written in the day before; the one that had found me in the most peculiar way. I shared the story with her, hoping it would inspire the trust, understanding, and optimism she needed to travel safely and with great luck.

"When I was packing, you know, figuring out the weight of things and all, I realized I'd only be allowed to bring one book. I thought about bringing a book on meditation or one about yoga and Pilates. I almost brought a novel by Dean Koontz. Then, on my last evening in Los Angeles, I went to dinner at Cafe Gratitude with a few girlfriends. When we were leaving, a book fell from a top shelf near the exit and landed in my hands. It was almost as if some ghost dropped it down to me. It's called *The Abounding River Personal Logbook: An Unfamiliar View of Being Abundance*. I'd like to share it with you if you're interested? Maybe we can do some practices to build our trust in knowing we live in an abundant universe? I don't know about you, but I could use some of that in my life right now."

She agreed to look into it with me. We flipped through the pages as we rode to Palenque, and our understanding unfolded right there on the bus. The suggested prompt for Day Two was: "I am worthy of everything wonderful. I am love expressed as me. I love being abundance me." I pulled out my journal and added it.

When I'd told a friend of mine this story, he'd said it might have been the "holy ghost" who dropped the book. He cited John 10:10: "The thief comes only to steal and kill and destroy. I came that they may have life and have it abundantly."[1] The thought intrigued me, as it's been a while since I'd last read the Bible. I attended Sunday school as a child while Mom was in mass, but I always felt something wasn't right with that church. I was eleven when I stopped going with her. It had been two decades since I'd conversed with God. *Could this be part of my problem?*

---

[1] Crossway Bibles. 2007. *ESV: Study Bible: English standard version.* Wheaton, Ill: Crossway Bibles.

Chapter Three

Gathering Rainbows

The bus dropped us off in the center of Palenque, where we joined nine other souls in the back of an old beat-up pickup truck on its way to the Rainbow Family gathering. Before the attendant tossed our larger packs on the roof, I found the charcoal and gave two capsules to Mimi, along with a bottle of water, and we climbed in and set off down an unpaved, pothole-filled road. Next to Mimi, a young woman with dreadlocks played a drum and sang a song about family. I stared out of the back of the truck at a man who hung like a sloth from the corner of its metal frame. Between each bounce over the holes and bumps in the street, he attempted to take pictures with a large DSLR camera. He was elegant in the chaos—steady, unwavering, and patient in his work. And handsome. I turned to Mimi.

"You OK, girl?" I asked.

"Not really. How long does it take for the charcoal to work?"

"Well, ideally, you should have taken it right when you started feeling sick. From what I understand, it works better the sooner you take it. We're slowing down. I think we're here."

The truck came to a sudden stop, and we piled out and gathered our things. A committee of volunteers welcomed and directed us toward a map of the land, which hung like an old animal pelt between two trees. The map showed where the river, fences, kitchen, camping, and toilet pits were. We learned that before the arrival of the festival celebrants, farmers used the land for growing plantain. Now it was "ground zero" for a huge celebration, with hundreds of people pouring in by the minute. Long-haired, dusty hippies with large packs just like ours surrounded us. The sweaty, musky scents of unbathed travelers permeated the air as drums played in the distance. People smiled and laughed. The sun was warm. It felt like home. We found a spot for Mimi to relax while I explored the area. *We need a great place to set up our gear.*

The farm was like a fairytale forest. A variety of lush ferns, bushes, small trees, and large stones lined a fast-flowing river. The dazzling, waterfall-fed pools here and there hypnotized me, beckoning me to jump in—to wash off the remnants of travel and relax in their care. It was the most beautiful place I'd ever been and, at that moment, I never wanted to leave. *We need a great place to set up our gear.* I snapped out of my daydream and found the camp center, where the outdoor kitchen, festive silk aerials, and central gathering circles were. From that point outward, I began my search. There were already a thousand people there and more arriving every minute. We got lucky. I scored a spot for my hammock on an island surrounded by those waterfalls. I also found a perfectly flat, shaded pitch for Mimi's tent right across from the island. After claiming the spaces, I went back to the entrance for my girl, who wasn't getting better with her stomach sickness. She was relieved when I told her the excellent news. We'd scored fantastic camping spots, and I could make some healing soup for her. After we pitched her tent, I pulled out my dehydrated vegetables, MSR camp stove, a small soup pot and got to work.

Once Mimi was fed and resting comfortably, I set up my hammock and went to help in the makeshift kitchen. It was surprisingly well-equipped. They had everything— huge pots the size of hot tubs along with all the tools needed to feed... What? Three thousand people? I jumped right in and learned that the entire system ran solely on volunteers. From giving money to purchase the supplies, preparing the food, cooking, and cleaning, the participants were involved in every step. *Fantastic*, I thought, as I diced up coconuts—which was more like trying not to cut myself while cracking stones with a dull chisel.

Suddenly, there was a loud shout from the kitchen. "Food is ready—ten minutes!" Seconds later and some distance away, another group yelled the same thing. This continued down the river—the voices traveling farther and farther, like an echo in a tunnel—becoming muffled until they disappeared completely. That's practical. I never considered how that was going to happen. Interesting....

Everyone started arriving in the vast open field next to the kitchen, and the volunteers instructed us to sit back-to-back in a humongous, spiral-like circle. Before volunteers served the food, all two thousand souls entered a ceremony together. The intimate unfolding of the community that was happening—that I was a part of—felt good in my heart. We sang, gave gratitude for the sustenance coming to us and for the opportunity to gather there.

As the rituals ended, the volunteers arrived, sliding the bathtub-sized bins of food along the grass. Salad, fresh fruits, and rice with curried vegetables were on the menu. Everyone waited their turn patiently while the servers pushed and tugged the bins along the winding paths of the circle. To say I was impressed would be a colossal understatement. After dinner, some of the group lit an impressive fire in the center of the field, and I roamed around, listening to various bits of conversation, laughter, and drumming. *Well, if this is the end of the world, I can't think of a better place to be.*

I sensed this beautiful collective experience was already changing me. I could feel it all around and within me. My spirits were lifting, and the excitement for life was returning. It was so welcome and it was what I'd been hoping for.

The next day I took in the incredible views, met more of the community, soaked in the natural pools, and let the waterfalls massage my back. *Today's the day. It's December 21st, 2012. I wonder what'll happen when the Mayan calendar ends. I can't imagine being anywhere else right now, and if my spirit soars from here, I'm OK with that.*

After the sumptuous dinner rituals and the usual dancing, playing, and laughing, I caught some dreams in my hammock. As I lay there in my cocoon, the sound of the trickling waterfalls soothed me as the gentle winds rocked me to sleep.

I woke up with a start. A wet chill was creeping from the crown of my head down my spine. Heavy rain had broken from the sky and was crawling into my hammock. The dribbling waterfalls sounded different. The sweet melody that had swirled around me earlier now sounded more like I was perched on the edge of Niagara Falls... *What's happening out there? I better check this out.*

I climbed out of my rain-fly-covered cocoon and fell thigh-high into the river. *Oh shit! Where'd the island go?* I stared into the darkness and was instantly aware of the mammoth flash flood—the thunderous water rose quickly to my waist. I clung to my hammock. Suddenly, a burst of blinding white light exploded into my eyes. *Uh, oh. Is this the end?* I laughed to myself... until my vision cleared. A man had appeared with a bright head-lamp around his head.

"We must get off this island right away!" he shouted.

I started laughing again. I looked up at the almost full moon and down at what used to be the docile river. "Do what? How are we supposed to do that? It's gone from half a foot deep to four feet deep already! I'm only 5 foot 6!"

He grabbed me by my shoulders, and though I couldn't see his shadowed face, I saw his blue hoodie tremble as he shouted.

"We need to cross, and we need to do it now!"

Before I could think any more about it, he took my hand, and we fumbled our way deeper into the onslaught of rushing water. As the river reached my chest, I stopped and looked back at my hammock. The water continued to rise and surge dangerously close to it. *My backpack, my passport... my gear!* But I realized there was no time, no way I could carry my huge pack through this raging flood. With a heavy sigh, I surrendered. I had to let it all go. Saving my life had taken priority over trivial material things.

Crossing a flooding river is no joke, people. The ledge between the island and the bank was narrow, and we struggled to keep a foothold as the water pounded against us. The energetic rush of adrenaline was maxed out when we finally landed, soaked through, yet exhilarated, on the bank. I danced and sang; happy the river hadn't dragged us along on its wild ride. My celebration was cut short when another man grabbed me by my shoulders. He shook my victory from me. *Oh, what the hell now? We're safe, right?*

"Are you insane? What are you doing? This is no time to play! You could've been killed!" he shouted.

"What the hell? Do you think I'm insane? I admit I'm a little crazy... but insane... noooo. You see that hammock there in the middle of the island? That's where I was sleeping when this all started—I had to cross. This man here gave me no choice." I looked around for the mysterious man in the blue hoodie. He was nowhere to be found.

The man released my shoulders, allowing me to turn toward the river. I bowed my head in prayer and heard the man who had accosted me mumble an apology. Ignoring him, I prayed the raging flood would spare my things, then set off to find Mimi.

Slipping, sliding, and crawling to the top of the muddied bank, I was relieved to see the water hadn't damaged Mimi's tent. I rushed over and opened it... to find her inside doing some interior decorating. Water from my soaked layers of clothes spilled all over everything as I fell inside.

Laughing at me, Mimi said: "What's happening out there? Why are you so wet?"

"Really? Don't you know we just survived the end of the world?"

She threw her head back and released a deep belly laugh, and I took her by the hand to show her what she was missing.

We spent a couple of hours watching the once-peaceful jungle sanctuary turn into a wild, dangerous jungle in what seemed like an instant, and the sun rose. Yep. It's damage control time. The first thing I wanted to see was if my hammock had survived. We reached the edge of the river and saw it hanging; my backpack resting inside it. *Thank you.* We retrieved my things carefully, using a thick tug-of-war kind of rope some generous soul had set up to help people cross the still-raging waters. Afterward, we walked along the river's new edge. Hundreds of people who had camped along the river's old border lost their tents, backpacks, passports, supplies—everything—and were left with nothing but the clothes on their backs. And for some of them, not even that! But they had so much more—they had a community of strangers who pulled together immediately to support their needs.

Participants were expected to be in silence on this sacred day, and a ceremony was to be held at the ruins to honor this time the Mayans had believed was significant. Yeah... well... that went out the window. People scrambled to find the things they needed and tried to decide whether they'd stay.

We helped in ways we could. We made lots of hot soup from our generous supply of dehydrated vegetables and assisted people in crossing the river. Then Mimi and I met with two other female travelers from San Francisco to discuss our next move. The first (and probably only) thing on all of our minds was the "shit pits." They were what they sound like—deep holes dug out in several rows for festival-goers to poop in. The pits had been placed strategically in four spots around the camp and river, and now there was literally shit everywhere. We made a unanimous decision: We'd leave today to avoid getting sick from all the poop we were sure was now all over everything.

We weren't the only ones who wanted out. Several hundred people were packing up. Somehow, magically, we scored a truck within an hour and hopped in the back with our gear. The girls laughed at how crazy the night had been as we bumped along the muddy road. I wondered what happened to the man in the blue hoodie who'd rescued me. *Where did he go?*

Back in Palenque, we met many travelers who had ventured out the previous night towards the ruins. Their stories were similar, but the endings were different. Of course, everyone got soaked (along with their gear, which had become quite heavy, they said). The guards who are usually at the temples weren't there, and a couple explained how they started a massage party inside one of those temples.

"There were about sixty people in there with us. We were totally soaked and freezing, so we took off our clothes to get warm," a man with ginger hair said, grinning from ear to ear. "Then I pulled out some coconut oil and started massaging my friend Scarlet. Next thing I know, everyone else wanted it, so we passed it around."

"Yeah—we thought the world was ending. It wasn't sexual, but definitely sensual. Everyone got in super close contact, and we loved it," the woman called Scarlet said. I was curious—I felt both comfortable and uncomfortable with the idea. I imagined the scene in my mind. *What would I have done? Yeah, there's a divide in me on how I feel about this. I guess I don't know much about sensual touch without mixing sexuality with it...*

The two young women from San Francisco, Mimi, and I shared a hotel room and thought about where we could find our next adventure. I told Mimi I wanted to go to a place called Lake Atitlan in Guatemala. I'd seen a flyer in a café for an event called the Cosmic Convergence New Year Celebration of 2013. I was curious. She thought about it, but as we had a week before New Year's, we decided to see San Cristobal de las Casas, a city located in the Central Highlands region of Chiapas, about a hundred and thirty miles from where we were.

San Cristobal de las Casas has a Spanish colonial design. Its vibrant yellows, oranges, and red and blue hues made it appear cheerful and pleasant, even in bad weather. We walked the cobblestone streets. Shops that sold ceramics and amber jewelry made by indigenous peoples lined the shady side of a narrow path. Donkeys hauled wood and what appeared to be milk canisters past us. The clip-clop of their hooves on the stones made me think of simpler times. We appreciated the small city's slower pace; it was a great contrast from the hustle-bustle of Los Angeles! I'd rather watch the donkeys over being stuck in traffic on the 405 or 101 for hours at a time just trying to get home from work.

There were foreign influences—mainly in the food and music—but little tourism (other than occasional backpackers like us). We learned that many tourists who once visited this quaint, modest village ended up staying and setting up shop. I couldn't blame them for wanting to stay. It was beautiful.

On our first evening, we devoured traditional dishes like saffron tamales, asado coleto (a pork dish made with garlic, chili, tomatoes, and spices), and a drink called "posh," made from sugar cane. After dinner, we found the Guadalupe Church (Iglesia de Guadalupe) and climbed close to a hundred yellow and white steps to reach its gated entrance. The gates were locked. At night, the church's hilltop view was impressive. The city lights twinkled like stars that had fallen to the ground. It was serene. We stood there, silent, taking deep breaths and enjoying the sparkling stillness for several minutes before walking back down to the village.

We took our time and marveled at the architecture and old-world authenticity of the city. The bright colors of the buildings beamed (even in the dead of night). I felt as if I were walking through a lively, celebratory town—

even when Mimi and I were the only two souls trotting along the back-alley streets. While we walked, I said, "I'd like to go to Guatemala. I'm ready to leave in the morning... you're welcome to join me."

Mimi thought about it along the way, and by the time we reached the hostel, she agreed to come along.

We met with one of the hostel staff members, and I attempted to explain (using Google Translate) that I'd like a bus to take us to Guatemala in the morning. The worker looked nervously at his hands and mumbled under his breath. We were making him uncomfortable somehow. A man sitting in a chair in a darkened corner of the room chuckled as he listened to our miscommunication. He rose slowly and joined us next to the computer and said in perfect English, "Iran is unsafe, and you should avoid it because of insects... or something like that?"

"What?" I asked.

"That's what you told this man here with your translation."

"Noooo."

"Would you like a bus to take the two of you to Lake Atitlan in the morning? Is that what you're after?" We nodded. He smiled and shot off our request in rapid Spanish to the confused hostel worker.

"I guess we can't trust Google Translate," I said.

"Ahhhh, sì. OK. El autobús llegará a las seis de la mañana. Por favor, prepárense para salir ya que no las esperará" the worker said. This translated to: "Your bus will be here at 6:00 a.m. Please be ready to go as it will not wait for you." We thanked both men and departed for some rest before the ten-hour-long journey to the lake in Guatemala.

Before I went to sleep, I felt it was an excellent time to use the goddess cards Mimi had brought with her. It was Christmas Day, and the 2013 New Year was approaching. I felt some guidance from the angels might be helpful. Here's the spread I drew that evening:

Card One
PAST - XVIII The Moon: Diana:
In ancient Rome, they honored Diana as the goddess of the moon and wild forests and animals. The changing moon reflects the cycles of nature and life.
Meaning: Support of women who genuinely care for you. Intuition. The receptive aspects of the Divine Feminine. Intense Dreams.

I thought of the women who had assisted me with my departure to Central America: Harley, Stephanie, Mimi, Cat, and Opal had all played essential roles in my breakout moment, and I thanked them silently for their support. Trusting my intuition even more was something I wanted to cultivate. I had to keep developing this sense that I would always travel safely and with great luck. Intense dreams? The daydreams I'd had in my hammock felt more like instructions than anything else, but they were intense.

Card Two
PRESENT - Ten of Pentacles:
An ornately carved gateway leads to a verdant landscape where there is more than enough for all to enjoy.
Meaning: Reversed - Discontent at home. Wanting greater prosperity, but uncertain on how to create it.

This card had resonance, as it described what I was feeling—a severe discontent at home. I felt there was more to life than what I was experiencing, but I wasn't sure how to create it.

Card Three
FUTURE - V Tradition: Juno:
In ancient times, Juno was honored as the patroness of marriage and other rites of passage in women's lives. This Roman goddess was believed to watch and protect all women from their first breath until their last.
> *Meaning: Following established social structures and traditions. In love relationships, the desire for marriage or declaration of intentions for the sake of security.*

This card didn't hit home, but I could see how I thought that was how my future should be unfolding... with my marriage and life desirable, trustworthy, and secure. It no longer was. I believed I was protected—that I'd be guided along the way. I told myself over and over, "This is true."

Card Four
OVERALL MESSAGE - XVII The Star: Inanna:
Clothed with the stars, Inanna, the great goddess of the Bronze Age, was honored with the title "Queen of Heaven."
> *Meaning: Follow your dreams without fear—don't be afraid to make them happen! Success, good fortune, creativity.*

This card sent chills through my body. Many dreams appeared as I trekked on through Central America. I imagined traveling far and fearlessly, using the journey to reintroduce myself to myself—whatever that might mean. *Success, creativity, and good fortune are possible for me.* There's no power in victimhood. I fell asleep that night with a renewed vigor and excitement for what was to come.

Chapter Four

The Convergence of the Cosmos

The bus dropped us off in Panajachel, Guatemala, at 4:00 p.m., and we were eager to explore the exotic new country. The currency conversion was 7:1 (quetzales [Q's] to US dollars), so everything was affordable, although we noticed some locals haggled well with foreigners. I bought a handmade, brightly colored fanny pack with three pouches and a wool blanket for twenty-five dollars—I've never been good at bargaining but thought it was fair. While wandering, we met a couple of other travelers who suggested accommodations across the lake in San Pedro. We'd need to catch a water taxi to get there, and it cost 25Q for non-locals (about $3.25 each) for the thirty-minute ride. It sounded like a good idea, so we checked this place out before the New Year's Eve party in Panajachel.

San Pedro was an exciting place full of backpacking hippies selling handmade jewelry, tattoo parlors, and accommodations. A plethora of lakeside bars with live music and dancing lined the main road, and after we found a suitable place to stay, Mimi wandered off with some new friends while I hung back. The camp we chose was minimal and cost us each only one US Dollar per day. Our ramshackle private rooms with dirt floors were perfect. A makeshift kitchen with a double-burner stovetop and sink stood under a tin roof in the middle of the courtyard. It was as basic as I could imagine basic can get, and I liked the simplicity. It was an opportunity to adapt. Suddenly, I thought of Jack. I felt a tightening in my chest and retreated into my cheap, dusty room. After a while, I picked up my pen and journal, walked outside to the shared courtyard, and found a shaded spot at an empty table. With a heavy heart, I sat down to write.

Why do I miss him so much? I couldn't come up with a clear, authentic answer. Everything I'd thought about our relationship felt wrong now—as if I'd been semi-conscious for the entire six years. I'd had narrow concepts about what "relationship" even meant. It wouldn't become clear to me until much later what had transpired in my marriage. It would take time to figure this out along the way, but some things became more transparent.

I loved him within my understanding of what love meant to me then. But I wasn't able to appreciate him. That realization stung. My inability to love fully (or be loved) and my lack of awareness would become part of my inner-work on this journey. *I need to know what's in the way....*

I looked closer, beyond my marriage. I've realized that I've always needed another's approval to feel complete. I must learn to feel complete in my solitude. When I can accept and love myself completely—break free from the idea that alone I lack something I can only gain from another person, then I'll live from a space of peace and tranquility. *I'll admit, these thoughts are unfamiliar territory. It scares me. Where does this aching desire and endless search to have another person determine how I feel about myself come from? Was it Dad's lack of compassion? His disapproval of me when I was a child? Does finding the source even matter? Is it necessary? What am I supposed to do?*

I heard, "What you have is now, regardless of the past—of your lack of awareness and the abuses and traumas experienced at the hands of others—of yourself. What you have is now. It's time to heal, forgive, devote your energy inward, and break this cycle. You are complete as you are. Only you can determine how you feel about yourself. Only you can judge yourself. Only you can influence who you choose to be."

Where is that voice coming from? I added that experience (and a poem that can be found in the appendix of this book) into my journal.

Mimi reappeared. I wiped tears away and closed my journal. We made tea, and I shared my experience and poetry with her. She put her arms around me, told me she loved me, and everything would be fine. I wanted to believe her, but at that moment, it didn't feel that way.

The following day, we were sitting in a little café sipping coffee. I complained to Mimi about how I longed for a Starbucks chai latte. I've always loved Starbucks. One of their stores was directly across the street from the apartment Jack and I shared in Los Angeles. I'd walk my dog over there almost every morning before getting into the car and driving to work. I missed our morning ritual.

A Slovenian man, who was sitting in a chair picking on a guitar, stopped playing and said, "You know, there's a market here that sells all the spices you need to make a chai. It's right up the road. First, you take that path there...."

I interrupted him. "Will you take me there?" I asked.

He smiled. "Yes, why not?"

I bought cinnamon, ginger, cardamom, cloves, sugar, milk, nutmeg, and black tea from various vendors. I searched for allspice. We didn't find it, but the Slovenian man assured me the tea would be just fine without it.

Back at the camp, I was eager to make my first chai latte in our outdoor kitchen and got started right away. The Slovenian man helped me, and we made an enormous batch for everyone there. It was delicious! It was almost as good as the memory of Starbucks chai, and everyone seemed satisfied with the results. We spent the rest of the day playing with the other travelers in our dirty camp, singing songs, and listening to stories, and I felt the veil of depression that had been creeping back in beginning to lift. I fell asleep that night with a smile as I imagined what other surprises awaited us in the following days. Before we left San Pedro, I bought enough spices to take with me on the road.

The next day, we arrived in Panajachel, where we'd camp for the weekend. Lake Atitlan was like landing in heaven. The lush, tropical feel of the place, coupled with its two massive volcanos and a large lake in the center, made it feel relaxing yet powerful. Giant butterfly wings hovered over the gathering place and provided cooling shade for the souls resting below them. Mimi and I stood at the entrance and took it all in. The shimmering aerial flags, shaped like butterfly wings; perfectly staged, gigantic papier mâché mushrooms; the reflection of the sun on the edge of the lake. It was breathtaking. People were setting up temporary dwellings to prepare for the event. Smiling volunteers directed us up the road toward the camping sites. We arrived in the center of one camping field and tried to decide where to post up for the next few days.

My smile faded. I felt a severe, sharp pain. Its fire covered the surface of both my legs, from my knees to my ankles. Shocked, I saw an army of tiny black insects on my legs. *What are these?* I jumped up and down and started screaming.

"What? Did you find the perfect spot or...." Mimi turned to me; her words trailed off. The look on her face turned from excitement to shock.

I was on the ground, rolling around in a panic, slapping myself on the legs and face.

"Mel... are you OK? I knew we shouldn't have accepted that water back there from those strangers! Oh, crap, is that going to happen to me too?"

My crying in pain turned into laughter. "I'm being eaten alive!" I screamed.

Almost magically, two trees appeared in my view—as if they'd just sprouted up, full-grown in that precise moment. I jumped up from the earth, grabbed my dust-covered backpack, and made a run for it. Mimi watched as I ran for the trees and the soon-to-be safety of my mesh-covered, biting insect-free hammock. Once I was set up, and after a few minutes of rest in which the burning in my legs subsided, we made our way back to the main grounds where the shade structures, butterflies, mushrooms, and music were.

The party was epic. We attended yoga classes, learned about Mayan culture, and took part in rituals to celebrate the earth. The insects didn't bother me again during those days, which was a relief. On the last day of the event, I met a gorgeous German man named Leon. He was lying on his back in the shade of a giant decorative mushroom. His eyes were closed. He was wearing white face paint and a huge smile. I sat down next to him and suddenly, I felt electric. My body buzzed and hummed with a current of desire. He opened his eyes and looked at me. My heart skipped a beat. The words rolled off my tongue before my brain had a chance to stop them.

"Hello." I said. "Can I kiss you?"

He cocked his head to one side before answering. "Yes."

It was the first time I'd kissed a man other than Jack in the last six years, and it was surprisingly welcome. The sudden newness of it, the warmth of his hand on the back of my neck, the taste of him. It felt dangerously delicious. I wanted more. We stayed up late and watched the sunrise: golden with hues of pink and orange that made the lake look as if it were made of glass. We held each other close and welcomed the new day in perfect silence. It was peaceful and serene— I didn't want it to end.

However, in the afternoon, after exchanging contact info with Leon, Mimi and I changed locations and took shelter in a small, simple hotel. We arrived exhausted. We both had quick showers and went right to sleep... but only one of us stayed that way. As my body relaxed, my legs itched and burned from the previous day's bites. Mimi was fast asleep when I decided to relieve the annoying itch of the bites. As I engaged in some pleasurable scratching, I guess I was enjoying it a lot because Mimi woke up. "Mmmeeellll... whaaaat are you doing?"

In the pitch black, I was lost in relief and only moaned louder.

Again, Mimi asked, her voice shaking, "Mmmeeellll, what are you doing over there?"

"Mimi... ohhhh, it feels so good! I can't stop because when I stop, it hurts...."

She was silent for a few moments, and I realized what she must be thinking. I couldn't help but laugh.

"Is everything OK, Mel?"

I couldn't stop laughing. "I can't stop scratching my legs!" I said between gasps. "When I stop scratching the bites, they just burn! It feels soooo good to scratch them!"

She burst into laughter, and I continued to claw at my legs until I finally fell asleep.

The next day, Mimi departed Guatemala to make her first solo trek to Mexico and then back to San Francisco. I hugged her, reminded her of our protection, and wished her a safe and fun journey home. *She's grown so much from this trip. She has more confidence and trust now. I think I do, too.* I joined Leon again and invited him to visit an Earthship high up on one of the mountains at the lake. Sam, a friend of mine, knew that I was in Guatemala and told me to go check out his sister Jax's Earthship. I was intrigued because, well, what is an Earthship, right? Earthships, I'd learned from Jax and her partner, who were building one along with the help of some locals, were initially created by a man named Mike Reynolds in New Mexico back in the 1960s. The walls are made of used tires packed with earth and stacked in a U-shaped pattern. The tires are then covered with thick mud, and recycled glass bottles decorate the non-weight-bearing walls.

Using these materials is beneficial because they're more durable than traditional building materials such as wood, and they're more stable in earthquakes. Also, insects don't care to eat them. The builders on site explained how an Earthship is an independent structure that can produce the power needed for heating, cooling, and water generation by using specialized modules that collect sun and wind energy to use in the home. Greenhouses can also be integrated into the building to provide food and help regulate the home's temperature. Now that's interesting....

Learning how these "Earthships" respected and worked with the environment further developed my interest in alternative living structures. I wondered what other possibilities existed in the arena of sustainable living. I wanted to know more.

But first? Tea. I set up my MSR Whisper Light Camp Stove, attached the bottle of fuel, and lit the burner. I filled my camping teakettle with water and prepared the chai spices and sugar.

"Thank you for sharing your day with us," I said. "I'd like to offer everyone chai before we go if that's cool? I only have two drinking cups, though...."

"That's awesome! We have cups! Some warm chai would be perfect!" Jax said. "What's on for the rest of your day?"

"We want to find Cacao Keith," Leon said. "A couple of passing travelers told us about his chocolate ceremonies, and we're curious. They said that Cacao ceremonies are helpful for inner work and processing, and they increase the heart's energy field."

"Yeah—and sharing cacao can bring us into the same energetic frequencies," I chimed in. "We want to try this medicine."

We found Keith and his cacao ceremony effortlessly. At his house, a young woman asked us to have a seat on the porch as volunteers inside prepared the magical drink. Many people gathered around—young and old—and more arrived through the gate as we took our seats. The patio filled up, and it was time to begin.

A few minutes later, warm cocoa with a dash of chili was served. I drank it and closed my eyes. Cacao Keith gave a sermon of sorts that I honestly can't remember. I was lost in meditation. When I opened my eyes, I realized that three hours had passed. Tears poured out in heaps, but without thoughts attached to them. Only a deep feeling of love and gratitude remained. It appeared as if I'd had an emotional release of old energies. I turned to Leon.

He'd had a similar experience. We looked into each other's eyes, and I couldn't feel anything other than radiant love. We reached for one another, and our embrace was pure magic. Coming back into the present moment lasted for some minutes. *Where had I gone? What just happened?*

We thanked our gracious host, and as we wandered away, I understood how powerful this cacao medicine could be. When we arrived at our hostel, as usual, curiosity got the best of me, so I did a little more research into this ancient ritual. I learned that archaeological evidence of cacao's use dates back to 3,900 years ago in Central America. Recent genetic evidence dates cacao's use to 5,300 years ago in the Amazon. But despite this long human history of using cacao, we know very little about ancient cacao rituals. Because of the massive genocide of the Americas' indigenous population beginning in the 1500s, and because ancient artifacts deteriorate quickly in wet tropical conditions, our chances of preserving that history have been vanquished. For the Olmec, Zapotec, Mayans, and Aztecs, cacao was a plant of central importance. It's mentioned extensively in the Mayan creation story and can be found in many engravings depicting ritual offerings. It seems we know that there were vast storehouses of cacao beans, that they were used as a currency and consumed as a drink. Today, cacao is still an essential part of Maya culture. It's used in midwifery, at weddings, and in social gatherings. *Fascinating*, I thought, as I closed my computer and drifted off to sleep.

The next day, Leon and I traveled to Rio Dulce on the coast of Guatemala, where we rented cabins built on wharves floating on a serene lake. We breathed in the stillness of the early morning and swam in the water as the locals sped past in their small fishing boats. On the third day, I told Leon I felt it was time for me to head north. He was feeling pulled to travel south to Honduras, so, after a quiet riverside lunch, we said our goodbyes and wished each other good luck on our journeys.

From there, I traveled on alone for the next few weeks, up through Livingston, on to Belize, and then to Tulum, Playa del Carmen, and Cancun, Mexico. Then I caught a flight back to San Francisco. This part of my trip was coming to a close. I drew one card from the deck Mimi had given me with the question "What does the future hold for me?" and received this as the answer:

MAGIC: ISIS - A growing awareness of the magic within yourself. A yearning to grow beyond perceived limitations. You can transform your life through the strength of your originality and power. All you need to do is OWN IT—a renewed creativity and vigor.

This card resonated deep within my soul. I had a profound desire to keep traveling. I wanted to see it all. I needed to absorb more fantastic opportunities, and it seemed I wanted this more than anything. As I flew from Mexico to California, I entered the last mantra from the workbook into my abundance log eight times: "I am fulfilled in this now moment. I am present to being abundance now." A new zest for life was emerging—an eagerness to learn more. It felt good. I smiled often, my energy increased, and curiosity and wonder returned. *There's that confidence. Nice to feel you again.*

Chapter Five

Setting Intentions

I arrived in San Francisco and met with my friend Jade to pick up my car. I'd met Jade several years earlier at a nightclub in Santa Monica. She'd been a supportive friend ever since. Her dark eyes shone as I told her about my sixteen-week journey and thanked her for keeping my Toyota safe in her garage.

"Of course. I'm happy to hear you had a good time. You look much better," Jade said, pushing her long, dark hair from her face.

"I feel much better. I think I'll keep going."

"Where to next?"

"I don't know. I only have $500.00 in cash left, enough for gas to get to Florida and a one-way ticket to Europe. And I still have credit cards to pay."

"What will you do in Europe?"

"I'm not sure. I trust it'll all work out. What else can I do?"

She smiled and raised her glass.

"To the unknown," she said.

"To the unknown."

The following day, I met with my friend David again. He suggested we head out for a traditional American breakfast: pancakes, eggs, bacon, ham, hash browns, toast, jam, coffee, and tea. *That'll guarantee a proper food coma.* We returned to his apartment and promptly fell asleep. During our rest, I heard a booming voice in my mind. It screamed, "You must leave San Francisco, now!" It was so loud; it woke me up. I sat there half-dazed, still groggy from the food. The voice came again, loud and clear. So, this isn't a dream... I shook off the sleep and woke David up. "Hey. I gotta go now," I said.

"What? You just got here! Aren't you supposed to meet Mimi and the girls at the art walk in Oakland tonight?"

The voice in my head grew even louder.

"I don't know how to explain this without sounding crazy, but there's a loud voice in my head right now screaming that I have to leave the city immediately. Trust me. I'm in no hurry to drive to Los Angeles to sign my divorce papers. I'd much rather spend some time here first."

He frowned.

"Oh yeah—that does sound crazy, but whatever. Do what you want. You always do anyway."

I called Mimi and apologized that I wouldn't be seeing her and the girls as planned. "I want to," I said, "but there's a voice giving me a headache with its shouting inside my mind: 'You must leave the city right away.'"

"I'm so disappointed. I really wanted to see you," Mimi said.

"Me too," I said. "But I have to go. Bye." I said goodbye to David, then drove south to Los Angeles. The more miles that passed, the quieter the voice became, until I couldn't hear it at all. *Thank goodness that's over.*

In Los Angeles, I met up with another wonderful woman in my life, Angelica. We stayed up till the early hours, and I answered all of her questions about my travels. Not long after I fell asleep, my phone rang and woke me up. It was Mimi, so I answered it immediately. She was sobbing uncontrollably for the first few moments; it caught me off guard. "Mimi... honey, what's happening? Are you OK? Mimi? What's going on?"

When she finally could speak, all she said was, "I know why you were being told to leave the city yesterday!"

"Wait. What? What do you mean? What happened?"

"Last night, at the Art Walk, we were shot," she sobbed.

Chills crawled up my back. "What are you talking about?" I asked, my heart racing.

"Last night at the art walk, we were standing there—me, Emily, and Becky. Then these two guys next to us got into a fight. One of them pulled out a gun and shot the other one in the chest! He died right there, Mel! Emily was shot in the back! Becky was shot in the leg!" Her voice changed to a high-pitched whine. "I told you! It's not safe! I told you, Mel! I told you in Mexico!"

I took a deep breath. "Mimi, were you injured?"

"Well... no, but...."

"Mimi, we're protected. You weren't hurt. The girls, they'll be OK, right? It isn't life-threatening, right?"

"Well... yes. But...."

"Mimi. It would help if you grew your power. Increase your bubble of protection to include those close to you. We did the practices in Central America. You haven't forgotten our trip. Grow your magic. Don't let this experience move you back into a place of fear. You have to be strong, enhance your magic. It's there waiting for you—the girls, too."

Just like when we'd traveled together, and spoken about abundance and effortlessness, I felt I was talking more to myself than to her. *If I'm going to do what I feel is next for me, I need to trust in and grow my magic.*

We spoke for a few more minutes before hanging up. The call left me with a confident yet simultaneously uneasy feeling. Part of me was curious as to why I'd been given this loud command to get the heck out of there; part of me was unsure if I'd continue to have such divine guidance on my side. *You are protected. Do not fear.*

I told Angelica the story over breakfast. We agreed it was unusual and that the warning was a gift. In the back of my mind, I knew I'd be meeting Jack in a couple of hours—and the thought of that encounter overrode any lucky feelings. The taste in my mouth became dry and sour. A surge of energy built up inside my chest. *Now's the time to be brave and accept what's happening.*

When I'd come back from my four-month-long backpack tour of Central America, I'd felt rejuvenated, alive. Free. The personal power I'd gained from the experience, I'd hoped, would carry me through. I drove to the office where we'd make our divorce final—a lump formed in the back of my throat. My hands were cold and clammy.

I entered a cramped, dimly lit office (that, oddly enough, smelled like my grandmother's house). I looked at Jack, my soon-to-be ex-husband. We exchanged glances that appeared to say, "I've always cared deeply for you, but our journey has ended." Our defeated smiles kept the sadness at bay. I signed the papers and walked out the door without saying a word.

As I drove away, I knew my life would never be the same. Central America had planted a seed that was growing steadily inside me. Tiny roots of hope, curiosity and adventure were spreading, but still, doubt carped at me. As I drove east from California, the voices in my head said, "You're crazy. Backpack around the world? Throw away all you've worked for? Then what? How will you survive? Have you lost your mind?"

My eyes grew heavy as the day gave way to the night. The miles rolled away, separating me from everything familiar. The flat plains of New Mexico mirrored my loneliness: they were dry, empty, void of color. In my side-view mirror, I watched my past disappear into the sunset.

Three days later, I reached the sunshine state and the warmth of Mom's arms. The delicate touch of her small, steady hand across my forehead brought me instantly into a place of comfort and calm. As she stroked the hairs from my face, I felt the muscles in my stiff shoulders and neck soften. A long sigh escaped my lips. I was falling apart and was grateful to have her there to catch me. There was something empowering about being in the presence of the woman who taught me the value of hard work and dedication. The goddess who took me camping with horses into the wild woods and connected me to nature. My greatest teacher and biggest fan. I admired her strength and knew this was a safe place to dance with the maniac shadows of negative self-talk that had ridden across the country with me. My chest was tight. My monkey mind jumped from one topic to the next. *All of this just from thinking about facing my fears?*

The following morning, I said goodbye to Mom, picked up my magical daydreaming hammock, and headed into nature to find my answers. As I sat at the edge of a nearby forest, a gentle breeze rocked me as I looked at the sky through a canopy of trees. Small and large puffs of clouds changed form as they drifted across the sky. I slipped into a daydream.

I dreamt I was soaring through the sky, sprouting large, iridescent wings from my back. They shimmered as if made of pure silk, and I danced among the clouds. My hair floated around me as if I were underwater. I felt weightless—as if every burden I'd ever carried had disappeared. This dream led to another: I was swimming through crystal clear water, but not with the awkward movements of a human swimmer. It was graceful, effortless. The clean, refreshing water spilled over my skin. *Is this how dolphins feel as they play together in the ocean?* The dream switched again: I stood on top of a mountain, surrounded by clean, fresh, powdery snow. I looked down and saw the snowboard attached to my feet. I jumped and sailed down the mountain, the wind nipping at my face. I flew quietly, precisely, fast–I was free.

I opened my eyes. The clouds had gone. I was looking into a limitless, bright blue sky. I stared into the boundless space, excited about my upcoming adventure in Europe. I took in a huge breath and released it. I smiled. I just wasn't sure how my trip would unfold, but I climbed out of my hammock, confident.

I returned to Mom's house and found her sitting with a cup of coffee. She grinned as I entered the dining room. She invited me to sit down. "I know the last few months have been hard for you, with Harley passing and your marriage ending. I'm proud of you for pulling through and finishing college with all of that going on. I think you deserve a gift."

"A gift? What kind of gift?" I asked.

Her face lit up. "How about some cash?"

Oh? I thought of the daydream I'd had earlier. Some cash would definitely get this trip going. I only had enough left for a plane ticket after the journey across the country and a wild dream in my heart.

"Melissa, you put yourself through college and haven't asked for anything since you left home when you were barely sixteen. I'd like to give you some pocket change as a graduation present. What will you do with it?"

My eyes were glimmering when I said, "Well, Mom, I want to do some more backpacking. I imagined starting in Europe this time."

The corners of her mouth curled into a smile, but her eyes showed concern as she said, "How long? One or two months?"

I closed my eyes for a moment. "Actually, I think it'll be closer to a year."

She sat back, sipped her coffee, and looked at me. "OK, honey, I hope it's not that long, but I can see you've made a decision. You know I'll support you even when I don't fully understand. Where to first?"

"I'm thinking Germany?"

"They have some language learning programs at the library," Mom said. "I'm going there today. I think they have the Pimsleur Technique, too. Would you like me to get you the German lessons?"

"That'd be awesome. Thanks."

With the surprise graduation gift, my crazy dream had just become real. I excused myself. I got into my car and drove. I didn't know where I was going until I got there—which turned out to be a tattoo parlor. I walked inside. The walls were covered in thousands of designs—I ran my fingers down them.

Two of the town's finest artists greeted me. "What are you in the mood for today?" one of them asked.

I sat down in the only chair available outside of the tattoo stations and closed my eyes. Immediately, an image came to mind—the one that would end up being the reminder of the trust I needed to have on this adventure. It was simple. It was clean—one word: *Believe*. I also wanted a saying that would remind me to stay in the present moment. But I wanted it in Chinese, so the meaning wasn't obvious to most others.

I opened my eyes, looked at the two men, and said: "I'd like the word *Believe* tattooed on my forearm. I want the B to be in the shape of a heart. And I'd like to have some Chinese characters to connect it like a bracelet."

Half an hour later, I left the tattoo parlor and drove to the beach. The fine white sand squeaked under my feet as I walked toward the turquoise water. I dropped my backpack, piled the soft sand into a cushion, sat down, and crossed my legs. Sandpipers pecked at the ground and ran toward and away from the waves. *What am I looking for? What is this trip for?* The answers appeared suddenly—I scrambled to grab my pen and journal from my backpack.

What are my travel intentions?

1. Trust in the universe and my power.
2. Learn new languages and ways to communicate.
3. Expand my cultural knowledge.
4. Learn about sustainability.
5. Seek beauty in everyday experiences through presence.
6. Enjoy being alone.
7. Listen more—talk less.
8. Change old patterns of thought.
9. Define my spiritual practice.
10. Learn to love all parts of myself.

At the end of the list, I wrote: "Be mindful and give consistent attention to your thoughts. What you think you become. Imagine who you are. Create your reality with intention. Be sure to make time daily for this. Let the world help you define your purpose and how you'll contribute to making it a more peaceful, loving place. Start with yourself."

After I accomplish these things? I want to fall in love again. First, though, I need to get right with myself. I'm open and ready to let the world be my mirror.

Before leaving the States, I decided to use a website to find hosts to volunteer with in exchange for room and board. In Belize, I'd met a young woman with a strong British accent named Deb. She worked at the bar at the youth hostel I'd stayed in, and I had to ask her how that was possible. She had told me, but I'd forgotten to write it down in my journal. Luckily, we'd exchanged contact information, so I called her out of the blue in the U.K.

"Oh, mate," she said. "Right, so there's a website called Workaway, yeah? You can find loads of opportunities all over the world. It's nice because you save some cash and sometimes make some cash. You're not just a tourist, you know?"

"That sounds great! What's the website again?"

"www.workaway.info."

I liked the idea. The agreements between volunteers vary from host to host, but generally, twenty hours a week are requested, and shelter and meals are provided in return. Some hosts also offered payment. I chose a small boutique hotel in Germany for my first exchange experience and sent the hosts a message. Two days later, they replied with an invitation. I was welcome to come. *Will they like me? Is it safe? Will I like it? And then what?* I closed my laptop, took a deep breath, and stepped into the unfamiliar.

Year One - Optional Questions for Self-Reflection: Investigation

What would happen if you made time to investigate your life? To take a deep look into what you have created and are creating? To look objectively at the situation you are living in? To notice what appears when you watch?

Is there something you want to work with? A failed relationship? Dis-ease? Unworthiness?

I invite you to sit quietly, focus on your breath, and simply listen to the thoughts that arise. Ask yourself a question. "What parts of myself do I dislike, judge, or fear?"

If you struggle to find answers, ask yourself a different question. "What parts of others do I dislike, judge, or fear?"

When you feel ready, pick up a journal and write what you notice. At this point, don't change anything—just notice what is there. This will be supportive for the journey that lies ahead.

Year 2

The European Union

Chapter One

I Reap What I Sow

I stepped off the train into the fresh, crisp air of the Black Forest in Germany. I didn't know where I was or how to get to where I was going. As I stood there, brooding over the choices I'd made, I saw an elderly couple on a narrow trail opposite me, looking at the brightly colored flowers growing everywhere. I became acutely aware of the present moment. I marveled at the variety and beauty of the flowers, inhaled the scents of the various shades of green, and tried to remember some of the German I'd studied.

"Bitte, Kannst du tell ich wo Studebaker Strasse ist?" I asked.

The gentleman pointed one way; the lady pointed the other way. They looked at each other and shook their heads, admitting they had no idea.

"Danke schön," I said. I continued wandering until, eventually, I found the boutique hotel. *Here goes: My first experience as a volunteer in a foreign country.*

Once I got settled, the hotel owner assigned me to work in the restaurant, bringing food out and taking dishes away. I also helped in the kitchen to prepare salads and vegetables. I enjoyed the work, but I kept staring out the window into the dense Black Forest beyond. Its darkness, shrouded in mystery and majestic knowledge, kept calling to me. On my first day off, I packed a small day pack with water, some fruit and snacks, my journal and tent hammock, and set off to explore. As I began my journey, I noticed that the air felt lighter here, fresher than in Los Angeles. It was delightful.

I ventured deeper into the forest, and the reason for its name became apparent. All the thinly stalked tree trucks were pitch black, as if they'd been burned long ago. The almost-fluorescent green moss below my feet felt like I was walking on clouds, its sponginess cushioning each step as I moved farther into the delicate, quiet space.

When I reached a point deep enough in the forest where the only sights and sounds I heard were from the creatures that called this place home, I set up my hammock and climbed inside. Rocking gently, I stared through the treetops into the mottled grey sky. I cried—I grieved for the loss of Jack, for Harley's death, for the condition of the planet, for my lack of connection to anything, for my family. I let it all out until I fell asleep and had a dream that felt oddly like a premonition. I was running with animals—I was a horse. We were running away from something through a field of long, golden strands of grass that were as soft as feathers against my body. Plumes of dust rose into the air as our hooves pounded against the earth. Then my body transformed into a seagull, which climbed into the sky, separating me from the ever-growing crowd of animals below and into the flock of birds above. I saw a dark shadow blanketing the earth behind us—it was as if the world was experiencing an advancing power outage—lights were blinking out in a sequenced fashion. Just ahead, I saw the brightest light. It contained infinite depth. The birds ahead of me disappeared into that light before the approaching shadow could devour what remained of the landscape. Looking behind me, I saw that not all the birds and animals would survive. My heart screamed silently, and I flew ever-upward into the light.

I woke up, breathing heavily, eyes wide. I forgot where I was momentarily. I looked around. I was back in the Black Forest, sitting up in my hammock, surrounded by dense silence and natural beauty.

Confused and slightly scared by the dream, I packed my things and made my way back to the hotel. The following day marked the end of two weeks of volunteer work in the hotel's restaurant, and I was ready to try something new. I'd found a farm three hours east of the forest and had written to the hosts. They'd replied that I was welcome to come and stay.

I got off the bus in Betzigau in Bavaria. The mother of the family I'd be volunteering with for the next couple of weeks, Katharina, met me there. "Hallo! Willkommen!" she said. "How was it getting here? Everything OK?"

She was a vibrant young spirit with short blond hair and a generous smile. I liked her immediately. I stubbed out my cigarette—embarrassed that she'd seen me smoking. "Yeah, great," I said. "It was easy, thank you."

"Great, great! My English is not so... aber... would you like to go to the market? I need some food for the family. You can choose something you like. Is this OK?"

"Of course."

We hopped in her car. Her instant acceptance made me uncomfortable. I'd been open and welcoming with countless strangers in my life and my home over the years, but I wasn't as open to receiving generosity. I squirmed in my seat.

After shopping, we drove to Katharina's home, and I met her husband, Norbert, and their three-year-old son Moritz. They immediately accepted me into their world.

They gave me a beautiful room to stay in and the freedom to choose what I'd like to do: I could help with the animals, assist with the daily household chores, or play with the children. They took me outside, and in the side yard, a caboose-style caravan caught my attention.

"That's for the pilgrims," Katharina said.

"Pilgrims?"

"Yeah. A pilgrim will pass through here now and then. They can stay in the caravan, and before they arrive, we put tea, fruit, bread, milk, and chocolates inside. Sometimes they leave a note or a couple of euros. Mostly we don't see them. They're on their way."

"Is it like a spiritual walk?"

"Mostly, yes."

I was curious. I hadn't heard of modern-day pilgrims and didn't know that pilgrim trails existed. The trails are all over Europe, with the Camino (or "Road to Santiago") from France to Spain being one of the most popular. In Betzigau, the pilgrims were few and far between, but occasionally, one would turn up and stay the night. *Maybe I should do something like that? I wonder what would happen if I just wandered alone for a while?*

The next day, the family invited me to meet the fifty cows they cared for. I was interested in learning how they kept these animals and met Norbert at the barn at 5:30 in the morning. We went inside, and a farm helper brought five cows into a holding area. He handed me gloves, a spray bottle, and some thick paper towels and led me down to a lower floor, where the cows' udders were at eye level.

"First, you have to clean the teats," he said. "You clean each one by spraying it and then wiping it off."

I put the gloves on, reached through the bars, took one of the cow's teats, and did as he said. At first, I was scared, but the cow didn't seem to mind, so I continued cleaning the other three. Then he handed me a set of vacuum cups.

"Just slip one onto each teat. This is a good cow—she'll let you do it," he said.

"Are there bad cows?" I asked.

"Some of them don't like it. They'll kick the cups off. We use this to stop them from doing that," he said as he brought out what looked like something used to pick up giant blocks of ice. One cow in those five was a kicker—he placed the metal vice across her back to where the dull hooks rested at her hips.

"That'll keep her from bringing her feet up," he said.

I continued to clean teats and put the cups on them, and after milking those five cows, I was done. I went outside and asked Katharina about how it all worked.

"Well, the cows are kept for milk, and the bulls are sold to be eaten when they are older," she said.

"And that baby cow?"

"The babies are separated after they are born but are given the milk from their mother."

The calf cried. It was sad to hear it calling for its mother, who mooed back at him. I watched as a farmworker fed the calf using a giant baby bottle full of the mother's milk.

I love cow's milk. I think it started when I wasn't yet a year old as Mom told me the story of how my older brother used to sneak into my room, reach through the bars of my crib, and take my milk bottle and drink it all before giving me the empty bottle. Mom said it took some time to figure out why I was always crying until one day, she caught him drinking the milk and putting back the empty bottle. Perhaps this is where my milk obsession came from? I'm not sure. Maybe understanding how it all works will change that?

I imagined this happening to humans, and it hurt. *What makes them so much different from us? We're all sentient beings, aren't we?*

After the early morning milking session with the cows, we sat down for breakfast, and that's when they brought the fresh, raw, super-cold cow's milk to the table. My heart and mind battled each other as I replayed the sounds of the calf crying and its mother responding, but my curiosity won. I sipped it slowly. Delicious! It differed from the regular organic pasteurized milk I was used to... creamier and sweeter. I was in awe. For the first time in my milk-drinking history, I felt conflicted—I didn't let it show.

We finished our lovely breakfast, and I spent the rest of the day playing with little Moritz and his friends in the garden, which I tried to do as often as possible over the coming days. Everything was going great. Then one day, the family left me at the farm alone for a few hours while they went into town on some errands. I walked through the seemingly endless open fields surrounding their property. It had rained, and the field was muddy, but the sun was shining, and the grass was dry.

Out of nowhere, an intense sadness filled me, and the hole in my heart rushed into my awareness. I fell to my knees. I slammed my fists into the soft earth. I screamed from the depths of my soul, and I prayed for the first time in a long time. I screamed at the sky, begging the gods and goddesses to help me. *I can't carry this any longer. I've had enough of suffering. This gaping hole in my chest hurts like hell. I want to be free.* "God, if you're listening, please help me! I need guidance!"

After what seemed like an eternity of lashing out and praying, I collapsed. Lying still, I continued to pray—for healing, understanding, liberation, abundance, and freedom. I prayed to know my true self again and to end this suffering. I'm not sure how long I lay there in that field, my face in the mud, but the sun set, and my body got cold.

I pulled myself up and wiped the mud from my face. I walked back to the house. The family had returned; I avoided meeting them. They seemed to sense that I was in a delicate space and allowed me to float by, up the stairs, into my room. I cried myself to sleep.

The following day, I opened my computer to search the Workaway website for the next volunteer opportunity. I found a unique hotel not far from where I was, sent a request to join the community, and closed my computer. I took a couple of deep breaths and went down the stairs to join the family for breakfast. After a quiet meal of fruit, cheese, bread, jam, and raw cow's milk, I joined Katharina on the patio for tea. She could see that I was troubled and was concerned for me. I decided to be transparent and share.

"Last year, my best friend died of cervical cancer," I said, as tears filled my eyes. "I was living in Los Angeles, and she moved to San Francisco to stay with her brother, so it was easy for me to drive up on weekends to be with her. The first time I went, I couldn't recognize her. She'd lost so much weight, all of her hair."

Katharina sat silently, allowing me time to continue.

"I visited her so many times in the last year of her life, and every time I had the same feeling of helplessness. She was in so much pain. I didn't know what to do for her." My heart grew heavy. My chest caved in. "The only thing I could do was be there. Touch her. Tell her I loved her. Seeing my healthy hands move about her frail body hurt me. Inside, I wanted to scream, but I didn't want her to know how sad I was. I just wanted her to know I was there."

Katharina reached out, placed her hand on mine, and looked into my eyes. "I am so sorry. I can see that this still hurts you."

She was right. It did hurt. I'd asked myself constantly if I could have done anything differently. *Had I done everything I could have? Had I been the best friend that she needed? Had I done what was right? Had I done anything at all to help her?* These questions continued to haunt me as I traveled. They inspired me to seek answers and understanding so I could heal the pain of losing her. I was still wrecked from the experience. "She died slowly and in great pain. It was awful," I said.

Katharina's face showed authentic compassion as she sat quietly and let me share what was on my heart.

"As Harley was dying, my marriage was falling apart. I'd come home from visiting her, and my husband, Jack, just wasn't available. I needed his support, and instead, he asked for a divorce. It was like the other half of my heart was being ripped out. Harley died in October. Jack left me that same month. I was confused and lost, so I decided just to let it all go. I quit my teaching job, closed our apartment, packed a backpack, and left for Central America four months ago. I felt like I needed to get away. I thought backpacking would help me heal. And it did—it has—in some ways. Before I came here, I felt pretty good about my decision—confident even. Now I'm not so sure. I feel a deep sadness. I need help sorting it out."

Katharina cried and took my hand. We stood up, and she gave me the warmest, gentlest hug. I was confused. How could this woman be so compassionate and kind to me? I felt her unconditional love, and it touched my heart.

"Yesterday," I said, "the reality hit me. No matter how far I travel, no matter how many beautiful experiences I have, there's genuine suffering below the surface inside me. Last night, I woke up, looked online for my next volunteer possibility, and found a spiritual retreat seminar hotel. It's not too far. I sent them an email this morning. Maybe it's the right place to get help."

My phone chimed. The hotel replied: "You are welcome to join our community."

That evening, as I lay in bed, I reflected on the past two weeks at the farm. I'd been free from all distractions and spent countless hours observing my thoughts, behaviors, and impulses. Many of the "Aha!" moments were more like "Holy shit!" moments. I'd started practicing Qi-Gong, chakra healing, and meditation every day—all of which were new to me. I'm a beginner. I'd like to know more. I need a teacher.

On the morning I left, I thanked Katharina, Norbert, and Moritz for gifting me such a beautiful experience. Katharina handed me a small box. Smiling, I boarded the train that would take me to the seminar hotel. Along the way, I opened that little box. Inside, I found a thank you note, some chocolate, and 150 euro. My heart fluttered, and I closed my eyes and gave gratitude to the family for continuing to support my journey even after I'd left. The money they shared with me would be enough to cover my travel expenses and feed me along the way, with a little extra leftover. The payment was unexpected, and I felt it confirmed I was on the right path. *You are supported, Melissa. You have everything you need, and right when you need it.*

Chapter Two

Strange Encounters

I arrived in Traunstein in south-eastern Bavaria, the closest village to the retreat hotel. That's where I first met Charles. With his long white hair and thick white beard, he looked like Professor Albus Dumbledore, the wizard from Harry Potter. His crystal-blue eyes sparkled. There was a calmness about him—as if a vast ocean of loving stillness resided within him. I felt nervous but intrigued by his powerful presence. He bowed, smiled, and said, "Welcome." He helped me with the larger of the two backpacks I was carrying and placed it gently in the car.

We stood in silence for a few moments and looked at one another.

"So? Are we ready to go?" He asked.

"I guess there's no time like the present."

The sprawling Jonathan Seminar Hotel looked more like a giant house and was nestled in a tiny village at the edge of a forest. Several team members and a few volunteers greeted me in the domed entranceway of the cavernous restaurant. We sat at a round table to share a meal, but before we ate, we joined hands—the right one palm down for giving and the left one palm up for receiving. I offered both of my hands, palms down, in full-on giving, until the woman sitting next to me pointed it out. *That's interesting.* As I switched my left palm up to receive, I recalled the discomfort I'd felt being welcomed so lovingly by the farm family. After a moment of silence, the person who had started the circle gave a few words of gratitude and welcome. Another moment of silence followed. I felt a slight squeeze in my hands: The circle was complete. It felt odd, as this way of coming together before a meal was new to me. But as time went on, I learned to look forward to these moments.

The following day, after a similar circle and breakfast, I asked how I could be helpful and was offered four options. I could assist in housekeeping, help in the kitchen or the restaurant, or volunteer in the maintenance department. I started with housekeeping as I had experience in this area from when I was younger. It felt appropriate—it took little mental power, and the repetition was meditative.

After a few days of cleaning, I searched for the wizard, Charles. A team member directed me to a back office to find him.

I found him sitting at a desk with two monitors, a heaping stack of papers piled high to his right, a small pair of glasses hanging off the tip of his nose. He stared at the computer screen and pecked at the keyboard. I entered the room slowly. He looked up at me, leaned back, pulled the glasses from his nose, and said, "Yes, hello. How are you enjoying the house so far?"

"The hotel is beautiful. It's interesting; you have so many trashcans. You guys recycle almost everything—cardboard, metal, glass, paper, organic material—in America, we don't sort the recycling like you do here. Everything goes into one can, and who knows where it goes. And the food? It's great! Your cook, Frank, told me you don't use any processed food, and almost everything is certified organic. That must be expensive, huh?" I realized I was chattering away, but I couldn't stop myself. I sat down. "And, in the housekeeping," I said, "you don't use any chemicals. It took me a minute to get used to the natural products—I mean using microorganisms from nature? What are those, anyway? I can see they clean just as well, but it took some getting used to. I also worked in the garden for a little bit. The volunteers told me everything's natural. You don't use any chemicals or pesticides there, either."

"Yes, it's not so difficult to live healthily and in harmony with the earth, or...?"

I thought about this for a moment and felt the disharmony within me well up. I felt a flush of heat hit my cheeks and looked down at my hands.

"So? It seems you're ready to look closer at your disharmony, or...?"

I looked up and almost couldn't believe what he'd said. *Did he just read my mind? Did my body language give me away?*

I sat still for a moment before answering. "Yes, it seems so."

He leaned back further in his chair and closed his eyes for a few moments. "Yes. It seems you have some themes to look at. It appears that there are authority, control, over-responsibility, food, sexuality, and self-worth themes playing in your system. In that order. Perhaps start with watching the authority and control themes first, yes? What does your belly tell you?"

I looked at him blankly. I had no idea what he was talking about or how to start this whole "watching the themes." *What did he mean by the "belly telling" thing?*

As I stared, he said, "So so so." He leaned forward, replaced the glasses on his nose, and went back to his computer work.

I sat there for a moment, perplexed but curious, before standing and leaving the room.

That evening, I couldn't sleep. What this strange wizard-looking man said kept playing over and over in my mind as I tried to make sense of it. *What was he saying? All these themes? Watching? What does that even mean? Did he mean noticing the noise in my mind?* I'd had some experience with this, but I was just a beginner. I knew I had disharmony inside; that was clear. I also knew I needed guidance. After all, I had begged for it in that cow field just a few days ago. *Was I ready?* He'd said I had six themes playing in my system—that sounded like a lot of work....

I learned more about the hotel and its vision. It was named after the book *Jonathan Livingston Seagull* by Richard Bach. The book tells the story of Jonathan, a seagull who grows disinterested in fighting over food and instead learns everything he can about flying. Two other gulls introduce him to a "higher plane of existence," where he discovers that there is a better world. He befriends the wisest gull in this new place, and his new friend takes Jonathan beyond his prior self-education and teaches him how to move throughout the universe. His mentor, Chiang, says that the secret is to "begin by knowing that you have already arrived."

This story inspired the hotel's creation, as it was built to serve others who had decided that they wanted more from life than just surviving. The hotel's written vision states:

The development, the unfolding of the human being, only seemingly happens through rules, struggle, and punishment. In reality, it happens through developing consciousness. We contribute to this unfolding by having realized this place, where the development of consciousness can take place both in the seminars and within the team. It is a practical exercise in our every-

day living—with ups and downs, which helps us learn and develop. We see planet Earth on the threshold where we humans either learn to live in harmony and hence respect existence or make the planet unsuitable for human life and destroy ourselves. Not by talking, but by taking action, we can change the world. And this daily practice can be a lot of fun.

This place is unique. I want to know more.

Charles and I met a couple more times in the following days. He'd ask me random cryptic questions that plunged me deeper into the core of my being.

"Are you tired yet of playing happy, and are you ready to be authentically happy?" he asked.

What is he talking about? Just ask anyone. I'm probably the happiest person they know....

"It seems you've mastered the art of being fast and of giving. What do you know about slowness and receiving?"

He's right about that one....

"Are you ready to touch that pile of repressed anger inside your system, or do you prefer it kills you one day? It might be helpful to meet these things now, or...?"

Again, I was perplexed. Meeting these things? What does that mean? What does it all mean?

I'd been working in housekeeping for a couple of weeks when Charles invited me to help around the hotel with repairs and upgrades. Someone had noticed I was knowledgeable about power tools, fabrication, and paint. I was excited to have a change of pace from turning guest rooms, dusting, and mopping the floors throughout the large house. Charles introduced me to the generous workshop in the hotel's basement, and I fell in love with it. The shop had everything—hand tools, power tools, bio paints, two large workbenches, and plenty of cables, ropes, cords, and boxes upon boxes of parts and supplies for the house.

As I progressed, they began to trust that I knew how to manage maintenance projects, and they gave me both responsibilities and challenges. The wizard (Charles) began to provoke me. I didn't know he was trying to help me "see" my authority and control patterns. I took the provocation personally. Over two weeks, when he'd pointed out something in me I couldn't see consciously, I internalized my anger at him and went into defensive mode. Although delivered gently, his constructive criticisms continued, as did the internal and external fighting. *You need to get the heck out of here. You're being brainwashed! These people are crazy. What's that man trying to do? What does he want from you? Go. Quick. Get out!*

The voice from San Francisco that had saved me from possibly being shot and killed entered my mind. This voice sounded different. I caved in. I left the hotel even though I felt it wasn't the correct move. After all, I'd been given free rein in the house, had many opportunities to advance my knowledge in project management, had the use of various tools, and was learning new building techniques—all these things added serious value to my experience. There wasn't a single person trying to harm, mislead, or misuse me. *Or was there?*

I decided to do some research before I left, so I could understand what Charles was saying. At the end of my agreed-upon four weeks of volunteer time, I started by reading online about "the shadow" and learned that the famous Swiss psychiatrist and psychoanalyst, Carl Jung, had coined the notion of "the personal shadow;" the unknown or dark side of one's personality.

I pondered before reading on and reflected on how Charles had attempted to show me something in myself I couldn't see. He somehow noticed things that were sabotaging me, keeping me from reaching my highest potential. The themes seemed to get in the way of me having a peaceful existence with myself. *Perhaps that's why my marriage failed? Why I felt helpless with Harley?* I didn't feel grounded—conscious even in my day-to-day life most of the time—I saw this all as if it were new. It stung.

The "shadow side" of ourselves consists primarily of what some consider "negative emotions" and impulses like selfishness, anger, desire, greed, or seeking the accumulation of power. There is a "positive" side to the shadow, but I wanted to focus on what was playing in my system negatively. I discovered through my research that anything we deny ourselves could become part of our shadow. *Maybe this was what Charles had said about repressed anger in my system? What if he's right? What if I've denied the angry part of myself? Can that make me sick?* I'd experienced too much anger from others during my childhood. I didn't want to treat anyone that way. *Had I eaten my rage?*

I began to understand that as we grow from children into young adults and beyond, our society, family structure, community, and especially how we feel about ourselves shape our understanding of "good" or "acceptable" behavior—and we come to understand that "bad" or "unacceptable" responses should be held within, not shared outwardly. We adjust our behavior to adapt to our external world. Essentially, we build walls inside ourselves and become inauthentic. Then, all the unwanted or undesirable parts of ourselves end up getting dragged around in our unconscious minds and continue to play out in our experience—usually through projection and without conscious awareness. I thought about the classes I'd taken for teaching. I'd learned some of this already… so I knew that the wizard was right.

Now, for me, the wall was cracking—and all the little things I'd held back had poured out, bit by bit. Apparently, Charles, this wizard, could see into it better than I could. *Or could he?* I listened to the strange new voice inside my mind and ran away as fast as I could. The whole situation frightened me. I thanked the group and packed my things.

A team member took me to the train station and handed me a small envelope. I hugged her and thanked her for the ride. I boarded the train, sat down, and opened the envelope. Inside, I found a postcard with signatures from the team, along with 300 euro and a heartfelt "Thank you" for my services to the hotel. Holding the card and the money felt strange. I sensed a conflict brewing: Part of me was afraid of these people, but another part wanted to love them completely and continue to work with them.

This was the second time on this journey I'd been gifted money when I hadn't expected it or asked for it. I'd just been of service and done my work with enthusiasm and heart. I'd learned excellent new skills, and those were payment enough for me. Again, the money covered my travel expenses, with a little leftover.

You always have what you need and when you need it.

Chapter Three

The Forgotten

A couple of days before I'd left the hotel, my friend Jade from San Francisco contacted me and asked me to meet up with her in Europe.

"Where?" I asked. "I'm in Germany but can go wherever."

"I've always loved Paris," she said.

"Paris it is."

We connected a few days later, wandered the city, sipped delicious coffee, and explored the Louvre Museum. One night, we considered whether to see the Moulin Rouge show while drinking at the bar next door to the theater. We were getting comfortable in our reunion—perhaps a bit too comfortable. I hadn't consumed alcohol in many months, so I didn't have the slightest tolerance. I was throwing drinks back.

The more we drank, the more relaxed and wilder I became. Enter some young, hot Polish guy, and the shenanigans were on. It'd been a while since I'd played with a man, and I jumped at the alcohol-fueled opportunity. Jade was not impressed. We stumbled away from the bar—she with a woman she'd met and me with this young man. It wasn't long before I started to see something in me—this "sexuality theme" that the crazy wizard had mentioned. I wasn't seeking an authentic connection... *what did I want? What's this all about?*

Ultimately, I ditched the man somewhere in the streets an hour or so after we left and made my way back to the apartment Jade had rented. When I approached the door, I began to shake uncontrollably. I called up to the room, and Jade sent the woman she'd left with to open the door. Once inside, I collapsed on the couch and fell asleep.

In the morning, Jade said she'd be going to England next—alone. I tried to understand this quick change of plans—but let it be. We'd been friends long enough for me to know that this wasn't the end of our friendship—just a little bump in the road. I'd lived in England as a child (but had no memory of the experience), and I turned to social media to find Rebecca, the woman who had babysat my brothers and me when we'd lived there during our preschool ages.

I found out that Rebecca had recently reconnected with Mom online, after almost three decades. I sent a message and told her I was curious to see where I'd spent some of the first few years of my life on planet Earth. I'd hoped the visit might shed some light on who I used to be.

She replied that her parents, Derek and Judy, were still in Ipswich, that her dad had adored me as a child, and that he'd love to see me again. They invited me to stay with them—I could sleep in Rebecca's room. I was excited to hear this and made my travel arrangements to England as well.

Derek and Judy picked me up from the train station and took me to the park Mom used to take my brothers and me to. "Your mother," Derek said, "would pack all three of you in a little red wagon and pull you here. Your dog, Lady, went too."

I stared across the freshly cut lawn toward the lake, where two geese paddled around each other in a circle. I watched the mid-day sun bounce off the ripples their dance created and tried to imagine what it had been like to play there.

"Your older brother hated those geese. What was he... Four years old? They always chased him," Derek said with a chuckle.

I don't remember anything.

"Your father worked an awful lot. Your mom was always busy with you kids. She took you guys everywhere. Would you like to see the shop?"

Derek's shop was behind an old bakery not far from the park. He pointed to the apartment above it where our family had lived. "When you were, I guess, three years old, you'd come down those stairs right there wearing only an oversized t-shirt and carrying a cup of coffee for me." He looked at the stairs and chuckled. "Yeah, I used to call you "bird legs." You had these tiny sticks for legs. Not much different from now, I see."

I looked down at my legs. Suddenly, I recalled something I'd written in a first-grade booklet where I'd recorded my answers to some questions. My mother had shared the tattered book with me when I'd last visited her. One of the questions was, "If you could change one thing about yourself, what would it be?" I'd written: "My legs." I snapped back from the memory. Had his innocent, playful remark made an imprint on me? I'd heard it from my grandfather as well, and I know in my heart that both Derek and Grandpa were stand-up guys; they meant no harm. *Was this one of the seeds I'd planted? The origin of my body shame that made me feel something was wrong with me?*

At the end of the first week in England, I lay in my hammock in Derek and Judy's backyard. *Where would I go next?* Judy called me in for dinner. I told them I was unclear about where my next stop would be. Derek looked at me sternly and said, "You know, you should go home. Stop all this crazy wandering. Your mother's worried, and I'm sure your pup misses you, too. Really darling, cut it out and go home already."

I understood his concern but sensed that my journey was not yet over, even though I didn't know where I'd land next.

Derek stood up and left to do something in the garage. Judy turned to me and said, "I don't agree at all with that old fart. You should continue to travel. See the world, darling—keep going. I'm sure whatever you're searching for will find you. If not, at the very least, you'll have some wonderful memories and stories to take back home with you when you're ready. Besides, I love watching you go. It's wonderful what you're doing—being so brave and bold. I wish I would've done the same. Now go on, get back in your hammock, and see what comes."

That's more like it. Her words resonated deep in my heart. I followed her advice. After dinner, I climbed into my hammock and fell into a daydream. I saw myself on a boat somewhere in the middle of a large body of water, no land in sight. I felt the wind in my hair, smelled the salt water, and saw the dolphins playing around the boat. I was reminded of the daydream at Mom's house before leaving for Germany some weeks ago. *Is this what's next?*

I climbed out of my tree sling and went into Rebecca's room. I opened my computer to search for volunteer opportunities on boats. I connected via Skype with an Australian man named Henry, who invited me to join him at the tip of Spain—in Gibraltar. He needed a crew to take a group of DJs from Ibiza down the coast. *No way.* "That sounds like tons of fun!" I said. "I'd love to join!"

Two days later, I arrived in Gibraltar and met Henry in person.

Chapter Four

Belly Talk

I stepped off the plane onto the tarmac and made my way into the small building to retrieve my backpack and meet Henry. I was excited to sail to Ibiza and eager to get going.

Then I met him. As we walked away from that tiny airport, an uneasy feeling formed in my belly. Is this what the wizard Charles was talking about when he said, "What does your belly say?"

Henry seemed decent enough. He bounced along on his 350-pound frame towards a dinghy; we made polite conversation along the way. Then it dawned on me. *Why were we walking to a dinghy? Didn't he say his ship was docked at the marina? I'm sure I asked that question during our Skype call?* To be clear, I asked again, "Henry, why are we taking a dinghy? Isn't your boat at the marina?"

"Well, it was, but I had to move it a short way out. We'll need the dinghy to reach it."

My belly tightened as we approached the small, air-filled boat that would carry us to Henry's large boat, somewhere out there in that vast ocean. The dinghy had about a foot of water in the bottom of it. "Ummmm, why is there water in this boat?" I asked, feeling even more concerned. *What had I gotten myself into?*

"Oh, just a small leak. Don't worry. We'll make it."

My belly contracted.

Henry attempted to start the small outboard motor for several minutes without success. Laughing, he grabbed the oars. "Well, we both know I could use some exercise," he said, and started rowing. The small rubber boat squealed under the pressure of his heavy frame, pushing and pulling the oars along its sides. Sweat poured from his brow, and my belly continued to contract and release with every forward and backward motion.

It took a good thirty minutes of continual rowing before we reached his boat. It was enormous, but it had been neglected for quite some time. When we climbed from the dinghy onto the ship, it was even worse than I'd thought. *This boat is nowhere near ready to take a group of anyone anywhere. What's going on here?*

Henry invited me into the galley for some food and showed me where I could put my backpack. I roamed around the inside of the beast and explored: four staterooms and two bathrooms. I made a mental note of the many things that were amiss. First off, there was a terrible smell coming from one end of the boat: not unlike sewage, not unlike rotting flesh, sort of a mixture of the two. My stomach turned. I looked into the staterooms. The beds were covered in pieces of scrap metal, old ship parts, and trash. There were no pillows, sheets, or blankets in sight. *Now I'm worried—this boat won't be picking up a group of DJs in Ibiza.*

I returned to the galley and found Henry stuffed behind the dinette table with what appeared to be a block of Velveeta cheese in his grubby fist. He took a huge bite from it and invited me to sit down across from him. I sat on the edge of the seat. I was ready to run up the stairs, onto the deck, jump off the boat, and swim to shore.

"Henry, you lied to me. You told me you needed a crew to sail this boat to Ibiza. You said we'd need to be there in five days to pick up the DJs. This ship is nowhere near ready to take on tour. What are your real intentions in getting me onto this boat? You told me you were docked at the marina, and we'd have consistent internet. That's not true either, is it?"

He seemed shocked at my bluntness. He took a bite of his fake cheese. As he chewed, he appeared to be thinking. He looked beyond me, into the hallway, then back at me. "Yeah, well, I was hoping you could help me get her ready to do a tour like that. I guess I've been a bit lonely and wanted some nice company. You seem nice enough."

I studied him for a moment before answering. "OK, Henry. Lying to me was very uncool, and I don't appreciate it. I'll help you clean the staterooms, remove some trash, and paint the upper part of the boat—if you have paint."

"I'm sorry," he said. "Thanks for the offer to help."

Before he could say anything else, I added, "I want to go to the Marina tomorrow first thing in the morning for supplies. Cool?"

"Yes, OK," he said.

I grabbed my backpack to make my way out of the galley and onto the top deck.

Henry stood up. "Where you goin'?"

"I'm going to set up my hammock on the deck and sleep under the stars. I'm exhausted from traveling. So? I'll see you in the morning, yeah?"

Before climbing inside my hammock, I pulled a Navy Seal knife and mace pepper spray from my backpack. I fell asleep with one in each hand, ready in case Henry intended to harm me. I was prepared to cut and blind him if necessary. Maybe a part of me, buried within, secretly wished he'd try something so I could unleash some ancient anger and hate on him. *Interesting.* I thought of the wizard in Germany and his comment about my repressed anger—how it could kill me one day. Right now, I may have to use it for protection.

Traveling with a knife and pepper spray was easy. I carried two backpacks—the larger sixty-liter pack I'd check-in at airports held my camping gear, clothes, and the knife and pepper spray. The smaller backpack I always carried with me was stuffed with the items I didn't want to lose. Things like my computer, journal, cameras—pieces I felt would be harder to replace. Some friends thought it was necessary for a solo female traveler to carry some protection and had gifted me the weapons. I'd hoped I'd never need them, but at this moment, I was happy to have them.

I woke up with the sun, enjoyed my morning yoga ritual, and waited for Henry to appear on deck, which he did a couple of hours later. "Ready to go to the marina?" I said with a huge smile.

"Don't you want breakfast first?" he asked.

"I'd rather grab something in town if that's OK with you? I've been up for a couple of hours, and I'm ready to see more of this area."

He seemed to consider this for a moment. While he pondered, I climbed down into the dinghy and waited for him.

At the marina, my first objective was to let everyone I met know, "I'm here in Gibraltar, with Henry, on his boat." I met a British man named Oscar, and an American named Gary in the first hour and told them my story.

"Oh damn, you're with that guy? Yeah, did you know his boat has been out there for the last two years?" Oscar said.

Oh shit, more lies he's told me.

"Sorry to hear that he's been bullshitting you, dear. Is there anything we can do to help?" Gary asked.

Actually, yeah, there is. "I told Henry I'd help him remove some trash from his staterooms," I said. It would be great if we had help with that—do you have dinghies too?"

"Sure, why not? We're all just kind of sitting here anyway, right? I mean, it's a few more weeks before we can make the fall crossing to America. Might as well do some good before we go." Gary said.

Oscar shrugged.

We made a plan right there at the water's edge while Henry was inside the marina, working on his laptop.

"Gary, can you help me find a store for supplies?" I asked.

"Sure thing."

I could tell he was relatively harmless and a bit silly, and after an hour of running around town together, we were friends.

When we returned, I filled Henry in on our little plan, and the process began.

Three properly working dinghies came out that day and hauled off the garbage. I spent the next two days painting the upper part of the ship a charming glossy white. On the third night, as I retreated to my hammock on the upper deck, I had that terrible feeling in my stomach. I said a protection prayer to the stars before closing my eyes—holding onto the knife and pepper spray.

I woke up as usual before the sun. I felt a slight panic—I saw fresh footprints in the dew on the deck floor next to my hammock. Henry had walked out to my bed while I slept, stood over me, and then retraced his steps! *I'm get-ting off this boat today. I kept my promise to help this man, and now I'm out of here!*

A couple of hours later, as I packed up my hammock and prepared my bag, Henry appeared on the deck.

"Good morning! Great job on the painting—she looks so much better. Thanks!" he said.

I looked across at him and said nothing. I listened to my belly as he walked toward me.

"What are you doing there?" he asked.

"I'm packing my things. I've done what I said I'd do to help you out. I still don't appreciate you lying to me. I'm leaving today."

He stood motionless. I waited to see what he might do. I held the knife behind my back in my clammy hand. I hesitated. The pepper spray was in my pocket. *Is this when my crazy fight for survival begins?* Suddenly, I heard a familiar sound in the distance. I turned slightly without taking my eyes off of Henry. *What is that?* It was Gary in his dinghy! He pulled up to the rear of the ship, tied off, and climbed aboard.

Thank God.

Gary started to say something, and I said, "Yep! Ready to go, captain!" and threw my bag into his dinghy. Gary looked confused, but followed my lead and joined me.

I looked up at Henry. His face was red; anger and frustration flashed in his eyes. His lips were pressed tightly together, a thin white crack across his burning face.

I turned away, and Gary started up the dinghy.

When we arrived at Gary's fifty-two-foot Catamaran, I explained the whole story from the beginning. From the first Skype call when I was in England to Henry's insistent requests that I sleep down in one of the staterooms each night to this morning's wet footprints, which had me freaked out.

Gary shivered. "Well, I know you came here wanting to learn to sail. I don't want to sound creepy or anything, especially after your ordeal with that weirdo, but if you want to learn, I'd be happy to teach you what very little I know about sailing."

Gary held his head low as he spoke. I noticed a boyish shyness about him that made me feel safe for the third time I was with him. "I'd love to join you on this adventure," I said.

For the next few days, we hung out close to the marina, gathering groceries and getting to know each other a little better. One day, there was some disagreement between the British and Spanish over coral reefs or something, and all foreign boaters anchored there (that's us) were asked to leave immediately.

I guess it's time to go!

Chapter Five

Throw off the Bowlines

We made our way from the harbor into the mouth of the Mediterranean Sea. Only one side of the double-engine motor worked, and there wasn't enough wind to push us out of that passageway. We spent several hours trying to leave and came within a few feet of slamming into a giant concrete wall. As it grew dark, we realized we wouldn't be getting out to sea that day. Instead, we looked for a new place to anchor for the night. Gary decided on a spot across from the harbor we had been kicked out of and dropped the anchor.

"Gary, I don't know about anchoring here... I don't have a good feeling about it," I said.

"Oh, it'll be alright, Puddin'," he said. (I'd earned the nickname Puddin' at dinner the night before; I'd eaten nine cups of pudding after the meal). "We have to stop because it's getting dark. I need to figure out how to get this motor running properly."

"OK, but I don't have a good feeling about this in my belly."

He was right, though. It had gotten late, and we were both exhausted from that long, crazy day of going almost nowhere. We said goodnight and retreated to our rooms. The sun hadn't come up yet when the first rogue wave hit the side of the boat. It knocked me out of bed. I jumped to my feet and ran to the helm to find Gary already running around the upper deck.

"What are you doing?" I shouted.

"Closing the roof hatches," he said.

I ran back into my room. As I reached toward the open ceiling hatch to close and lock it, another rogue wave hit the boat so hard it knocked me to the ground and dumped about fifteen gallons of seawater right into my face. I couldn't help but laugh. I scrambled to my feet, reached again for the open hatch, and slammed it shut.

"Puddin', you alright?"

I locked the door and wobbled my way to the helm, soaked and laughing so hard I could barely breathe. Gary's hands were on the steering wheel. "Oh shit!" he said. "That rogue wave broke the anchor lines on the front of the boat! We're drifting!"

I climbed up past him. Weren't there floating docks somewhere near us last night? I looked at the water. The docks were now only six feet away.

"Gary! The docks! There're RIGHT HERE! We gotta move left, now!"

Gary struggled to control the boat, and as with the concrete wall the day before, we barely escaped smashing into the floating fishery docks. Thirty minutes after it all started, it was over, and the sun began to rise—damage control time. At the front of the boat, we saw that the rogue wave had indeed ripped away the anchor line—and had taken a piece of the fiberglass with it. *Damn.*

"Well, we'll need to repair that part and get another anchor set there, I guess," Gary said.

We both broke into laughter.

Once we'd calmed down, I looked at him all serious-like, brow furrowed, hands on my hips.

"Don't even say it," he said. "Next time you have a bad feeling about something, I'll know to listen to it, OK?"

I smiled. Even though it was dangerous, it was also fun.

We retreated to the lower deck, prepared breakfast, and discussed the problem with the motor. Gary thought it had something to do with the hydraulic system, and after we ate and had coffee, he got right into it. I watched him from above.

A couple of hours later, the sun was fully awake in the sky. I stared off into the horizon and noticed a tiny dot in the distance.

"Hey, Gary! Is that Africa?" I asked.

He joined me at the front of the boat.

"Oh yeah, it is, isn't it? What? You want to go?"

"I do, I do!" I said, jumping up and down, clapping my hands with girlish excitement.

"Well, OK, I guess we go then."

We were off. It took us a day and a half to make the crossing, with very little wind and only a partially working motor, but we made it. Gary taught me several things, like how to read wind maps and GPS navigation, what nautical miles are, and how to tack and jibe the sails. He also pointed out that I sleepwalked and found and ate cookies while asleep. *No way. Mom told me I did that as a child. I had no idea it still happened.*

When we arrived at a marina in Morocco, a man searched the boat before we were allowed to stay. He nodded his head in approval and exited, just as another man appeared and offered to be a guide for us on a sight-seeing tour.

"What do you think, Gary? I'd love to see some of this city's history—how about you?"

"Sounds good to me, Puddin'," he replied as he shouldered a small daypack filled with water and snacks.

As we followed him into the city center, the guide told us a bit of history about the Berber people. "The Berbers are famous for handmade carpets, colorful clothing, spices, tea, and jewelry," he said.

"That's cool. We're interested in seeing the architecture and learning more about the culture, not so much into shopping. Can you show us some historical sites?"

Our request fell on deaf ears. Instead, our guide took us into a shop, where we were accosted by two men who insisted on rolling out every one of the hundreds of carpets they had stacked along the walls.

"Ummmm, he lives on a boat, and I live out of a backpack," I said to the persistent men.

"Yeah, we aren't interested in carpets. But they are nice," Gary said.

The men elaborated on how we could easily "Send them home to your families. Wouldn't your mother just love one of these beautifully handmade rugs?"

I ended up buying Gary a tiny yet costly ($150) Berber rug as a gift for his boat before we left that store. The guide continued to take us in and out of shops, and Gary ended up buying fifty dollars' worth of mint tea and a couple of other things before we'd finally had enough and split. We just turned away from the man and ran. The city's seemingly endless ancient architecture of white walls and blue doors intrigued us. Homes, stores, and markets were all mixed together and sat side by side along the twisting, turning alleyways of the medina (the historical heart of the city). The scents of perfumes and incense wafted through the narrow walkways, assaulting our noses as we trotted along. It was a maze of dark and light, musty and bright spaces. The contrasts were dizzying. I noticed that the locals seemed to neither like nor hate us—they appeared indifferent to tourists in general.

At the harbor, we made friends and danced in a local hot spot until way too late before we returned to the boat. We left the following morning. We drifted into the expanse of the sea and headed back toward Spain. The wind vanished at one point, and the calmness of the deep ocean beckoned us. The Catamaran had two levels, and we climbed to the top and jumped into the bluest waters I've ever seen. After a while, we settled back into drifting, and again, I started to feel heaviness within me.

"You alright, Puddin'? You seem a bit down, even after all that fun. Wanna talk about it?" Gary said, reaching for a package of cookies.

I was feeling a bit down and did want to talk about it. Gary had earned my trust, and I felt safe sharing with him what was again in my heart. "It's just... well, I think I'm heartbroken. Or maybe, just broken in general. I'm not sure." I said, looking down at my hands.

"You don't seem broken to me. I haven't had this much fun... probably ever. Why do you think you're broken?" He joined me at the stern of the boat with the sweets.

"I have this pain in my chest, and no matter how far I go, what beautiful things I see, how much I enjoy myself, I have these shadows that haunt me. They're inside—I can feel them, but I don't know why they're there—or what they are."

"Shadows, huh? I think I have some too," he said as he opened the package of cookies.

"Really? What do you mean?"

"Did I tell you what I used to do before I got this boat?" He said, handing me a cookie.

"No. What did you do?"

"I worked as a prison guard for twenty-five years. It's why I like being out here on the boat." He looked at the horizon. "I can't stand people," he said.

"I guess that makes sense—I mean, if you spend your life in that kind of place with the worst of the worst. I can see how you wouldn't want to be around people. What do you mean by having shadows?"

"Well, Puddin', I was married once. We separated. My wife committed suicide and left a note saying she couldn't live without me. I've carried that guilt with me all these years...."

I couldn't believe what he'd just said. As I watched him, an incredible sense of sadness came over me, and I wanted to hold him and tell him it would be OK, that it wasn't his fault that she took her life. Instead, I just sat there in silence. I thought about my guilt, shame, and shadows; how I couldn't imagine any words that could comfort me. "I think somewhere deep inside," I said, "I believe I'm not welcome here. I keep hearing words that were said to me as a child: 'You're an embarrassment, a waste of space, you have nothing to offer—in my mind. I think some part of me believes those words." I dropped the cookie into my lap.

"Really?"

"Yeah. The more time I spend alone, in silence, the more I can hear these stories. I think about Harley dying and my divorce, and yeah, the stories kind of fit, don't you think?"

"No, I don't think so. I think you're bright and funny, and I sure have had a great time playing with you. I don't think your stories of having nothing to offer are true at all," he said.

Gary and I spent hours sharing what we felt weighed us down and kept us from enjoying our lives to the fullest. *Trying to develop a sense of self-love is difficult. I grew up in an atmosphere where my very existence wasn't fully appreciated, so why am I surprised?* We leaped into that deep ocean, attempting to rinse off any remnants of guilt or shame that might still be hanging on.

As we approached Spain, a pod of about ten dolphins joined us. I was reminded of the daydream I'd had at both Derek and Judy's and back at my mom's. I was swimming with the dolphins—no, I was a dolphin in those daydreams, wasn't I?

I watched the pod from the boat's netted front end; they rolled playfully from side to side below me. I was mesmerized. As they glided through the waters and swam sideways so they could look right at me as we cruised along, they seemed to smile. I wondered if I could be like them—so playful and at ease in this world. The dolphins seemed familiar to me somehow, like we shared some forgotten common ancestry. I enjoyed their animated display of interest in us and the boat.

Once we reached Spain, we decided to take the dinghy to explore the marina before pulling the big ship into it. Neither of us was skilled at handling the Catamaran, and we wanted to be sure we could easily get in there.

On the way, the dinghy ran out of gas, and we crashed-landed into a closed port in the city of Malaga, Spain. We had no choice but to climb the locked fences to purchase gas, and naturally, to climb them again after we'd found some. It was when we "broke back into the port" that the police captured us.

Standing there inside the locked port with a can full of gas didn't look right. There was a woman officer there. In the little Spanish I could remember, I attempted to explain what happened and where we were going. "Nuestro barco está ahí," I said, pointing to the dinghy tied to the end of the dock. But the officer kept insisting that we had broken the law when we'd jumped the fence and entered the property.

"Pero… el barco no tiene gasolina. We didn't have a choice," I said.

She wasn't interested. She was out for blood, and I couldn't understand why. She called three other officers to the scene, and again we explained our situation in Spanglish (a mix of English and Spanish) to the men. They asked to see what was inside our backpacks, and after some explosive laughter, one of them said: "You're free to go."

We were relieved when we heard those words, and as we turned and began to walk to the boat, I couldn't help but notice that the woman officer was not pleased with us being released. She appeared to be insisting that we'd broken the law, but the male officers waved her off and walked away. *Why could she only see the legal, not the human, side to the situation? Why did she want us to endure punishment for this mishap?* Gary wagged his behind toward her and stuck his tongue out as if to say, "Na Nah Na Nah Na. You didn't catch me."

We filled the dinghy with gas, and I asked Gary what he thought her problem was.

"Hell, I don't know, Puddin', but it sure did seem like she wanted revenge, didn't it?"

I could only agree. I tried to make sense of it in my mind without success as we sped back to the Catamaran.

We enjoyed three wonderful weeks on that boat before I felt it was time for me to move on. During our time together, Gary and I shared many deep conversations about our experiences that exposed some painful realizations of our current dramas—what we struggled with now. He couldn't stand to be around others because of what he'd witnessed as a prison guard, and I couldn't love all parts of myself because of the inner dialogue I believed to be true. We also shared what we hoped for in the future. Those little talks were part of why I felt it was time to go. I realized through our sharing I still had searching and inner work to do.

"Are you sure you don't want to do the crossing with us?" Gary asked. "My brother and his wife will be here in a couple of weeks. We'll install the water purifier, do a couple of repairs, and we'll be off. I mean, it's not every day an offer like this comes along, is it?"

He was right. It isn't every day I'm invited to make an epic six-week-long sailing trip from Europe to America on a roomy Catamaran. I knew in my heart that this was not for me at this moment. My mother was terrified at the idea of me being out of reach for that amount of time. I told her that a few hundred boats would make the crossing simultaneously (it can only be done twice a year, from what I understood). She didn't like the idea. I knew something else was waiting for me; I just wasn't sure what. I thanked Gary for the exciting adventures and wished him a safe journey across that big ocean. "I hope to see you again sometime," I said.

"You better return my messages, brat, and I love you, too."

Year Two - Optional Questions for Self-Reflection: Raising Emotional Awareness

The next step is raising your awareness about how you are feeling. How do you feel when certain thoughts arise? Do you blame or shame others? Play the victim and accuse others? What do you feel physically? Does your body contract or relax? Make time for this. Invite the feelings in for a conversation. Everything is welcome. Nothing is right or wrong. You are simply inviting your awareness to expand into the field of the emotions that arise from the thoughts. When you are ready, add your findings to your journal.

Year 3

Africa

Chapter One

Turkish Delights

It all began with a family who lived in a large penthouse flat on the top floor of a seventeen-story building in downtown Izmir. Before leaving Gibraltar, I'd found them on the Workaway website and asked to join them as an au pair and help with their children. I thought the experience would give me a glimpse into their culture, and I wanted to play. Seven days came and went. I was with the children and did not see their pediatric-doctor parents once. When they finally did appear, I sat down with the mother.

"I'm sorry," I said. "I don't feel that this is what a volunteer exchange is all about. I was hoping to learn more about your culture and this area—not to become a full-time replacement for you and your husband. I've decided to leave tomorrow. I wanted to talk about it with you both, but you were never here," I said.

Her eyes grew dark and burned with anger. "What am I supposed to do now?" She screamed and slammed her fists on the table.

I sat, frozen stiff. Then, I said, "Well... I don't know, but I don't feel right about this. It's not good for me—or your children," I said.

She jumped to her feet and started pacing the room before swinging at a cup that rested on the counter, splashing its contents across the kitchen floor.

"I wrote you a letter. Here you go," I said, placing the note on the dining room table. "Perhaps I should go now." I stood up.

The children appeared and began to cry. They ran to me and threw their little arms around my legs. I knelt and hugged them. "Thank you for playing with me," I said. "It was a lot of fun. I'm sorry I have to go. My mother isn't well," I said. I didn't feel good about being dishonest; I just wanted to be sure they didn't think my departure had anything to do with them.

As I left the penthouse and stepped onto the elevator, I thought about the letter I'd written to the parents. I'd shared my observations about how the children were affected by their constant absence. I wrote about how I'd seen the eight-year-old girl taking money from my wallet and the housekeeper's purse and the night before, from the mother's bag. I shared how it appeared that she was learning that money was the most important thing to have and that it saddened me. I also shared how the three-year-old boy was so desperate for attention that he'd thrown a tantrum at every opportunity, several times during the week. When his father had returned the night before, he'd come through the door with a small gift—a toy of sorts—had patted the boy on the head and then disappeared into his bedroom. I said I felt that the parents were unaware of how their constant absence affected their children, but I didn't know how to help them see it, other than by writing this letter.

As the elevator doors closed, I bowed my head and cried. *Had I done the right thing?* I hoped that perhaps sharing my observations might help this family in the future, and I silently gave thanks for the opportunity, even though it wasn't what I'd hoped for. *What now?*

My phone chimed. It was my friend, Eric, in Los Angeles.

"Are you still in Turkey?" he asked.

"Yeah, I'm leaving Izmir today. What's up?"

"I took a Turkish guy named Salih to Burning Man. He loved it. He asked me if there was anything he could do to repay the favor. Naturally, I thought of you."

Burning Man is a festival held in the Nevada desert, and if you are keen on the arts, it's a spectacular display of creativity to behold. The mutant vehicles, costumes, performances, center camp, bicycles, playa art, and DJs will blow your mind. I'm sure he loved it. I know I did when I was there in 2004.

"That's awesome! Is he cool? I'd love to meet him."

Eric made the connection, and after a brief Skype call with Salih Saka, I was on my way to Besiktas, Turkey. From the very first day I was with Salih, he swept me off my feet—fancy meals, VIP parties, a private driver, and a beautiful home to sleep in. We even ended up on the cover of a famous Turkish magazine! Salih was a kind and gracious host. He took me all over the city and introduced me to some of its "top one percent." I felt awkward and out-of-place most times, as I was often asked, "What business are you in?" and "What assets do you hold?"

"I'm just backpacking around the world. I don't own anything. I gave it all away," I'd say. The noses on those folks turned up faster than you could say "Shazam." Assets and wealth defined who they were, and after my comment, their interest in talking with me disappeared. I watched Salih as he observed their reactions. Something was shifting inside him. A distaste appeared to be forming for his old lifestyle, and a glimmer seemed to emerge inside him of what other possibilities might be available for him on planet Earth.

One morning, Salih told me he'd be leaving for Rome for a few days. He introduced me to my driver, a couple of shopkeepers, and showed me which market I could buy food in. In the evening before his departure, he took me to a nightclub. Salih waltzed through the room and shook hands with everyone. *Who is this guy?* I took a seat at the bar, and that's when I met Emre—a bartender at the club. He moved awkwardly behind the narrow bar. His broad shoulders and sturdy frame made the already tight space appear even tighter. He leaned into the light between us, revealing his smooth forehead and kind eyes.

"You speak English. Salih told us. What would you like to drink?"

Salih told you? Didn't we just get here? How'd I miss that?

"I'll have a Coke, please. Hey, how does Salih know so many people in Turkey? It's like, everywhere we go, someone wants to shake his hand."

"Oh. Uh. Yes, everyone knows Salih. He has a radio station. He owns a couple of nightclubs, too. How do you not know who you are with?" he said with a smile.

"It's a long story. Listen, I want to do something tomorrow. Maybe you can help me?"

I described my plan to Emre about what I intended to do the following day. The smoothness of his brow was replaced with deep worry lines, and fear showed in his eyes.

"That's not a good idea. I don't think... no, you shouldn't."

I laughed. Emre didn't. *Wait, is he serious?*

"Well, I'm going. If you really think it's dangerous, you can come along and protect me."

"I don't think you should go. But I'll come because you might get into trouble."

The next day, we went to Taksim Square. The street hummed and buzzed with motion. Swarms of people carrying boxes, bags, and purses flew in and out of posh boutiques, fancy restaurants, and high-end hotels. We zig-zagged through the mob of busy bees until we found a small swatch of motionless terrain. *Here looks like a good spot.* I pulled out my sign, a four-foot by four-foot piece of bedsheet with the words "Free Hugs" written on it in different languages. I'd met with a childhood friend and her two young daughters for lunch at their home in the States before leaving on this crazy trip. I told the girls about when I was in Las Vegas in 2012 and gave away 182 free hugs on the Strip with another friend and her then four-year-old daughter. Their eyes lit up as I explained that I'd start backpacking through Europe next, and they quickly left the room. They returned with one of their old bedsheets and asked if we could make a free hugs sign that I could take with me. I was thrilled by the idea, and as Germany was the first stop, we decided to write it in German and English first.

I'd pulled the sign out several times during my travels, and people added their languages to it along the way. The sign now included German, English, Korean, Spanish, Dutch, Arabic, Italian, Turkish, Mandarin Chinese, Hindi, Farsi, Swedish, Indonesian, and French. It's said somewhere that we need four hugs a day for survival. We need eight hugs a day for maintenance, and we need twelve hugs a day for growth. What I learned is that when I hugged a hundred or more people in a day, I could ride that endorphin high for nearly a week. I loved it. I was ready to do it again.

I held up the sign in the square, and everything was going well—really well—as something was happening that hadn't happened before. Not only were people open to the free hugs, but they were also taking the sign from me and giving others free hugs too! This is awesome. I pulled out my camera and started filming. Then, two men approached me with gloomy looks. One of the men said (in English), "I'm the police. You must stop what you are doing right away."

I started laughing. I thought he was joking. The look on his face told me otherwise, and my friend asked in Turkish for their identification. They pulled out their badges—they were Turkish police. I looked at the one who had asked me to stop and said: "Are you serious? Can't I hug people? Why can't I hug people?"

"You must have permission to do this," he says.

Permission? Are you kidding me? OK. OK.

"So, where do I get permission?" I asked. He pointed to the gang of police behind a small barrier a few hundred meters away that I hadn't noticed before. "OK, I'll ask permission," I said.

Emre and I walked over to the police and explained that we were told we needed permission to give free hugs and would like to have that permission. Reluctantly, we were granted the authority, so I continued joyfully hugging people. A few minutes later, we were approached by another plain-clothes policeman.

"You cannot do this here," he said.

"We have permission."

"Yes, I know. I'm the one who permitted you. Now I'm saying that you cannot do this any longer."

"OK, OK," I said. We walked away—but only a few hundred feet. "I'd like to do it again, Emre," I said.

He shuffled his feet and stuffed his hands into his pockets. "I don't think this is a good idea," he said.

His disapproval, naturally, didn't stop me. Another policeman approached us and told us to stop. My little game of moving around and getting caught by the police happened around Taksim Square a couple more times—until the last time.

A policeman approached me from behind and grabbed my arm aggressively.

"If you don't stop this right now, I will arrest you!"

Oh shit! I understand those words! I shook free of his grip and yelled to Emre, "RUN!"

Away we ran—laughing and dancing through the sea of people as we escaped the police. Never in my life would I have imagined that someone could be arrested for spreading what we thought was simply love and kindness to fellow human beings. It took me some research and time to understand a few things I'd been ignorant about then.

First, the police were present because recently, there had been heavy protests and riots over plans to destroy the local park. The Gezi Park Protests were much more critical than I'd known then. The wave of demonstrations and civil unrest that it sparked around the country had been compared to the Worldwide Occupy Movement. It also addressed a range of concerns from the citizens, such as freedom of expression and freedom of assembly. It was considered the spark because of how the police had handled a peaceful sit-in protest at the park when the urban development plans were released. It had been pretty violent and caused ripples that some might say were the most challenging events for President Erdoğan's eleven-year term and the most significant nationwide disquiet in decades.

No wonder the police were still on edge.

Secondly, after posting the video from that day online, I received a comment about how I didn't respect Muslim culture—that I should be ashamed. I decided to research and educate myself. I mean, he was right. I didn't know about Muslim culture. What I found was interesting, and, thanks to the internet and its reach, I could see where he was (and wasn't) coming from.

I learned that the appropriateness of hugging isn't explicitly defined and that there's a range of beliefs concerning this act of closeness. Some people believe that nothing in Islam forbids hugging the other gender and that nothing in the Qur'an says anything of the sort. (I've never read these things, so I can't comment on whether this is true). I also learned that all Islam says on the matter is that we should be modest and that from this, different cultures and societies have determined what modesty means for them. In some cultures, the appropriate behavior of women out in public is to be covered and escorted by a man. I didn't wear a scarf over my head or cover my ankles and wrists. I was, however, accompanied by a man.

As a Muslim, if one chooses to hug or not hug, their basis of doing so is not because there's something in Islam that says "No" explicitly. I read that it's because of social norms, shyness, and modesty, and how they choose to express those things while obeying the prescription of decency in Islam. Either way, I decided that Taksim Square wasn't the best place to play, and that was that.

Salih returned, and we spent a week enjoying the city. Then I received an email from that wizard, Charles. He invited me to join him and a group of others on a journey into the Sahara Desert called "Zeit für Freiheit" (which translates to "Time for Freedom").

When I read the email, I felt a slight pull from my heart to go.

What the heck? Why would you go there? You have access to a personal driver, the finest foods, and great company here. The Sahara can't compare to this kind of royal treatment, can it? Yeah. I didn't think so. It seemed that my ego was not yet finished being stroked with all this luxury and attention. I sat with this push-pull of my heart and mind for a day before calling my friend Talula, in the states. She answered on the second ring, and I explained my dilemma and asked her to pull a goddess card.

"Oh, of course, Mel. Let's see what the angels have to say about this," she said.

I heard her ask whether I should accept the invitation to go into the Sahara several times as she shuffled the cards. She pulled a card and said: "Oh Mel, it's the Hanged Man."

I already knew what this card was and what it meant. The Hanged Man is suspended from the branches of the Tree of Wisdom and represents making a temporary sacrifice to achieve a greater goal. This could mean sacrificing time, energy, comfort, resources, old habits, or an outdated attitude. He is gaining a new perspective by hanging upside down, and he looks at the world from a different vantage point. The Hanged Man is suspending his regular routines to focus his energy. His face is calm. Although he is not "comfortable," he is not suffering. He knows that sacrificing his usual stance of keeping his feet firmly on the ground will free his mind to consider new solutions.

The appearance of the Hanged Man is often a good sign—if one is willing to be courageous and make the proper sacrifice, that is. He represents looking at one's life through the lens of transcendent wisdom. Viewing one's experience from a different point of view leads to breakthroughs.

"I have to go into the Sahara, don't I?"

"It seems so."

Damn.

I replied to the email and said that I'd accept the offer and would see them in a couple of days. I was excited but also apprehensive. *Was this the right choice? I mean, Jesus wandered the desert, and it was good, right?* I wasn't so sure....

Chapter Two

The Sahara Desert

Iarrived at the hotel in Germany three days before the adventure began. We prepared a monster truck with fresh fruits and veggies and bins full of rice, quinoa, wheat, and other goodies. We drove from Germany into Italy and onto a ferry at Genoa that took us across the Mediterranean Sea into Tunisia. I slept almost the entire two and a half days—and woke up in Africa. During the drive south from the capital, Tunis, to the edge of the desert, I asked Charles about the Sahara's significance on this "Time for Freedom" journey.

"Think of it like therapy times a thousand. The Sahara is a place where old patterns and stories playing in your system can be seen and integrated quickly, without much else," he said.

Really? OK, that's interesting. I wonder what the Sahara will show me....

The southern part of Tunisia lacked any actual color (other than beige-brown). Its plainness was unappealing. After an eight-hour drive, we parked in front of a tour office called "Sahara Event." I jumped from the truck in knee-length shorts and my 'Miss Lucky' t-shirt, eager to explore this boring sand-colored town. Slipping into my headphones, flag poi by my side, I started walking toward the town center (which is called a souq). The village was dusty. Dry. Weathered, ancient-looking men peered from open doorways with curiosity. I turned on the music, and the sweet melody of Lindsey Stirling's violin put my body into motion. I danced with the flags for the four minutes into town. I hadn't seen one woman. There were many men gathered at the plentiful "coffee and shisha" cafes. There were four cafes on this short street—you could walk from one end to the other in just a few minutes. *That's odd. Where are all the women? Have they all gone to some kind of women-only party? I'd like to meet them!*

I returned from my mini-tour and asked Charles, "Where are all the women?"

"Oh? Don't you know? They're at home minding the children and cooking and cleaning as expected," he said.

"Are you freaking kidding me?! That's a joke, right?"

Stupid, naive girl.

Charles told me that women don't have the same rights as men here. They must cover their bodies head to toe, even in 100-degree Fahrenheit heat. When they do get to leave the house, they must be escorted by a brother, father, or husband. There were some exceptions, but their families ostracized many who demanded their freedom. Shunned women were considered unworthy of marriage and were treated like aliens—which was worse.

No freaking way. I wouldn't last two days. How awful that must feel. And the rules—how a woman must behave, what she can and cannot do? How she must dress and present herself to the world? Was a woman's existence not worth sharing openly? This is nuts.

We loaded some supplies—tents, sleeping bags, and whatnot from the office and picked up Yasmine (the only Tunisian woman I'd met so far) before Charles said it was time to go shopping at the souq for fresh local fruits and vegetables. I purchased some bananas from a fly-covered bin and turned toward a moaning sound behind me. That's when I saw him. His wide eyes and slow shift-

117

ing from foot to foot caught my attention. I walked closer. Something was wrong. This young, majestic-looking dromedary (like a camel but with one hump, not two) had fear in his eyes. A sense of panic came over me. *Why are you so afraid, little guy?*

A rope around his foot secured him to a concrete slab. Ten feet behind him was a dromedary's head, hanging on a steel spike. Next to it, its legs swayed in the wind. I froze. I was sickened and stunned. I couldn't move. I stared at the baby dromedary and understood its panic—I was feeling it, too. After what seemed like an eternity, I fled, clutching my bananas. That image haunted me. It replayed in my mind over and over again. The shifting of the dromedary's feet, the darkness in his eyes, and the remains—*was it his mother?* —swinging in the wind behind him.

We loaded the truck with our fruits and vegetables, and Charles invited us to purchase some Sahara-appropriate clothing (brightly colored turbans and loose-fitting shirts and pants). In one of the boutique shops, I met a second Tunisian woman. Her name was Jihene; she spoke excellent French, Arabic, German, and English.

I asked her about the culture here concerning the women, and she shook her head and said, "Yes, it's true. Women here are not treated the same. They work harder, make less, and do not have the same rights. It is unfortunate. I work in this shop twelve hours a day, seven days a week, and make only 400 dinar per month." That's only $130... I felt ignorant. Conflicted.

"Have you ever been in the Sahara?"

"Oh no. Women are forbidden to go there. The devil lives in the desert."

Does the devil live in the desert?

"Thanks for helping me with the clothes—"

A Tunisian man leading three dromedaries met us at the edge of the village. The twelve of us poured out of the truck in our fresh, new, unscented, loose-fitting Sahara dress. The dromedaries were loaded with what we learned from Mabrouk (the lead) was food and water for them and his supplies. Makeshift seats were strapped to the one large hump on their back to carry a passenger should it be wanted or needed. He left the dromedaries with us to admire and joined Charles at the front of the truck. We were in awe at how large they were. Standing at what seemed to be ten feet tall, they towered over us and shuffled their tied front feet from side to side. When Mabrouk and Charles joined the group, I asked Mabrouk why the creatures had their front feet tied.

"So they don't go too far," he said. "If I let them free, we don't find them later."

He picked up the rope tied to the first dromedary. The other two were attached to the first with longer cords and quickly followed suit, and they walked into the desert.

The vast emptiness of the desert shocked my senses: the brightness, the absence of smell, the silence. I plunged my hands into the sand to get a feel for where I was.

So it begins.

Charles gathered the group and offered everyone handheld compasses and GPS navigation devices. "For those who have a GPS, they are already set to the meeting point. The compass direction is 112 degrees for eight kilometers," he said. "You can also ride a dromedary if you need or want to. Mabrouk is here to help."

Eight kilometers? Ummmm, OK.

The truck rolled away, and the group splintered off, each person taking their own path across the sand. The landscape didn't change. It was like walking through the pores of the skin of the earth, up and down, up and down. Small bushes sprouted up in the sand like tiny hairs. In the distance, the others looked like small insects rising and disappearing from view as they trekked along. Halfway through that first journey, I stopped in the only piece of shade I'd found in two hours. I dropped my head into it. *I feel heavy....*

The burden of sadness became more than I could bear. Harley's death and the death of my marriage hit me at the same time. My body contracted—pulled in on itself as if to protect against what was coming. But it didn't last long. Just a teaser. A trailer for the premiere.

The group met, arriving at different times, eight kilometers later. Everyone looked rough. Quietly, everyone set up their sleeping places—some chose to sleep under the stars in just a sleeping bag, while others (myself included) erected small two-person tents. Then everyone gathered at the fire to enjoy the food Charles had prepared. The desert grows surprisingly cold at night, and we huddled around the fire and ate in silence. I was lost in my thoughts and, after dinner, I snuck quietly into my tent, wrapped myself up in two blankets, and fell asleep.

For the following week, we walked our own paths across the hot sand—it slipped into my Teva sandals and burned my feet constantly. Ripples of heat radiated from the ground as far as the eye could see, giving the desert an eerie underwater effect. The turban kept the sun off my face and the sweat out of my eyes, but nothing could keep the sand out of my mouth. The constant grinding of grit in my teeth reminded me of where I was, even while I slept.

Each day as I walked, to sustain my process, my thirst, and my hunger, in my small backpack I carried a pen and journal, one liter of water, a handful of nuts, and a couple of pieces of fruit. I walked alone—struggling during the day, resting at night. The desert was dry and unforgiving and appeared never to end. Eight days in, after yet another arduous hike through the heat, Charles told us we'd be camping in solitude for four days. We huddled around the fire while Mabrouk made dinner, and Charles explained what was to come.

"You can set up at least 400 meters from the truck, but not beyond those dunes two kilometers in the distance," he said. "It's suggested that you fast, and there are bottles of Spirulina and Chlorella in the truck. There is also fruit, bread, and nuts if you need them. I suggest you take at least four liters of water with you. There are also teapots, lighters, and miso soup you can take."

The group appeared pleased with the news that there would be a break from walking each day and were eager to be still. I, on the other hand, wasn't looking forward to it. *Fasting? Eating only algae and water? How will I survive?*

"And if we get hungry, we can come to the truck for food, right?" I asked.

"Yes, you can come to the truck if you need anything at all." He said. "We will have breakfast together in the morning, and then you each can find your place for the next four days."

During those four days, I did nothing but cry. Hard. It lasted for hours until I was exhausted and fell asleep, only to wake up and start sobbing again. On the fourth day, I woke up without tears. I'd finally poured all the repressed sadness out of my system. But in reality, I hadn't poured anything out—it had been pulled out of me.

I gathered my things slowly and made my way back to the truck. My body was weak, and I dragged the large sack that held my gear (blankets, teapot, small pack with journal and pens, and minimal trash) behind me. I returned for my tent, which folded up into a disk, and double-checked that I hadn't left anything behind. Back at the truck, we waited until everyone from the group had arrived before sitting down together to eat. After three days of fasting, when the covers were pulled from the resting bowls to reveal an abundance of fruits, vegetables, bread, and pots of soups and teas, I was surprised to find that I wasn't hungry. I stared at the food, and my body didn't react. So, to ease back into eating again, I had a bowl of soup and a tea. We shared stories of what the time had revealed to each of us and took time to rest before packing the truck and moving on. That evening, we all rode in the truck to a new destination about thirty kilometers away and camped as usual in the desert.

The following day, I walked naked and alone. I've never had any issues with sunburn, and the emptiness of the desert had me convinced that I wouldn't be seen. My backpack cradled my journal, pen, water, and clothes, and the sun kissed every exposed bit of skin. All of a sudden, I felt a presence behind me. I turned, worried, but saw nothing. But there was something. Or someone. Yeah, it was someone. I felt their presence. Right there. Standing behind me. For a moment, I thought my mind was playing tricks. I turned around and looked over the endless miles of dunes. I continued to walk, and I felt that same presence walking beside me. I turned toward it. *Is it you? Harley?* I thought it was her. My now-dead best friend. I felt her presence walking with me.

I crumbled to the hot sand and began to sob. After purging even more sadness, I gathered myself up. I was alone again. I continued walking toward the group meeting point, but couldn't shake what I'd experienced. When I joined the group, I told the wizard what I'd felt.

"Yes, it seems that your friend is stuck between the worlds," Charles said.

"Stuck between the worlds? Why would she be stuck between the worlds?"

"Sometimes when things are unresolved before death, the soul must sort them out before being able to pass on."

That evening, as the sun was setting, I lay on a dune and looked into the horizon. I saw Harley's face, and she was pissed off—I mean, really pissed off. I couldn't remember one time in our twenty-four-year friendship when I'd ever seen her that angry. *Am I really seeing this?* I couldn't figure out why she was upset and asked her. I fell asleep that night without an answer. The next morning marked the end of a two-week journey that crossed at least a hundred kilometers. We packed all of our gear into the truck and drove back into the village. We needed to re-up on supplies and prepare for another small group to arrive— and then do it all over again. On our second day in the village, as I sipped tea at a men-only café a few doors down from the office, I saw a woman watching me from a kitchen window in the only restaurant on the street. When I waved and smiled at her, she ducked from the window and disappeared. Foreigners had special permissions here, although not all agreed with these exceptions. This particular tea shop owner, Ramsey, didn't care what others thought and welcomed me openly.

"The woman is an essential part of our community," he said. "When will these men realize that without her, we are nothing? That if we continue in this way, we will remain a third world country?"

I couldn't agree more. It was obvious who disagreed. Some men argued with him at the front door next to where I sat. They pointed at me and screamed in his face. His response surprised me. He threw them out! *What a brave man. Standing up for his beliefs—risking his business in the name of fairness and equality.*

I wanted to meet some of the women here. I hoped I'd get the opportunity. Yasmine said she'd take me to some of her friends' homes so I'd get that chance, and she delivered. I was curious about how they felt being here. I met eight different women, and whereas some of them were completely accepting of their circumstances, there seemed to be an equal number who were definitely not OK with it. Many of them cradled a smartphone in one hand while waving the other hand while they talked. *Did their access to the internet make them more aware of the restrictions in the women's lifestyle in Tunisia?*

I returned a couple of days later to the Sahara Event office. I sat outside at a table and listened to music openly, wrote on my computer, and sang and played with my flag poi in the entranceway. There were people decorating the town with festive banners. When I asked what the decorations were for, I found out that the town center was to be the finish line for a race. Several people appeared with TV cameras. One man in particular caught my attention. He was young, handsome, and dressed like a movie star. I had to meet him.

"Hey! What's going on?" I asked.

His thick black hair shimmered in the breeze as he turned to me and smiled.

"The runners are almost here, and we will film their finish," he said.

He joined me for a cup of tea. His name was Karim, and he was from the north of Tunisia. We had a similar, familiar energy. "When is your birthday?" I asked.

"June 21," he said.

"That's it! We have the same birthday! That's why you seem so familiar."

As we both had work to do, we exchanged numbers and went back to it.

A day passed, and Yasmine arrived, saying that some women would like to meet with me.

"Wonderful! Let's get some tea and cookies and have some girl time," I said, excited. I had no idea what this seemingly simple request would become. The following morning, six women met us in the Sahara Event office and shared how they wanted the same level of freedom I seemed to have. They dreamed of singing out loud, dancing in the streets, and choosing a partner versus having their family decide for them whom they'd marry. Being born in America, I had no idea what to say to these women. What I did have, though, were a couple of GoPro cameras and the ability to edit digital footage. We met twice more, created a storyboard for a video, and talked about shooting it when I returned from the Sahara.

I contacted Talula, my oracle in America, who had been good friends with Harley for many years. I told her what I'd felt and seen during my previous trip into the desert and how I didn't understand why Harley was so angry. Talula's voice dropped to a whisper. "Oh Mel, I know... You don't know."

I was confused. "Know what? What don't I know?"

She took a deep breath before telling me a secret that Harley had kept from me during our entire friendship. It broke my heart—even more than when she'd left her body a little over a year ago. Her words hit me so hard I thought I might lose consciousness. My heart sank, my head spun. So many emotions hit me at the same time, I wasn't sure what to say next.

"Mel?" Talula said. "Are you OK? Do you think that's why you saw her so angry?"

Was it? Had she not processed that trauma? Had it killed her in the form of cervical cancer? Is she stuck between the worlds?

I thanked Talula and hung up. I felt nauseous and retreated to the bathroom. I cried for Harley. The intensity of sadness was followed by a wave of genuine, wild anger.

I sat with this intense mix of emotions. Then I heard our desert guide, Charles the wizard, calling for me. It was time to go. I went to the truck where the new guests and team waited and remained silent during the ride into the Sahara as I processed what Talula had told me—and what I was feeling.

The following day, I went to Charles and told him what I'd learned the previous day, how it affected me and how I felt helpless for my friend.

"She's still here with you. You can still be here for her now. Talk to her; certainly, she will hear you," he said.

I did just that. After about ten days of walking and processing more pain, we entered the three days of solitude. During the first night, I searched the sky for Harley. I didn't see her as I had before, but I felt her. I raised my hands to the sky—tears burned my cheeks.

"Harley, my love, we've shared so many things over the years. I'm sorry I didn't know how to help you when you were dying. I see you now. I can feel you. I know what happened to you when you were a child. I was mad that you hid this from me, especially when I remember all the times you were there for me. Why did you hide your hell from me?"

I choked on the words.

"I'm here with you now in an attempt to sort through my shitshow. Let this be the last thing we do together before I see you on the other side. Please, let me be there with you. You were there for me through so much during our friendship. Let me support you in passing over."

I held my hands out toward the stars.

Tears flowed down my cheeks, vanishing into the soft sand. I'm not sure how much time passed. I fell asleep and woke up just before sunrise. I called out, "Harley? Are you there? Hello?" Nothing. I couldn't see or feel her. I cried again as the sun broke above the horizon. I wanted to see her again, talk to her, laugh, dance, and play together. But I'd promised to support her in passing and to let her go. As sad as I felt, I also felt good—like I could finally help her somehow. It had helped me.

I opened my journal and a small yellow piece of paper slipped out and fell into my lap. It was from Talula. She had given it to me before I left the States. Lifting the note, I read it out loud. "Remember what Harley said to you? She said 'Rite' (as in ritual), 'Right' (as in make things right) and 'Write'."

I held the note to my heart and bowed my head.

"Yes, I will Harley. I will."

That morning felt light and airy, but after a sunrise meditation, I was consumed yet again. But this time, it was anger. Red hot. I screamed into my pillow and slammed my fists into the sand. My body twisted tightly, then relaxed. I sighed deeply. In the shadows of the desert dunes, I was dancing with the shadows of my anger.

This experience was just as exhausting as the three days of sadness I'd experienced on the previous trip. It ended on the fourth day. After three days of fasting and purging, I returned to the group. I felt lighter but sensed that I'd just opened Pandora's box. *Would there be more of that coming in the future? Ugghhhh, I hope not.*

In the evening, we gathered around a fire and shared our experiences from the past few days. I shared how Charles had asked me, several months ago when I first arrived at the hotel, if I was ready to meet the angry little girl within me and if I was prepared to let that anger out before it did some real damage to my system. I'd had no idea what he was saying. I told the group about the anger that had bubbled up when I'd been alone in the desert and how I'd released it. As I spoke, I felt myself getting upset—but to a lesser degree. At least I had removed some of my anger.

After the sharing was complete, we ate a huge meal, and Charles surprised us with banana ice cream. Yeah. This wizard was somehow able to make ice cream in the desert! It turned out there was a small fridge/freezer in the truck, and the ice cream was just frozen bananas and rice milk Charles had kept hidden until then. It wasn't "magic," but still, it surprised us. It was a wonderfully refreshing treat after days spent in both extreme (external and internal) heat.

We must have looked like a small army of leaf-cutter ants to the birds that flew above us. Our brightly colored turban tails waved in the wind as we covered several kilometers of ever-changing scenery over the next few days. On occasion, the dunes would open to rocky, flat terrain with dead or dying bushes that housed lizards, beetles, snakes, and scorpions. The walking became easier but more dangerous as some of those creatures were deadly. At the end of the last day, I saw what I thought was a mirage in the distance. The image rippled in the heat: a collection of green palm trees surrounding a pool of water. I recalled old cartoons in which characters imagined an oasis in the desert and ran toward it, only to dive into... more sand.

In the distance, I saw a few jeeps appear between the trees surrounding the oasis and continue into the dunes. It is real! I leaped up and ran through the hot sand toward the trees. I arrived at "Ksar Ghilane," a well-known oasis and campsite for trekkers. I was delighted to see a pool of water there—and we were allowed to swim in it.

The rest of the group arrived as I changed into a swimsuit in our waiting truck. My skin was dry and wrinkled, aged because of the dry desert air. I was eager to quench its thirst. I walked into what I hoped was the fountain of youth. It was warmer than I'd expected or imagined it would be. Everyone shared my relief—the group plunged into the water and celebrated surviving the desert heat. After floating for about half an hour, I left the pool. The deep wrinkles I'd seen in my arms were now smooth and looked even better than before I entered the desert. *It is a fountain of youth!*

I joined the group at a long table that had been prepared with sweet and savory delights from the truck. We shared the abundant meal, laughed and talked, then sat in silence together one more time. I'd grown closer to this small group in two weeks than I had in some of the friendships I've had for years.

There was something special about sharing and processing pain together—about being vulnerable and naked in a way that brought us close. Not naked in a literal sense, but metaphorically. Unapologetically, we let the cloaked layers of our souls—our fears, most naïve hopes, and deepest regrets—fall away. I felt a genuine authenticity and connection in this journey, and again, I was happy to be a part of it. I was learning how to be with my emotions.

When we returned to the village, Charles told me he'd be going to Germany for six weeks and that I could stay here in Tunisia. I was thinking about this when Yasmine said, "Yes, sister! You can stay with my family. Yes! Please stay!"

I didn't care much for this place, primarily because of how they treated women, but Yasmine reassured me that foreigners were different and that her family would take great care of me. I agreed to stay and help the two Tunisians who ran the Sahara Event office to understand how to work with foreign tourists and grow the business. It was the least I could do in exchange for the opportunity

I'd had to free myself from decades of repressed emotions, thanks to the desert tours.

I wished Charles a safe and joyful trip, and Yasmine and I made our way the short distance from the office to her parent's house, where she helped me prepare a room for my stay.

Chapter Three

Support for the Goddesses

My time in Tunisia was not at all what I expected. First, Yasmine's family was unusual for this part of town. There were three sisters, each of whom had chosen unique paths for themselves. The youngest, Farah, was married and had a beautiful daughter. She and her husband ran a clothing store in the center of town and seemed happy. We had long conversations about Southern Tunisia's culture, and Farah got excited when she talked about the potential opportunities Muslim women might have in the future. She believed that women were as important as men and deserved the same rights. She got angry when she saw them being mistreated.

The middle daughter, Meriem, was charming and timid. She shared Farah's feeling that women's power should be respected, not feared, but wasn't very vocal about it. The oldest daughter, Yasmine, was like a unicorn here. She traveled with us into the desert for weeks to support Charles on the tours. Occasionally, she walked through town with her hair uncovered and carried herself with a proud, upright posture. She had big dreams of living in Europe and wasn't afraid of what the townspeople whispered about her behind her back. I admired her; her attitudes and behavior were uncommon, bold, and brave.

Their parents were wonderful people; they accepted me into their family. I learned how their daughters' unorthodox ways of being had brought much stress from the community upon them over the years, but their father said, "What am I to do? They're my daughters, and I want their happiness." I admired him. Yasmine's father was kind and loving, unlike some of the fathers here, who forbade their daughters from deviating from the norm and who, on occasion, beat those lessons into their flesh. I heard many stories about women being abused for following their hearts and instincts and appreciated that the family I was lucky enough to stay with wasn't this way.

One day, two of the sisters invited me to the Hammam. In Tunisia, a Hammam is a traditional public bathhouse—a place to bathe, relax, and socialize. When we got there, a woman told us that it was jam-packed inside. Meriem said, "Oh no, I don't like it when it's busy like this. I'll wait out here."

"Are you sure?" I asked.

"Yes, sister. Go on. It'll be fine for you."

The primary languages spoken in Tunisia are French and Arabic, and after Yasmine and I entered and disrobed, a woman started screaming at me in French. Yasmine just laughed. I was clueless about the woman's problem, and Yasmine couldn't stop laughing long enough to translate for me. I was standing there almost nude—except for my sandals and G-string panties—as the woman continued to yell. Finally, Yasmine caught her breath and explained that the woman had a problem with my thong underwear. No one here (especially this woman), she said, wants to see my butt. Yasmine had a solution—she brought me not one but two pairs of regular panties to choose from.

Phew! Saved!

Next, we entered the "hammam," a series of dark, steamy rooms. The main room was packed with women; splashing water echoed all over the place. I followed Yasmine to the water trough, and she handed me buckets-full to throw around. After filling them with way-too-hot water, we moved into another room where she pointed to a free space and told me to sit. She made me put my feet in one of the buckets before she left to get... even more water.

When she returned, she gave me some soap and a shower puff and instructed me to scrub myself. We spent about ten minutes in this super-hot, super-steamy room before she disappeared. I decided to meditate. Then I heard a tiny voice close to me ask—"Are you meditating?"

I opened my eyes and saw a curious girl leaning in close to me. "Yes."

"Mmmmm..."

"Do you meditate?"

"I don't know how."

After a quick conversation about meditation, she left, and I went back into my trance. About five minutes later, I heard, "Pssst! Psssst psst!" I opened my eyes. I was the only one left in the room, and the same woman who'd yelled at me earlier about my G-string pointed at me, then at the door.

Time to go, I guess...

I searched for Yasmine. Finally, I found her near some stalls, and she asked if I'd like a massage.

Hell yeah, I would!

She pointed to a burly woman who fired off rapid French at me. Yasmine started laughing as I looked at the woman, utterly confused. Yasmine explained to her that I didn't understand French. The woman let out a hearty laugh and gestured that I should sit in front of her. Now, this is where it got interesting.

Yasmine left me again, and this woman started scrubbing my hands and arms with brute force and a semi-steel glove. Then again, she said something in French. I looked at her like a dog cocking its head. *Are you going to give me something?* She laughed, spun me around, pushed my face into her crotch, and continued with the steel glove scrub down. She scrubbed away all the dry-desert-damage until I was squeaky-clean and fresh... though I swear she took an extra layer of skin off just for good measure. She finally said something to me that I understood as she pointed to all the crud she had scaled off of me. "For you— 10 dinar!" Then she flipped me over and continued the assault with a strength reserved for gladiators.

Finally, it was over. She covered me in some kind of mud, and the same girl I spoke to about meditation appeared and explained what was next.

"Go in there and wait five minutes. Then wash off."

When I was done, I retreated into the hallway, where Meriem waited with my clothes. "What do you think, sister?" she asked.

"Well, that was by far the most unusual massage I've ever had. I don't know that I'd call it that. It was definitely different. How do I look?" I asked.

"You look beautiful, sister. Would you like a facial?" She asked.

"Ummmm, OK, sure."

We entered a small room with a single chair and a glassless window that looked out into a waiting room. Several chairs lined the wall, but only one woman sat there. Another woman entered the room behind me, rolling a golf-ball-sized gob of what appeared to be ear wax between her fingers.

"Just relax, sister. You will look beautiful." Meriem said with a giggle.

Oh no. What have they gotten me into now?

The woman approached and smudged the waxy substance from hand to hand before stretching it into a snaky roll. *Ewwww... what is she going to do with that? What is that, anyway?*

She smashed the snake across the side of my face and, with a quick flip of her wrist, ripped it off. I screamed. She laughed. Then she did it again. *This is a facial? Why do these beauty treatments hurt so much? This isn't at all what I was expecting....*

More women gathered in the waiting room to listen to my tortured screams and seemed to enjoy it—their laughter grew louder each time I cried out. *Is this normal?* When it was over, I peeled my fingernails from the arms of the chair and looked in the mirror. My face was bright red, with sunflower bursts of broken blood vessels on my cheeks.

"You look beautiful, sister," said one of the women.

"Yes, very nice," said another.

I wasn't so sure. My face felt like it belonged to someone else. I didn't recognize the strawberry shortcake reflection in the mirror, but I paid the 10 dinars (about $3.50). As we left, I thanked the women. On the way home, my friends asked about "Hammams" in other countries.

"Well, this is the first time I've ever been to a 'Hammam,' but from my experience with massages, they're mostly relaxing and gentle, and I've always managed to keep my skin when I've had one. And facials are usually done with mud or creams, not... what was that, anyway?" I said.

"It's sugar wax," Meriem replied.

"Right. Sugar wax. Well, it hurt. All of it. But it was fun because it was different. And I like different. I think that's what makes life so interesting. All the possibilities."

"You look beautiful, sister. Beautiful," Yasmine said.

I continued over the following weeks to help the office team understand how to work with foreign visitors for tours, and the women slowly reappeared to work on the video script. Even the shy woman from the Hammam who asked about meditation joined our growing group. At the end of the first week, it seemed that we were ready to shoot the video. We intended to submit it to Madonna's "Art for Freedom" campaign. Her project was a global initiative encouraging creative expression to bring awareness to human rights violations. It was designed to fuel free speech and address, protest, and respond to persecution worldwide. We all loved the idea and wanted to contribute.

We hoped our video would be selected and featured on Madonna's BitTorrent site so these beautiful women would know that the world was finally paying attention to their voices. Getting the women into the desert to shoot the video would be another challenge as they're forbidden to go there. They're forbidden to play in their own back yard. I had a hard time accepting this.

We enlisted the help of two trusted men to pick the women up in taxis with dark-tinted windows. Another two men rode on horseback around where we'd be filming to keep anyone from viewing our forbidden act or to warn us to leave if necessary. We were ready to go.

We arrived at a destination where we were least likely to be discovered or disturbed. Five Tunisian women and two French women joined me on a walk into the sand. We spent the next four hours shooting as the men on horses circled the perimeter as security lookouts. When we finished, we jumped into the same taxis that had brought us there. The women were returned to places of their choosing that they felt were safe and where they wouldn't be seen disembarking from a cab.

For the next three days, I edited the video footage and assisted the foreign visitors that came into the office. I'm an amateur video editor with basic skills, but did my best to help these women out. On the fourth day, I invited all the women from our group to view the final edit before submitting it to Madonna. As we watched, some of the women cried, some screamed in pure joy, while a couple of others had a genuine fear of posting the video online. "Sister," they said, "What if the people here see it? I mean, this would be bad for us, sister."

"It'll be online, but the odds of the village people here seeing it are super low. This all started with the desire to have your voices heard, right? I get that you're scared. Do you not want to submit it to Madonna?"

Somewhat reluctantly, the women agreed to send it.

It wasn't long before we received a reply. Our video had been selected and would be featured on January 2, 2014—right in alignment with the New Moon. The women wanted to celebrate. To shout from the rooftops, "Can you SEE ME NOW?" But they weren't ready for that. And I wasn't prepared to lead them into the revolution their hearts were so desperate for.

A couple of days later, as I closed the office, I heard that voice again in my head: "Leave now." It was just like the time in San Francisco. I locked the doors to the office and went straight to Yasmine's house. "Yasmine," I said, "can you please call for a car to take me to Tunis?"

"Now, sister? It's eight in the night. You want it now, sister? Not in the morning? It will arrive in Tunis very early—like 5:30 in the morning."

"I'm getting a signal that I need to leave right away. I think this voice protects me, and I have to listen to it. I don't know what's coming, but I shouldn't be here for it."

"OK, sister. I will call for you. Ten minutes. It will be here, sister. Prepare your things."

That's precisely what I did. I went into the house, greeted the family, then made my way to my room and packed a small backpack. I returned to the front gate as the van pulled up. I hugged Yasmine and thanked her and was on my way.

During the long ride north, I thought quite a bit about that voice in my head and where it was coming from. I also thought about the women of the Sahara and their desire for freedom. On that trip, I realized that even though I was born in a country that provides more freedom to women, although it is still unequal, here I was in Tunisia, on a "Time for Freedom" tour. I mulled this over in my mind as the miles separated me from that small village. *What does freedom mean?* I was free to choose more than these women were for sure, but inside I didn't feel free.

I called my new friend Karim and arranged for him to meet me, then continued to mull over women's rights… not just in Tunisia, but everywhere.

I saw how many of my issues were related to stories and situations created from interactions with men. *Is this why the women here are not afforded those same choices? So that the possibility of them suffering at the hands of men in other ways wasn't possible?* This topic of women and freedom repeatedly played until I arrived at 5:30 a.m. at the drop spot where my friend Karim was supposed to meet me. He'd said for sure he'd meet me, but I couldn't find him. I waited for about half an hour and then decided to take a taxi to his house. During that ride, the driver pulled out some pepper spray and pretended to spray it at me. I'm not sure why he did it—was it because I was an American? A woman traveling alone? Was he just playing around? It wasn't clear. I told him to stop the car. I grabbed my bag, threw some dinar through the open window, and walked away in the direction of Karim's house.

Thirty minutes later, I arrived and rang the doorbell. I left the dates I'd brought as a gift for his parents and walked away. I was halfway down the street when he came out the door and yelled, "Melissa, stop!" I was pissed.

As Karim ran down the road to catch up with me, I turned away, walked toward the beach, and sat in the sand.

Karim sat down beside me. He was still half asleep and quite worried.

My anger flew out of me like a tornado. I screamed at him: "You didn't meet me, and you'd promised. A taxi driver threatened me with pepper spray! I had to walk to your house, in a foreign land where it's standard for men to treat women with disrespect. I'm pissed about having to fight, internally and externally, for freedom and equality."

Karim sat there, listening as the barrage continued for a good five minutes. When I was done, he apologized. "Please," he said. "I'm sorry. Come back to the house, let's have breakfast, and relax. I'm sorry I wasn't there. I fell asleep. I didn't leave you there on purpose."

Begrudgingly, I agreed.

While we were having breakfast with his family, my telephone rang. It was Yasmine. "Sister," she said, "The police are here, looking for you. They want to speak to you. Sister, were you talking about Jesus? This is very bad. You must not talk about Jesus. Only Mohammed, sister. No Jesus."

What the heck?

"Yasmine, I never spoke to anyone about Jesus. Why would I?" In an instant, the reason the voice had told me to leave the night before became crystal clear. The authorities were coming with a severe charge and wanted to take me in for questioning. Apparently, someone was on to the meetings and didn't like it—enough to send the police after me with a false charge. I was being protected yet again. *Where are these warnings coming from?* "Yasmine, you can tell them I did no such thing—that I'm gone. I won't be returning for their questioning. This charge is absurd." I thanked her for the call and said goodbye.

I told Karim and his family about the conversation. His mother shook her head and said, "Yes, this is very bad to speak about Jesus here. These people, especially in the south, are close-minded and only pray to Mohammed. They see other possibilities as a threat to their way of life. Not all are this way, but many have this belief."

I told her about the women in the village and the meetings and making the video.

"It most certainly was a man who felt threatened. You need to be careful," she said.

Am I in danger? Is this a bad idea? I am protected. I trust that I'm protected.

"I am happy to hear that the women there want a revolution—that they want their freedom. It has been too long," Karim's mother said.

I smiled. We finished our breakfast in silence.

I spent a few more days in Tunis with Karim and noticed that the north of Tunisia was much different from the south. I saw women out and about, and the locals seemed more tolerant of tourists in general. Yasmine told me the heat was off at the end of that week, and it was safe to return. I thanked Karim and his family for having me as their guest and made my way back down south.

Chapter Four

Magic and Mayhem

Once I returned to the south, we'd begin to have secret meetings again, and more women joined. The more we met, the more I realized I was becoming frustrated. Their pace of growth was painfully slow, and I couldn't get why they didn't understand me when I suggested they take the next step. It wasn't until Charles returned several weeks later, and I explained my frustration to him, that it all started to make some sense. Calmly, as usual, he asked, "Are you speaking to them at their level? Because it sounds to me that you're not. Can you see that you're at a level eight, and they're at a level one? And some are even at zero? And perhaps in the negative? Do you notice how you're speaking to them as if they have a level four understanding? Perhaps this is why you're finding yourself so frustrated, and they're not growing as quickly as they could."

I sat with his words and reflected on all the meetings we'd had while he'd been away. He was right. "Yeah, it seems it is this way. I'm not sure how to speak to them at level one, and I have no idea what the negative levels look like. I don't think I've ever known those levels in my life. I have what they seem to be seeking. I mean, I was born into it, so how do I speak at a level one? Or below, for that matter?"

He smiled. "The first step in understanding what a level one looks like," he said, is to ask questions and listen, without trying to do or change anything at all."

Uggghhhh. Another one of my weak points. I was acutely aware that I wasn't the best listener, so this certainly would be an excellent exercise. *Didn't I say I wanted to be a better listener? Wasn't it in my travel intentions?*

Charles supported me as I practiced leveling up my acknowledgment of where the women were at. My frustration faded, and the women seemed to be growing faster in their understanding. One day, a few of us were sitting in the office enjoying tea and cookies when one of the women's husbands appeared. He screamed, ran to his wife, pushed back her headscarf, grabbed her violently by the hair, and pulled her toward the door. Charles was there and knew this man. "Is this treatment really necessary?" he said. "The women are here to...."

"This is *my wife!* You don't tell me what I can and cannot do with her!" He dragged her out the door.

Charles followed the man, trying to calm him down.

The women sat for a moment in shock. Fear rippled through the meeting—they gathered their things and bolted.

Head in my hands, I cried. For what had just happened. For the memory of Dad throwing Mom around. For all women whom men mistreat.

Charles returned and sat beside me in silence. When I was done, I walked outside, put on my headphones, played poi, and sang as loud as I could.

The only way to overcome this imbalance, this madness, is to become so free that nothing can ever get in the way and stop it.

When I finished expressing what freedom looked like to me, I returned to the office. Charles asked if I'd ever heard of a growing global women's movement called

One Billion Rising. I hadn't, so he showed me a video. There was to be an event in Tunis around the time the last Sahara tour would finish.

"Would you like to check it out?" he asked. "I think it could be interesting."

His invitation couldn't have come at a better time.

"Absolutely, yes," I said, still angry about this country's blatant disrespect for women.

I wanted to learn about and support women's rights, not just in Tunisia, but in general. I wondered when the goddess had been dismissed from her nurturing role and why this had happened in the first place... I was looking forward to attending the event. But first? We were to go into the Sahara one more time before heading back to Germany, and I asked Charles if I could invite Karim to join us.

"Yes, this feels fine," Charles said, "but we're leaving today. You could take the KTM motorbike and meet us near Ksar Ghilane in a few days after he arrives if you like."

Yes! I saw the group off, then contacted Karim in Tunis. I waited in the village for a couple of days for him to arrive. The morning we were to set off together on the motorbike, Charles called. "So? Are you ready to go?" he asked.

"We're getting there. We should arrive in Ksar Ghilane around noon."

"So so so... Remember to check the tires on the bike before you go, and we're out of dates."

"Yeah, OK, I will," I said and hung up. Karim and I finished preparing the one backpack we'd carry with us, and as we approached the bike, I kicked haphazardly at the tires. I wasn't really sure what to look for—did they need more air? Less air? "They're fine," I said, eager to get on the road. "Hey, Karim, since this bike is super tall, when we stop, I'll need you to put your feet down first because your legs are longer. If you don't, we'll fall over. It's important."

He nodded and climbed on the back. He kept his feet planted on the ground as I jumped on and started the bike. I steadied myself against the outer wall at Yasmine's house. "Put your feet on the pegs." I released the clutch, pulled the throttle back, and we rolled down the road towards Ksar Ghilane.

Outside the village, we pulled into a gas station to fuel up. The next hundred and sixty kilometers between here and the oasis would be mostly void of anything—or anyone. When we approached the pumps, Karim forgot that he was the kickstand, and instead of putting his feet down, he pulled off his helmet. The bike fell slowly to the left and crashed to the ground. We both jumped clear.

"Karim, honey," I said. "Remember this step. I can't hold this heavy-ass bike up with you on the back. My legs aren't long or strong enough, so please, take me seriously. Do this one thing, yeah?"

He looked down at his feet. "I'll remember next time," he said.

We picked up the bike, filled it with fuel, searched without any luck for some dates, and set off for the long haul down the highway to Ksar Ghilane. About sixty kilometers into the journey, the back of the bike broke into a sideways slide. Time slowed down. I took a deep breath, let the bike lead. I didn't touch the brakes. I released the throttle and steered in the direction the bike was taking us—to the left side of the road. A lump formed in my throat. I was genuinely afraid that the bike would flip over, tumble down the road, and pitch us headfirst onto the hot pavement.

When we came to a complete stop, Karim put his feet down and removed his helmet. "What happened? Did we slip in oil or something?"

My heart was racing. "No."

"Was it the wind?"

I felt the heat rise in my chest and yanked the bike's kickstand into place. "Karim, the back tire blew out."

He looked surprised.

"Don't believe me? Take a look." He climbed off the bike and saw what I knew. The tire was as flat as it could be.

We stood there in the middle of nowhere. I prayed for cell reception and was relieved when I saw a couple of bars at the top of my phone. Panicked and frustrated, I called Charles and explained.

"Yes, just wait for the truck, and we're out of dates," he said.

"Wait for the truck? We haven't seen a single car or truck in the last sixty kilometers since we've been on this road. What do you mean?" I said.

Just then a truck appeared in the distance, headed toward us. "Oh, wait. I think there's a truck coming. I'll call you back."

"Yes, and we're out of dates."

I hung up the phone. A few minutes later, the truck stopped for us, and three young men got out. Karim can speak French, Arabic, and English, so he explained what had happened. With wide eyes, they listened in a sort of amazement I couldn't understand. *What is Karim telling them?*

"They'll take us and the bike to Ksar Ghilane," Karim told me. "They were going to Matmata and missed picking up the things they were supposed to have in the back of this truck because they were late. They think that happened so they could be here to help us now."

I pulled Karim to the side. "Ksar Ghilane is at least a 200-kilometer detour from Matmata. Are you sure it's OK for them to take us all that way?"

"I said the same thing. They insisted on taking us and the bike. They feel this is why things happened the way they did."

"Well, OK."

The ride was smooth. I couldn't help but think of what Charles had said during our two conversations so far today. "Check the tires, wait for the truck, and we're out of dates." Well, he got two out of three. *How'd he do that? It's like he knew this was going to happen.*

An hour and a half later, we arrived at the oasis, and I asked Karim to translate my thanks to the guys for helping us. "If they can wait a few minutes," I said, "at the very least, I can bring them some gas money."

"No, no, no," they said and told Karim that it was their duty to support us—that they'd been given this divine opportunity and were happy to help us out. *Seriously? Wow.* "That's nice, thank you," I said.

After Karim translated my gratitude for their service, one of the men grabbed me by the arm as I turned to walk away. He said, in English: "Gift." He reached behind the driver's seat and handed me a cellophane-wrapped, flower boutique-sized package of dates.

No freaking way. That's it. Now I KNOW this wizard-turned-magician could see all of this coming. But how? How could he possibly know?

We thanked the men again and made our way to the truck. After handing off the dates to Karim, I pulled Charles off to the side and asked, "So. How'd you do it? You knew the tire was going to blow, you knew the truck was going to arrive, and you knew that we'd be gifted with dates. Tell me; I must know how you did that magic."

He smiled. "So so so," he said. He turned to the group and said something in German, which must have been a cue to pack up because everyone began loading their gear. At the front of the truck, I stopped him. "Can you teach me this level of magic?" He smiled, climbed into the truck, and prepared the GPS for the next leg of the trip.

The week that followed was relatively relaxed for me. We trekked through the desert—yet again. There weren't many of the cumbersome processes I'd experienced during my previous trips.

When the tour ended, we returned to the village and finished our duties, said "See you later" to our friends, and made our way up north to Tunis. I invited Karim and his family to join me at the One Billion Rising event in the capital. It was impressive. Lots of people attended, and there were many diverse events for women's rights: spoken word poets, musicians, dancing, and generally, a good feeling. I met several women who no longer wore the traditional headscarf (hijab) even though they'd once preferred it. To them, it was a symbol of the repression of women. I also met women who felt otherwise. To them, it wasn't that way at all. Even though they disagreed with some of the views on how to treat women, the hijab didn't symbolize repression to them—it represented protection.

We stayed for the entire event, and afterward, Karim and I sat outside a coffee shop and talked about how "to be the change we wished to see in the world." Suddenly, I had an idea. I grabbed my notebook and a pen. I wrote in large, bold letters, "Do you speak English? Speak to me," and sat the notebook on our table where those who walked by could read it. I grabbed my camera and set it up to record. Karim looked confused, so I explained what my intention was for this little experiment.

"I want to know what the people here would like to see change in the world. We can call it the "Spare Some Change Tour," if they ask. I'm curious. Let's see what happens."

For two hours, we sat there and recorded the many people who bravely took the hot seat without knowing what they were getting themselves into. They were curious. I only asked two main questions. The first was, "What would you like to see change in the world?" The answers ranged from wanting equality, more freedom, less fighting, more rights, and the like. These answers came quickly and with ease from nearly every person who sat with us. The next question was, "How are you going to be the change you wish to see?" I was surprised: Most people had plenty to say about what they wanted to see change but had no idea how to influence it. We discussed possibilities of how people could get involved. While the social experiment was fun, it reminded me of a cartoon meme I'd seen. A group of people were asked: "Who wants change?" Everyone raised their hands. Then the group was asked, "Who wants to change?" All the people let their hands fall by their sides. Why? Did the people feel powerless? Were they unsure of what was needed?

Charles arrived. "It's time to go," he said.

I packed up my camera gear. "See you later, Karim," I said, and hugged him. We set off to the dock to catch the ferry to Europe.

Chapter Five
Radical Releasing

Back at the hotel, the team invited me to take on the role of "House Meister." My two main jobs were coordinating volunteers and overseeing projects. We all got busy upgrading some of the hotel's systems, adding fresh paint, and building structures in the garden. I learned to "see what was needed," and I scheduled volunteers accordingly. This opportunity brought me another great lesson. As Charles pointed out, I'd viewed the team as equals and expected them to perform as such, even when it was evident this wasn't the case. I'd work harder to make up for what was lacking in some of the volunteers' work. Again, as in the village with the women, I'd end up frustrated. Charles reminded me that I'd benefit from recognizing what levels people play from and working from there. *I thought I'd already learned this....*

Over the following weeks, as volunteers came and went, I practiced over and over again. One day, after a working guest had destroyed a couple of beneficial tools, more of my repressed anger appeared. It wasn't directed at the tool-breaking man—he was just the trigger. As the situation needed damage control, I swallowed my anger. I carried on with the tasks at hand.

Charles appeared, and somehow, he saw that I was destroying myself from the inside out by eating my anger. "So so so. You chose to hold it again, or...?" he said.

"What? What are you talking about?"

"Did you notice you ate your anger?"

Utterly unconscious of the pattern I had so meticulously spun within myself—and thinking that unconditional kindness is the only way to be—naturally, I argued with him (politely). Until I got mad—outraged. I was so upset, I spent three days stuck, yet again, in the one emotion I'd avoided for so long: full-on anger. At the impressionable age of thirteen, I realized that I'd committed to never getting angry with anyone. Ever. I'd made this decision because I'd lived through too many violent experiences. I'd kept that promise for two decades.

On my fourth day of "mad," I felt a bit lighter. I was ready to cooperate and listen to what Charles had to say. Through an enlightening conversation with him, I learned that eating anger can be as unhealthy and unnatural as eating socks for breakfast. I gained a new perspective: Anger isn't necessarily a "bad" or "undesirable" emotion; it can be healthy when experienced appropriately. *How does one do that? What is a healthy way to express anger?*

My answer was to come just a few days later. On my birthday, I received a sweet electronic breakbeat mix (dance music) from DJ Phooka in Dallas, Texas. Naturally, listening to this got me excited, and I wanted to go dancing. That's what I wanted as my birthday wish. I asked my friend Tony, who was sitting next to me while I was blissing out to the beats, if he'd join me on a trip to Salzburg, Austria, and dance with me. His response was all it took to reignite the repressed anger within me. It went something like this: A prolonged, heavy sigh, followed by, "Really? You want me to go to listen to that? Uffff, oh well, it *is* your birthday. I guess I could go just for that."

Bam. I slammed my computer shut and retreated to my bed, where I attempted once again to eat the anger welling up inside. I lay there under the covers for a good twenty minutes, hyperventilating and trying to calm myself. I realized that it wasn't going to happen. Somehow, I was unable to eat this anger. Not only that, whatever unprocessed anger I'd eaten before was about to be regurgitated. *Oh shit. What to do? Take a walk. Take a step before someone approaches you, and you knock them out with this energy coming up.* So, I did. I walked away from the house toward the forest.

I never made it to the forest. Something between the house and the trees caught my eye—a stack of weathered wooden chairs that were to be used as firewood. One by one, I pitched the chairs down the hill to the fire pit. I stared at the pile of chairs and the basketball-sized stones that circled the hole. I picked up the first chair. I held it by two of its legs, raised it above my head, and, screaming primitively, I slammed it onto a stone. With a loud craaaack, it broke in half. I picked up its remains and smashed them. This continued for four more chairs. *So this is anger—pure, hate-filled rage. I need to release it.* With even more power and intention, I grabbed another chair and slammed it on the rocks. After fourteen chairs, I ran out of chairs to destroy. I stared at the carnage. I observed what was coming up within me. There was nothing left. I felt bright, clean, relaxed. Somehow, I was happy with this mess. As I sorted the broken pieces and stacked them into piles, I laughed an uncontrollably hearty laugh. Releasing the anger hadn't killed me. Instead, it had created an opening that hadn't existed before. Space had grown inside me. I felt good. Happy even. I was grateful the chairs were there for me to pulverize. I spent a few minutes admiring my carefully sorted destruction, then walked back to the main house—floated, really. I informed the team that we now had plenty of firewood—and that I might need a back massage to roll out the knots that were sure to appear after all that effort. Everyone cheered for the firewood (we burned a few mangled chairs that same night). I was offered assistance for the knots in my back in the form of energy work—and by that, I mean working with energy, not massaging the mess out with their hands on my body. The healing would take place without any touching whatsoever.

This should be interesting.

The following day, Vukosava, a working guest at the hotel, saw me wandering around the garden with incredible difficulty. She approached me. "How are you feeling today?"

I turned toward her. "Not so good. My right shoulder is almost touching my ear, and I can't turn my head at all."

She laughed a little. So did I. She said: "Would you like some of that energetic help I mentioned last night to sort that out?"

"Yes, please."

"Stay right here. I'll be back."

She returned to the garden with a pillow and blanket. Every step hurt, and the paralyzing pain in my neck and shoulders was intense. I dared not move another step. "You'll need to lie down here, face up. Have you ever had mental healing energy work before?"

I collapsed to the blanket like a heavy stone and looked up at the sky. "No."

"Just close your eyes."

I closed my eyes and listened to her soothing voice.

"I won't be touching you with my hands, but I will be touching you with some very real energy. Don't worry. We'll work those kinks out in no time."

She made a kind of hissing noise. I opened my eyes a little. Hers were closed, and her hands were pointing over my shoulders. I closed my eyes. A minute later, I felt the tension, like a Kung Fu grip on my neck and my shoulders, loosen. After about twenty more minutes or so of this "energy work," I was free from the Hulk-like squeeze. It felt incredible.

I opened my eyes. Vukosava was sitting quietly. When she opened her eyes, she asked, "Are you ready to sit up?"

"I think I'm ready to do backflips even though I don't know how."

"That sounds great, but I suggest you take it slow the next couple of days while this works its way through your system."

I took her advice. I walked slower, talked slower, and worked slower for an entire week. I was impressed. The healing had opened up another door to magic I wasn't aware existed.

A few days after my body felt right again, I received an invitation from Charles to a BioDanza event that would be held at the hotel in a couple of days.

"What's BioDanza?" I asked.

"Oh, just a new way of meeting others and coming into deep contact through dancing. I think you'd love it."

Forty or so guests arrived to create the BioDanza. I joined with apprehension. It was a bit awkward. I'm used to dancing in my own space, usually on a platform in a loud nightclub to bass-filled electronic music. But this was different. In this class, I was invited to gently and loving- ly connect with strangers, and it tested my comfort level. Getting up close and personal with strangers was some- thing I'd grown used to through traveling. Yet, this dance intimidated me at first. Once the music started, though, the energy became infectious.

The BioDanza classes ranged from an hour and a half to two hours long and usually started with high-energy exercises and gradually slowed in intensity. Each day had a theme. One day, the theme was friendship, and the dances touched on solidarity. One dance that was moving for me started with finding a partner and approaching them slowly. Once we were face to face, we'd look into each other's eyes. As the music changed, we'd turn away from one another. We'd walk slowly in opposite directions until we'd almost reached the far ends of the room. Then, turning toward each other and holding eye contact for a beat, we'd turn and walk away again without looking back. These actions impacted me because, as a traveler, I'm used to meeting new people and developing beautiful contacts. But when it's been time for me to move on, I've always had the impulse to run away. Through this dance, I became aware that during many of those times, my leaving was usually not as heartfelt as it was in this dance. This taught me how to appreciate and respect every meeting.

BioDanza means "the dance of life." It is a self-development system that uses music, movement, and positive feelings to deepen self-awareness. It seeks to promote one's ability to make a holistic link with oneself and one's emotions and express them organically. BioDanza also claims to allow one to deepen bonds with others. That's exactly what it felt like.

When I looked up this style of dance on Wikipedia, the article said that "BioDanza" could be defined as a "human integration system of organic renewal, of affective re-education, and re-learning of life's original functions." It's a method that aims to assist participants in developing their human capabilities, promoting feelings of happiness, developing communication skills, and improving relationships. It was created in the 1960s by Chilean anthropologist and psychologist Rolando Toro Araneda. During his work at the Centre for Psychiatric Research in Santiago, BioDanza was born, as he intended to create something that would re-educate our broken gestures—that we would re-learn at an affective level and give life to a view that we all matter, that we are all connected, our cells are all working in perfect harmony within us, with each other and with the universe.

By the end of the three-day-long event, people in the group were no longer separate beings. We'd danced together, and we'd danced with our shadows. We'd become a community that could see the value and love in one another and we'd actively helped even more of that to surface. The last dance wasn't a dance at all, but a giant cuddle puddle, where all forty souls simply lay down together in close contact, doing nothing but being: no aim, no desire, no need to change anything—just surrendering into being in close, deep connection. I loved it.

On that final evening at dinner, this group of strangers had become like family. We chatted during our last meal together as if we'd known each other for years. All in all, it's a great way to get in touch with yourself, as well as with others, in an entirely uncomfortable—yet comforting way.

I felt that Rolando Toro Araneda understood what was missing in our way of relating to one another. He'd created a way to remember the natural, organic way many of us seem to be afraid of now. I was fearful to some extent, and I appreciated this opportunity to change. Bio-Danza helped me to walk a bit more gracefully alongside my fellow human beings.

I'd like some more of that, please. I want to walk with as much peace as possible.

I stayed at the hotel for another month and learned more about how everything operated. I attended some "awareness" workshops and worked on myself. Then I felt the impulse to visit India with a British man named Tony. We'd been introduced while I was in England, and afterward, I'd invited him to work at the hotel. (Yeah—THAT Tony. My trigger man from the chair therapy, remember?)

Before I left, I asked Charles, "So, what's my homework?"

"Yes, just continue to watch the authority and control patterns that you can now see playing in your system. And pay attention to when you are acting in a role of over-responsibility," he said.

I knew I had my work cut out for me, but I was stoked to use my newfound skills out there in the "real world." *You've got this, Melissa,* I said to myself as I headed for the plane to India.

Year Three - Optional Questions for Self-Reflection: Talk to It

When you find that place of discomfort, talk to it. Ask questions like "What is it you need?" and "What are you trying to show me?" Take time to listen and record in your journal what you hear.

Year 4

Asia

Chapter One

Incredible India

From the air, the mist that blanketed Mumbai made the city look like a vast graveyard of ghosts gathered around jutting tombstones. The airplane descended to 10,000 feet, and the thick white cloud dispersed. As we approached the airport, I saw a collection of decaying wood and scrap metal—I realized with shock that I was looking at the Mumbai slums—shanties lined the airport fences and stretched as far as my eyes could see.

From my window, the slum looked like several old cardboard puzzles thrown together haphazardly. As we approached the runway, I saw what appeared to be a lake, filled with what I could only imagine was foul-smelling garbage, human waste, and who knows what. Luxury high-rise hotels surrounded the slums—it was eerie. A stark contrast between deep poverty and incredible wealth. *What's it like to live there? What kind of work do they do? Are there schools? How many families are down there?*

We touched down at 8:00 a.m., and as the British put it, I was knackered. I collected my additional forty pounds of gear, and as we had five hours before our next flight to Goa, Tony and I decided to try some traditional Indian cuisine. We found a suitable-looking place—it had the proud face of a lion on the wall and comfortable-looking red-booth seating near the exit. We chose our seats; then

I went to talk to the chefs at the counter. "What's the best thing to order?" I asked. "Not too spicy?" I ordered samosas (I know what those are), and one chef suggested I try something else. "Is it spicy?" I asked. "I don't have a high tolerance for spicy food." I saw a sparkle—*was it mischief?* —in his eyes that told me: *Don't trust him.*

"Oh, spicy? No, no, my friend," he said. "This is not spicy. Maybe a little bit. This is all."

So, I ordered it. We nestled into our corner booth. We had a view of both the inside of the airport terminal and the street outside. I took a bite of the mystery food. Holy moly! It was literally the hottest food I'd ever put in my mouth. My nose ran, my eyes watered, I started sweating. I looked toward the chef—he was nowhere to be found.

I finished the samosas. I dropped the crazy-hot food in a trash bin. "I'm going to roam outside and explore for a bit," I told Tony.

"Right. I'll stay here and read a bit." He said. "Come get me when you're done."

I arrived at the exit, only to have a police officer step in front of me. He wore a khaki uniform and navy cap with a yellow band, a thick leather belt, and sported a gun on his hip. He held up his hand to stop me. "You cannot leave the airport," he said.

I started laughing. I thought he was joking and tried to step past him. His associate stepped up to block me. I mean, where in the world are you *not allowed to leave* an airport? Playfully, I said, "Um, I'll be going outside. I have no intention of staying in this airport for four hours, waiting for my next flight. Chase me if you want."

One of the guards smiled. The other looked at me like he imagined sticking a knife in my eye. A third officer stepped forward. "You must go to the airline attendant, sort this out."

"Okay," I said, "but I'll be back. I'm going outside."

I walked up to the Air India counter and was greeted by two lovely women and one man and explained the situation. They asked to see my flight itinerary, so I handed it over.

"Well, you'll be going outside because your next flight is not from this airport, and if you don't go now, you'll be spending New Year's here."

Ha ha! Wait... what? Where do I go then? I better get Tony... and fast!

They wrote down the information on my itinerary, and I headed to the restaurant to get Tony. Then we went back to the exit—and the police blocked both of us. I explained that we must go and handed them the papers. While they looked it over, I thanked them for sending me to Air India.

"Sorry, miss," one officer said, handing me the papers. "You cannot leave."

Seriously? I threw him a very dirty look.

He stepped in front of me.

I turned, stomped back to the Air India counter, and asked the agent to come with me to the exit. *Stopping me once? That informed me I was at the wrong airport. Okay, thank you for that. But stopping me again?* This time, I let the Air India man talk to the police. Two minutes later, Tony and I were free! Not only free to leave the airport, but free to catch the right flight to Goa.

After our New Year's Eve was saved, effortlessness and divine timing unfolded. We caught our flight to Goa on time, and when we landed, we found a woman to share a taxi with, reducing the cost of the ride—and our carbon footprint—by half. I'd reserved a flat in Cortalim on

Airbnb, and after a great night's rest, we decided to trek up to Adjuna Beach to welcome in 2015. I grabbed my small backpack, and the next step was to find our way up north. After we were quoted ridiculous prices for taxis (2000 rupees [rs] to get there—roughly $35.00), a kind gentleman told us about the bus stop right across the street and that by bus we'd spend roughly 100rs each (about $1.50).

At the bus stop, I started to play with my flag poi—twirling and dancing as I spun them around my body while we waited. As usual, I played for quite a while, headphones on, eyes closed. Suddenly, I heard Tony laughing loudly and people shouting. I opened my eyes—traffic had come to a stop. The local Indian people took photos of me, and traffic police were screaming for them to move on.

"Oooopppsss! Sorry!" I packed up the poi, and just then the bus arrived.

We crammed into the overcrowded bus like sardines packed in a tin. I laughed. A sign above the driver said, "Max Capacity: 35." We easily tripled that number. It was that way on all three of the buses—which we found with minimal effort—that took us to Anjuna Beach. On the last bus, Tony had his wallet nicked. It contained all the money he'd brought out for New Year's Eve, and his bank card. No worries, I had enough for both of us. He was still visibly upset from the loss.

After we got off the bus near the beach, we went to a roadside restaurant. I ordered a smoothie for Tony to remind him that we were still okay. Then to get into the groove of New Year's Eve, I took some makeup out of my bag and painted his face. After I'd applied the glitter, his heaviness faded. Then, after I painted my face, we wandered through a maze of markets and shops to an event called NYEX at a fantastic beachfront nightclub.

We bought the tickets at the door and went to the bar to order food and drinks. We were early, and the outdoor club was practically empty. Look at all this space! I started playing with my LED poi. A handsome Turkish man named Mustafa approached us and said his wife loved poi. Would we like to join them at their table on the edge of the water? We accepted and followed him down the maze of steps. We met his wife, Kara—a lovely soul from Boston, along with Paul the Aussie, and two girls from Canada who were, simply put, our kind of people. They commented on our face paint.

"I've got body paint and glitter," I said. "Would you like some?"

After they were all painted up, we spent the evening/morning singing, dancing, playing with strangers, and wandering around the beach, tripping over the occasional person buried up to their necks in the sand. Our night welcoming in the 2015 New Year was flawless.

At 6:00 a.m., Tony and I said our farewells to our new friends. We took a bus, then a taxi, back to Cortalim. Later that day, after some rest, we found a roadside cafe about a block away from our Airbnb. Tony sipped chai and wrote in his journal, and I retreated into music and poi. An Indian man watched us from across the four-lane street that buzzed with buses, mopeds, bicycles, cars, and the occasional animal-pulled cart. He paced back and forth for some time, seemingly trying to decide whether to cross the street. I smiled at him and waved. In that instant, he hopped his way over.

He introduced himself as Samuel. He appeared intrigued by Tony and me. We invited him for tea, and he shared his story. He'd pick up a Russian woman in the morning, and they were going to travel by motorbike to Palolem Beach. Tony and I traded surprised glances. "That's where we're going to be volunteering in a few days! It would be epic if we could travel by motorbike too—you know, to check the place out ahead of schedule."

Samuel couldn't hide his excitement. "I can get a motorcycle for you and would love for you to join us," he said.

"No way. Really? Amazing!" We finished our tea and traded contact information.

The following day, I met with Samuel, and he drove me to pick up the other bike. When we arrived, I noticed that, yeah, it was a motorcycle, but it had no mirrors and a defective back brake. I decided that although it was a bit beat up, it would do. We took the bikes back to pick up the Russian girl and Tony and started our unexpected (but welcome) journey.

The ride from Cortalim to Palolem Beach was fantastic. The landscape changed dramatically as we rode through forests, over giant hills, and crossed small and large rivers over simply crafted bridges. We stopped halfway for tea and snacks, and when we were ready to travel on, Tony announced that he'd ride the bike sitting backward, facing the rear. His excited screams and childlike playfulness as we whipped around curves and through the hills and valleys kept me laughing through it all. When we arrived at the mile-long beach, I was surprised to see how beautiful it was. It appeared as though the British ex-pats had taken over Goa; it was clean and refreshing. Brightly colored huts and shanty shacks lined the beach. Foreign backpackers strolled lazily through the souvenir shops and enjoyed the fresh seafood found everywhere. We parked our bikes and ran straight for the water. It was as warm as a bath and felt lovely against my skin. The place was new; I was in awe. *So, this is India? Wow. Incredible. It's so clean, friendly... and cheap!*

Later that day, I met a photographer named Michael from Los Angeles who invited me for tea at his place. He had a laid-back attitude and a mischievous smile, so I agreed. His house had pastel-colored curtains that flew in and out of the windows on the whims of the breeze, and there were large, plump pillows on his terrace. The air smelled like citrus. Against one wall in the living room was a low shelf filled with books. When he went into the kitchen to prepare tea, I sat on the floor to look at his library.

"Do you like chai?" he asked.

"Actually, it's my favorite! A Slovenian man taught me how to make it from scratch in Guatemala when I was having a Starbucks chai withdrawal."

"Really? A Slovenian man in Guatemala?"

"Yeah. Weird, huh?"

"Indeed. What were you doing in Guatemala?"

"Learning mostly, I guess. Hey, Michael, you wouldn't happen to know anything about the slums in Mumbai, would you?"

He returned with the tea. "Funny you should ask. That book right there, *Behind the Beautiful Forevers* by Katherine Boo, is a story about the slums."

No way.

I picked up the book and held it in disbelief. I'd been thinking about the slums from the moment I'd seen them and was curious about the story of that place—and here and now, that story was resting in my hands.

"I flew into Mumbai and saw them from the airplane. It was crazy—the contrast, I mean. The divide between the rich and the poor right next to one another. May I borrow this book? I'd love to read the story."

"You can borrow it, but you better bring it back. I normally don't let my books out of the house."

"I promise I will. Give me a week to finish it? I'm volunteering at Paradise School for a month, so you'll be able to find me."

"Paradise School? With Shilpa? You're going to love that place. All the groovy parents around here and their kids will be there."

Tony and I stayed and played in Palolem Beach for a couple of days, found the school where we'd be volunteering, and attended a silent disco at Neptune's Point. At the disco, we were given headphones with a button on them to change between channels—Green for Breakbeat and Jungle music, Red for Ambient Lounge, and Blue for House music. I loved watching the sea of people as they swayed to the different tides of the tunes. There was an eclectic mix of both energy and sound in the atmosphere that felt good. Tony and I were delighted with the area and its community.

Back in Cortalim, we thanked Samuel for his kindness, hospitality, and generosity and packed up the rest of our belongings. The bus arrived, and again we were gifted when the conductor offered us free seats as his special guests for the day. Tony and I smiled at one another, placed our hands on our hearts, and thanked the driver for his generosity. We couldn't ignore the effortlessness and flow and continued to bask in gratitude as the bus rolled on. *Maybe the abundance journal I've been keeping is working? Is it the inner work of changing my belief systems? Is it India? Are we just getting lucky? Could it be something else?*

The Indian people were incredibly friendly and welcoming. On the bus ride back to the beach, I wanted to know more. I read the book about the slums that Michael let me borrow. It was so well written and had such incredible detail, and I couldn't put it down. I almost couldn't believe it was nonfiction. Six hours later, I was finished and had my answers about the Mumbai slums—which only brought more questions. *How did the world get this way? Why is the divide between the rich and poor so wide? There seems to be enough for everyone. Why isn't it shared?*

I went to the beach to meditate on these questions. I sat and listened to the waves flow in and out. Suddenly, I felt a wet nose touch my cheek. *Sweet. A little dog is welcoming me.* I didn't open my eyes. I heard a growl and opened my eyes, just in time to see that a pack of wild dogs had encircled me—and they'd grabbed my fanny pack and my sweater and were running away with them.

Oh shit! My passport!

I jumped to my feet and chased the dogs down the beach. The one that carried my fanny pack dropped it, and with relief, I picked it up and snapped it across my waist. Two more dogs in the group of six played with my sweater, and I heard it rip. "I only have two sweaters! Give it back!" I shouted. The dogs stopped running and approached me, their heads low to the ground. The pack circled me. I panicked. They were growling and snapping at me as I turned in circles, looking for help. Out of nowhere, an Indian man came running to my aid. He was carrying a large stick, and he swung it wildly and shouted in Hindi. The dogs dispersed, and I fell to my knees. He came to me, lifted me by my arms, and I hugged him.

"Thank you. That could have been bad." I said.

He smiled and wobbled his head from side to side before walking away.

I watched the dogs playfully pick up my sweater again and run away with it.

Just let it go. You'll find another one when you need it. Trust the abundance. Let go of lack. You have just what you need and right when you need it.

Paradise School was run by two British women and catered exclusively to the ever-growing group of British ex-pats and their children living in Goa. Around twenty young souls played here five days a week, and Tony and I were eager to get started on the projects they had in mind for us.

Our most significant and challenging creativity task was to build an outdoor play area in the spacious but overgrown yard. For the next two weeks, we took what some might call "useless trash" and turned it into treasure. We repurposed old tires into a climbing wall and rolling benches. Broken umbrellas became shade structures, and we used donated fabrics to create vibrant reading teepees. Some of the tables needed resurfacing and lots of paint to bring them back to life. Curious Indian children peeked over the walls as we worked. I invited them to help out in the evenings, and over the days, while we hand-sanded and stripped tables together, they taught me some Hindi in exchange for English words. The local children worked hard, were eager to learn, and were a pleasure to be with. The monkeys that hung around in the cashew trees, on the other hand, were not so helpful. They stole food, tipped over paint cans, and scattered supplies every time we took a break. They always left a trail of disaster behind them… and taught us to be more careful with our things.

Tony and I loved every moment of the unpredictable unfolding. I watched as this "over-responsibility" theme that Charles had mentioned played throughout the building process. There were times when I took on more than necessary, and sometimes I even overlooked others who could have helped. However, I saw all of that in hindsight. I even tried to convince myself that this theme "wasn't all bad"—it enabled me to do great things for the school. I realized later, though, how taking over the potential contributions of others wasn't a great thing for everyone. *I need to watch this. I can only imagine what gifts lie within it.*

The women who created the school inspired me greatly. What they developed and were directing was terrific. The children loved to be there and learned well together. In particular, one of the founding women, Shilpa, impressed me. She had this presence—this determination about her—I knew that she'd continue to do great things (and she has). I studied her grace, poise, and fierce-yet-friendly "I will not take no for an answer" attitude. She always knew that the seemingly impossible was possible—and she proved it over and over again. I loved to watch Shilpa in her power and hoped secretly that I'd also create brilliant things one day. *Now that's the feminine divine in action. It's beautiful.*

Several months after I left India, I learned that Shilpa was a speaker at an education summit where she'd described to a room full of top educators the story of why she created Paradise School Goa. I also read her tributes to her father when he passed. She wrote: "I'm proud to carry on the legacy. He showed me to be a freedom fighter and truth seeker. He always said, 'just be yourself, Shilpa.'

With that, you can do anything. It's the ultimate free-dom." I read her post online about when she was flipping through an old journal and reading the notes she'd written to herself before setting up a new school. She wrote:

> *Why am I doing the school? What do I love about it?*
> *I like changing the game.*
> *I like leading the way.*
> *I like seeing a deeper truth and acting on it.*
> *I like shaking things up.*
> *I like moving, growing, expanding, and learning.*
> *I like the adventure of it.*
> *I like finding like-minded players on a world-class level.*
> *I like bringing in the new.*
> *I am good at it.*
> *I like showing what's possible.*
> *I love miracles.*
> *I love shining.*
> *I love giving.*
> *I love making a difference.*
> *Clearly, I am my own life coach! And this self-talk works."*

Clearly, it does....

I tried to remember the travel intentions I'd written in my first journal three years earlier. I thought of the abundance log I'd been keeping and the daily gratitude practices I'd developed. *I think Shilpa is on to something. Thoughts and intentions really do create our reality....*

Shilpa continued to inspire me as I followed her online and gave thanks for being allowed to help to create a part of her brilliant dreams. I watched her continue to rise, and it made me think of the women in Tunisia. I wondered what they might do for their community if they were allowed the same freedom that these warrior goddesses and I, in our own way, seemed to have access to. I asked myself: What would happen if all the world's women were to step into their authentic selves—into their full power? If they broke the chains with which their cultures, religions, communities, and personal beliefs have kept them shackled? *That would be something beautiful. How did it ever get this way?*

Before we left the school, I happened to be on the same beach where the dogs had taken my sweater. As I walked along, I saw a hint of black ... and there it was! I expected it to be torn to shreds, but it wasn't. There wasn't a single hole in the fabric. I was surprised. I was pretty confident I'd heard the two dogs tear it up as they pulled it between one another. I held the sweater up in astonishment and thanked the universe for allowing it to come back to me in perfect condition. This feels like another lesson in surrender. I should remember it.

Chapter Two

Sri Mooji Satsang

I met another lovely soul at a silent disco on a rocky headland just south of Palolem Beach. Petar was American but had been raised in Switzerland. He worked in Goa, running a restaurant with some Austrian friends. In our conversation, he shared that he was also a seeker with levels of discomfort similar to mine that needed sorting out. So, we decided we'd meet up and attend a ten-day Vipassana meditation retreat together. But before attending this retreat, I'd agreed to go with Tony to Sri Mooji's Satsang in Rishikesh, India. ("Satsang" means "fellowship in truth.")

As human beings, we like to be entertained and distracted, and we are full of thoughts and ambitions. I am, anyway. There's nothing wrong with that—until we find ourselves waking up one day thinking, "What happened? This is not my beautiful house. This is not my beautiful life!"

Being distracted reminded me of the old story in which a boy asks his father how much he makes in an hour so he can save up enough paper money to buy some of his father's time before it passes by. We are timeless, but in this human form, we're here to remember something before we trap ourselves in routine, thoughts, and distractions that take us further away from the truth.

Being in the moment is not always easy. I understand this well. Being in the flow of each moment requires the absence of thoughts from the past and desires for the future and letting things occur naturally. No attachments, no judgments. Because of my journey, I've realized that it's taken me time to find this sweet spot in my life—and it seems to be taking even more time to be able to hold it.

Located in northern India in the foothills of the Himalayas, Rishikesh is known as the "Gateway to the Garhwal Himalayas" and the "Yoga Capital of the World." The sacred turquoise-colored waters of the Ganges River flow through this serene spiritual town; Hindu saints and sages have visited here in search of higher knowledge since ancient times. The "street sadhus" (or "devout holy men") appear on the streets in the mornings, dressed in simple saffron-colored clothing, carrying donation jars as they wander through the town. Having denounced worldly possessions, they've devoted themselves to the spiritual practice of attaining liberation from the cycle of death and rebirth, and they rely on handouts to sustain their physical bodies and continue their spiritual endeavors.

I walked along the Ganges. People bathed, washed clothes, and prayed in or near the waters. I entered the 800-year-old, thirteen-story-high, pyramid-shaped temple. It's a place where one can worship all the gods and goddesses in one place, and I was amazed at just how many gods existed here. There are deities for health, luck, fertility, companionship—just about anything you can think of. Each deity is staged in a cell of sorts with a small black box attached to the cage bars. The ritual is to offer money to the God you are praying to—not to give it to

God, but to the temple, so they can continue serving God. I walked through the labyrinth of candle-lit cages and climbed a dark, musty staircase to the twelfth floor, where I met two ancient-looking men. One man asked if I'd like a prosperity and protection prayer from a priest. He invited me to sit on a pillow opposite the other man, who lit an incense, adorned my neck with a lei of orange flowers, and bowed his head. He murmured some kind of prayer before he lifted his head and bowed again. The man who offered the invitation tied a simple red string to my wrist and suggested donating some rupees to the priest. I gave them 500 RP and thanked them for the prayer by bowing in return. "How do I get to the roof?" I asked.

One of the men pointed to a staircase to our left. I bowed again, one hand on my heart, and climbed the stairs.

The view was incredible. A long, crowded suspension bridge that spanned the Ganges bustled with people from all walks of life. Indian women dressed in brightly colored sarees and salwar kameez, backpackers, older men pulling carts, street dogs, and tourists with cameras trotted over the river on their way to somewhere. I sat down and closed my eyes. I gave silent gratitude for everything that had brought me to where I was. I prayed I'd continue to have divine guidance on this journey. I opened my eyes and gazed into the setting sun. I thought about the sadhus and what spirituality meant to them. They aimed to seek "moksha" or liberation. (Moksha is derived from the root "muc," which means, variously, "free, let go, release, and liberate.") I wanted liberation as well but wasn't ready to relinquish ties with society and all worldly things to obtain it. *There has to be another way, right?* To me, spirituality was a practice I was developing, and for me thus far, it wasn't clearly defined. I wanted understanding. I wanted peace within my heart and on planet Earth. I wanted to be the change I wished to see in the world. This

I knew. So far on this journey, I'd seen many of my inner conflicts—stories I'd told myself about this world and my place in it—that were not peaceful and loving. I'd learned how to love these shadows into submission, dance with them, and integrate them, but there was more work to do. *Does it ever end?* Before I left the temple, I asked the gods and goddesses to continue to show me the way and thanked them for their support.

I set out to find Tony, who'd found a class he wanted to attend. As I walked the streets, I noticed that spirituality was for sale here. There were brightly colored, western-style yoga mats, t-shirts with the Om symbol, and "Yogi" banana bread available everywhere. *How is this helpful? I mean, if the aim is to relinquish an attachment to worldly things, how is this spiritual paraphernalia making it any easier for seekers? It seems it's just another distraction—a way of saying, "Look how spiritually evolved I am."*

I found Tony sipping a chai at a "Yogi Café."

"Oh, hello, darling," he said in his sexy British accent.

"How was the meeting?" I asked.

"Right," he said, "so the Satsang started four weeks ago and lasts another week. Would you like some chai?"

"I'd love some. Do you want to stay the week here?"

"That's a good question. Why don't we just allow things to unfold and see what happens?"

That's what I loved about traveling with Tony. He was so laid back—so kind and open. He had taken a different path than me, but we were reaching the same destination. He focused on the "I am" instead of dancing with shadows, as I'd been doing. It seemed to be serving him well. Sri Mooji was one of his teachers, and he was delighted to have the opportunity to attend a live Satsang meeting. I was curious—his path was gentler than mine—drudging through past trauma to find liberation. Before retiring to our hostel for the night, we sat in silence, enjoying our chai, watching as people from all walks of life passed us along the dusty roads of Rishikesh.

The following day, we entered the Satsang. We watched, along with hundreds of other people, while Mooji delivered the goods. Several people came to the microphone with questions, and I noticed that my tolerance for what I perceived to be *ignorance* in some people was waning. I realized I was making judgments, not allowing my fellow human beings the space they needed to get themselves sorted out. Then Mooji said something that snapped me out of my mood.

"It's essential," he said, "to make and hold space for others who are in their process, at their level of experience, so that they too can grow from their journey into being."

Was he speaking directly to me? His words resonated. Some new level of understanding shifted within me. He showed me something about myself, something that dams up the flow inside. He also spoke about the mind being "in full sabotage mode" and explained that this is not a sign that you're on the wrong path—it's a sign that you're on the right one.

Thoughts can be mischievous. They love to sabotage balance and efforts and finding peace, and the ego likes to fight for control. I thought of Charles back in Germany and how afraid I'd been of the people there, how my mind had told me to run away as fast as possible. I was beginning to see my ego's attempt to remain in control, how it wanted to sabotage anything that might expose it. Learning this was my motivation to continue dancing with my shadows when I felt like giving up and sinking back into the comforts of ignorance. I needed to meet my resistance.

We attended four of the final five days of the Satsang. On our last day in the city, we decided to hike to the Garud Chatti waterfall. I wanted to contemplate the takeaway message I'd received: *Being the observer of your life—the witness who can observe all the thoughts, habits, and actions—allows you to arrive at the truth of your existence—(which is pretty simple in the end). You are light. You are love. You are that which cannot be named.*

Tony and I each packed a small backpack with water, fruit, and nuts and began our walk along Neelkanth Road toward the waterfall. Along the way, a street dog joined us. A few minutes later, another one tagged along, and by the time we'd reached the entrance to the hiking path, we had a pack of three street dogs by our side. They climbed the narrow dirt paths with us and stopped to allow us to catch up to them. When we reached the top, we saw that the small waterfall dropped from seven different levels into a perfect swimming pool. The dogs took the lead and plunged into the water. I sat on a rock and watched them play before I kicked off my shoes and jumped in with them. I imagined the cool, refreshing water rinsing off any stagnant energy I might be holding. Then I played with the dogs. Some other hikers arrived and watched us from the side of the pool.

"Are those your dogs?" one of the hikers asked.

"No. They followed us here from Rishikesh. One at a time, actually." I said.

"That's a very good omen of protection."

"It is?"

"Oh yes. You have protection with you on your journey. This is proof," he said, nodding toward the dogs.

Really? I thought about the priest who had offered me a prayer of protection at the temple, and in my mind and heart, I thanked him again. I was feeling lighter, more confident, and even more trusting in what was unfolding. The Satsang had left me in a state of peace and presence, and I felt grateful for all the experiences I'd had in Rishikesh.

We walked back into town, and just as they had appeared, the dogs left us. One by one, they wandered away, just a few minutes apart, as we approached the town center. As each dog departed, I thanked it for providing us with its protection. Back at the hostel, I looked up our intriguing guru, Sri Mooji, online. I found many videos in which Mooji discusses the self's identity, what can get in the way of one's seeking, and what can aid in growth. He believes there is a simple truth about one's existence: there is no body, no birth, no death—that the thinker and the thought don't even exist. That was the main message from his Satsang, but I found it challenging to grasp.

Some of Sri Mooji's followers had taken past talks he'd given and remixed them to music. He spoke over reggae and psychedelic trance, and over minimal and otherworldly sounds that were soft in the ears. The music was new to me, and I added some of the songs to my playlist. Mooji speaks from a place of "I am," which I see as a different path to the same destination. While I'd been led through my unconscious shadows and I'd danced with them, bit by bit, Mooji explained that another way was also possible. To focus on the "I am" of being and know that all the rest are illusions and shouldn't be given any importance.

I'd already given loads of ideas quite a bit of emphasis and importance. What does it mean that everything outside of the "I am" are illusions? Are the illusions the stories we tell ourselves? What about the beliefs we hold so close and protect as our truth? Are those the illusions that shouldn't be given so much of our precious energy? I thought again about the shadow dancing I'd done. I recalled the many times I'd observed my thoughts—without reacting to them—and through that non-judgmental observation, the tight grip they had held loosened. Many times, they had disappeared. Was this the same thing? Recognizing that these thoughts, this conditioning, and these beliefs aren't real?

I'd watched Tony follow Mooji's style of teaching, and it taught me to honor everyone's path—whatever it may be. I thought of Yasmine's family in Tunisia. They had accepted me even though I didn't share their faith.

Why do people fight so much about God?

That evening, I started to prepare for what I'd committed to next: to attend a ten-day Vipassana meditation. I wanted to understand on a deeper level what becoming that witness meant—to see whatever else was residing in my unconscious. I wanted to shed the light of consciousness into those shadow spaces and dance with whatever appeared from the darkness. Tony was preparing to meet with a friend of mine, Zoey, who was flying in from the states. She had sent me a message and said she wanted to come to Asia. I suggested she meet Tony; I just knew they would enjoy one another. I met her at the airport and introduced them before I left.

Before Vipassana

The hands gripped tighter around my neck. I struggled to swallow. The throat-crushing force has held me for four straight days. When will it finally either suffocate or release me? My mind has been let loose like a runaway herd of wild horses.

Deep within, I cry out, but no sound leaves my lips. My mouth is glued shut from the inside. My body wants to kick and fight, but my energy has been held hostage by – Who? Me? Realizing that I'm the cause of my suffering doesn't change anything.

Yesterday, I begged the universe to cut me some slack. To help me return to the bubbly, entertained, laughing little girl I remember hanging around with once but can't seem to find anywhere anymore. She's been trampled, too. Tomorrow, I'll be sitting in silence as I attend the retreat. No books, no internet, no disco balls, and no dancing girls. Just me and my shadows. During the journey to the Dhamma Center in Punjab, where I'd take the next step along my path, I watched the full moon from the open train doors. Interesting timing... I'm curious about what secrets will be revealed – and if I'll leave with some new insight.

Chapter Three

Vipassana Meditation

One of India's most ancient meditation techniques is called Vipassana, which means "to see things as they really are." Gautama Buddha taught Vipassana more than 2,500 years ago as a universal remedy for universal ills. This non-sectarian technique aims to eradicate mental impurities and is a way of self-transformation through self-observation. It focuses on the deep interconnection between mind and body, which can be experienced directly by disciplined attention to the physical sensations that form the life of the body and that connect and condition the life of the mind continuously. The observation-based, self-exploratory journey to the common root of mind and body is said to dissolve mental impurity, resulting in a balanced mind full of love and compassion. The scientific laws that operate one's thoughts, feelings, judgments, and sensations become clear. Through direct experience, one comes to understand the nature of how one produces suffering or frees oneself from suffering. Life becomes characterized by increased awareness, non-delusion, self-control, and peace.

Vipassin-on...

Disclaimer: I don't expect everyone who reads this to relate to it or even understand it, as it was new to me. The following story is an account of my personal experience with Vipassana Meditation in Punjab, India.

The night before Petar and I started our retreat, our journey through the Hoshiarpur District of India was quite a ride. We arrived in Punjab, and there's little I can say about this city, as we were only there for an evening. Still, it had all the usual India scenes: horns blasting, cows blocking the streets, chaiwallahs everywhere, street stalls carrying the typical jars of sweets and long, tentacle-like bags of chips that hung from its corners like giant swimming squid.

That night, I thought it would be safer (and more hygienic) to eat at a KFC (which I was shocked to see in the first place) than to tempt fate and eat at one of the many street food stands. Wrong. Waaaay wrong. I spent the entire night running to the bathroom, my body rebelling from both ends. A blanket of sweat covered me from head to toe; I shook miserably. *It's 4:00 a.m., and Petar and I are about to start this thing at 3:00 p.m.? I'm in trouble.*

Day One: Introduction

Vipass-ana: Very Impatient Person Asked to Sit Silently – ana whole lot of nausea.

I arrived at the center an hour early in a poor state and sat outside to gather myself. Half an hour later, I felt a bit more confident and strolled into the office. A man (who was clearly harassed and dealing with hassles) greeted me, rushed me to a chair at a desk, and handed me some papers. As I filled out the required forms, I noticed that the other participants were from all around the world—the UK, Israel, America, Spain, and, of course, India.

A young girl named May caught my attention. There was a quiet desperation in her eyes and a nagging cough clutched at her chest. She sat beside me, and the clerk asked her the same questions he'd asked me: "What is your profession?" "Who is your emergency contact person?" She declined to provide answers to either question.

I leaned over and said, "May, what about saying you're a professional time traveler with contacts in the stars? At least this man can write something down...."

May stared blankly beyond the office walls.

Not a good time for jokes, I guess.

I finished my application quietly and handed it in. After the frazzled man relieved me of my electronics, he asked me to take the rest of my belongings to my shared room and return in an hour for orientation.

I arrived at my room to find I'd been paired with a young girl from Spain. We snuck out of the center and shared our anticipation about the days to come—and some tobacco. Then it was orientation time, which consisted of watching an old video of an Indian man on an eighties box television (I learned later that he was S. N. Goenka, the man who revived Vipassana in the modern world). He described with great emphasis what to expect and how the program would unfold over the next ten days.

The video ended, and the man leading the meeting mumbled something that I missed. I asked another woman leaving the office what we would do next, and she replied (sternly), "Go to your room."

Ahhhh, great. I was exhausted from the travel and sickness and eager to rest. After a quick brush of my teeth and wardrobe change, I fell asleep in the sparsely furnished and dimly lit room before my head even found the pillow.

Day Two: Frustration

Vipass-ana: Violent Intentions Permeate All Sacred Spaces - ana I'm confused

The bell sounded at 4:00 a.m. I wiped the sleep from my eyes. *Where am I? Right. Meditation. Gotta go now.*

The hall was divided; men on one side, women on the other. It appeared that I'd missed something as everyone was taking what seemed to be pre-arranged seats (pillows on the floor). I took one in the back corner, as it had yet to be claimed. The first two hours went by effortlessly, minus the food poisoning discomfort, but it went from a little bit bad to worse as the day progressed. If that wasn't bad enough, I had a severe case of "monkey mind"—it was wild and on the loose and throwing poop in my face.

Many thoughts arose in my mind. Most were fueled by anger. First, there was anger at my dad, then at Jack, then at myself, and the world, and this place, and all of humanity...the list went on. The relentless onslaught from my past welled up inside of me—I felt like I was going to explode. Finally, the bell rang for lunch. I was so grateful for the break from this madness—until I arrived in the dining hall.

The food was as uninteresting and unappetizing as any I've seen in India. I stared at the plate. *What the hell am I doing here? Is this the right thing for me?* Just then an overwhelming sense of sadness and loneliness took hold, so I took a walk.

I strolled through the grounds, trying to find anything beautiful. All I saw was dust, dying flowers, and waves of heat rising from the ground. *This place isn't helping.* Step by step, I sunk deeper into depression. I realized I was giving real importance to my thoughts instead of observing them as if they were happening to someone else, and I was watching from a distance.

I returned to the hall with the group for another two hours of silence. The noise in my head had calmed down dramatically... until we began the meditation. Suddenly, I heard the drama happening in everyone present in the room. It was loud, painful, and disturbing. I stuck with it, though, and listened to the noise for what seemed like an eternity.

I finished the first day lying on the edge of the flowerless, round concrete planter in the middle of the women's area's gray stone grounds. I stared up at the stars and daydreamed. Then, out of nowhere, an overwhelming feeling of suffocation hit me. I choked and struggled to catch my breath. I retreated to my room. Once there, I couldn't ignore this incredible feeling that death was taking me somewhere, and it was coming soon. Then, suddenly, the sensation stopped. I fell asleep, and two hours later, I heard the wake-up bell chime.

Day Three: Suicidal and Homicidal Tendencies

Vipass-ana: Varying Identities Present A Special Session – ana I'm dying in here.

Shit started getting scary. I hadn't slept and was tired when I stumbled out of bed and into the courtyard. I stood in my PJs, looked into the still-dark sky. I took some deep breaths. A door slammed. The women's assistant rushed past me out of the courtyard. Moments later, two men appeared and entered room F6, across the yard from me. They left the door open.

One of the men screamed, "May! Maaaay! No, no, noooo!" I could see through the open door that he was frantically shaking a body on the bed. Then he crumpled to the floor, sobbing. I remembered the feeling I'd had a few hours before, like I was suffocating; that death was coming.

The other man looked out the door and saw me standing stiffly in the courtyard. He waved his hand as if to say, "Please, go away."

I tried to react, but I couldn't move. My feet were glued to the courtyard stones; there was a disconnect between my brain and body. May had tried to reach me. I had met her in the front office just two days earlier. She'd needed help, but I didn't know. I felt incredibly sad. *I didn't realize. I'm so sorry. I'm so sorry, May...*

I can't remember how or when I arrived back in my room. The women's assistant appeared and escorted all the women to the hall for morning meditation. My body was present, but my mind had disappeared into a wasteland. Throughout the day, the death theme haunted me. At one point, death turned on me: *"Try it out, you know, all the things troubling you will cease."* Do what? Is this happening? Did I just offer to off myself? Did it seem more appealing than looking at my shadows or staying in the present moment? This can't be real. What the heck is all this noise in my head about?

After morning meditation, I couldn't force myself to eat the unappetizing breakfast set in front of me. I decided to sit in a meditation cell in the pagoda instead of joining the others in the hall. I entered the tiny space, sat quietly, and paid attention to my thoughts. They had diminished in intensity (compared to when I'd been sitting with the others) but still came, as if the volume had been turned down momentarily. I felt anger (hatred even), sadness, and confusion: all the ingredients for a crazy cake. *There I go again, making judgments. I've slipped out of observation mode yet again.*

The flow of thoughts continued for three hours, and it was time for lunch. Still, I couldn't seem to eat.

The women's assistant approached me. "Why weren't you in the hall this morning after breakfast?" she demanded.

I pointed to the schedule painted in giant blue English letters on the wall behind her. "We have a choice," I explained. "We can meditate in the hall, in the pagoda, or in our room. I chose the pagoda. So please, back off."

She huffed off.

After lunch, it was time again to choose where to meditate. I chose my room. I was exhausted from my upset stomach, the lack of nutrients, and from realizing that when I'm in the hall with the others, I can feel everyone's shadows (which is overwhelming enough).

The assistant entered my room and slapped my bed with her hand. "You should be in the hall with the others," she said meanly, "not in here sleeping. This is not Vipassana."

I looked up at her—into her—and saw that she couldn't see or respect my state of health. That kept me from exploding, getting up, pushing her out of the room, and slamming the door in her face. I ignored her and rolled over. A half-hour later, I joined the others in the hall for group meditation at the scheduled time.

The reflection went OK, but again, playing in the background, this darkness of hatred and anger was troubling. I watched, but it scared me. I witnessed warlike thoughts and feelings. Profound, dark destruction—as if the world and everything in it were being annihilated.

The bell rang. I retreated to the pagoda cell again, attempting to regain balance. I fell asleep, and that suited me fine.

We finished the day watching another video on the eighties TV, the volume so loud it sounded like the master was talking with a mouthful of marbles. I didn't gain anything from it (other than more confusion and frustration).

Day Four: The Great Escape

Vipass-ana: Vipassana Isn't Providing a Spiritual Sensation - ana I'm ready to go.

The day started at 4:30 a.m. I shuffled to the meditation hall to join the group. After missing breakfast, lunch, and dinner for three days, my body felt weak. I was also mentally exhausted. I looked for Petar. When his eyes met mine for the first time since we started this thing, I felt a connection, and tears fell. I didn't want to sit in this hall anymore, now that I knew all the crazy thoughts were a part of the collective energy that I was tuning into somehow. I wanted to be held. I wanted to cry out, to kick and scream and slam my hands into the earth. I wanted to focus on my inner work—not digest the thoughts and feelings of others.

I managed a smile. *I'll connect with him soon.* I closed my eyes to meditate. The "show" started again, bigger and wilder than before. My monkey mind was having a jungle party. I sat with this for two hours.

After an unappetizing meal, I decided to retreat to the pagoda to meditate for the next three hours—alone. After a calmer meditation session by myself, I went to my room to lie down.

The boss-lady arrived, yet again. "If you're not here to practice true Vipassana, then...."

"Yes," I said. "I'm leaving. Your job here is done."

She stood there with an expression of confused satisfaction on her face.

I turned to the wall and heard her walk from the room.

I got up, packed my things, and walked through the courtyard toward the office—but I didn't make it. I collapsed in tears. Petar appeared and held me in his arms. I felt like I was falling to pieces. "I can't do this," I said. "You can stay, but I can't do any more of it," I said.

"Let's go then. I'm ready, too. This center is not the best place to do Vipassana. Trust me, I know—I've done this before and have something to compare it to. Look around. Everything is dead or dying. The food is terrible, and the organization is practically non-existent. It's not a good center for this process."

I was relieved.

We began our departure procedure. It took time because a couple of the program's facilitators confronted us as I dug for some rupees to donate to the center. I explained that I appreciated the opportunity, but it just wasn't for me.

One of the facilitators said, "It's not recommended to contribute if you didn't complete the program and receive its benefits."

I stuffed the money into the donation box hanging on the wall. "I did learn something," I said. "I know I need to explore further, so I thank you for the opportunity to experience some of this lesson here."

There were two detectives in the office—no doubt they were investigating May's death. They overheard our conversation and offered us a ride to the bus station. We accepted.

As we rolled along in the car, one of the investigators lifted a large envelope from his lap and poured some photos on the seat between us. "What do you know about May's passing?" he asked, sifting through the images of her lifeless body.

May's face was blue, speckled with black dots. Her eyes were wide open—her hands curled into fists at her waist. I felt a wave of sadness. I closed my eyes and attempted to shake the images. I didn't share with the detective that I'd felt her death—that she was somehow calling out to me—I kept quiet. I would probably sound like a crazy person and create more questions. I shook my head and looked out the window.

Petar and I arrived at the station and boarded the bus to Dharamshala. That's where Tony and Zoey were. I needed to be close to people I knew and loved; a return to familiarity was essential. As the miles between us and the other sixty meditators at the center increased, I felt calmer. I was glad we'd left.

Vipassana is touted as a highly effective meditation program for self-inquiry seekers, and I had been curious to experience it. However, after four days, I realized it's not for everyone. Or better yet—not for everyone in every stage of experience. I learned (in hindsight mostly) that I have yet to master the art of not eating others' energy. The process was bizarre—it left me feeling in need of guidance. I asked the universe for help, let the request go, and got ready to journey into the Himalayas.

Chapter Four

Dharamshala and The Dalai Lama

When we found Tony and Zoey, they told us they'd found the Dalai Lama's temple complex, and they'd heard he'd be there in four days to give a speech to the monks. I was thrilled to have a chance to see such a highly revered spiritual guide and spent the next three days in eager anticipation of going to his temple in Dharamshala. "Dharamshala" means "a spiritual dwelling," and after the darkness of Vipassana, I was happy to be in a place considered to be a rest stop for pilgrims. I felt like a pilgrim needing rest!

Surrounded by a dense cedar forest, Dharamshala became the center of the Tibetan world in India after the 1959 Tibetan uprising; many refugees had followed the Dalai Lama there. The city is divided into Lower Dharamshala, where the bazaar (shopping street) and markets are, and Upper Dharamshala, where the Dalai Lama lives. We didn't spend much time in the lower part, but instead headed for the hills. The trek was arduous. The farther we climbed with our heavy gear, the more the crowd thinned. I climbed what felt like a thousand narrow steps up a steep hill and rested at a café near the top. An Indian man with bleached hair and too many necklaces offered me tea and cookies. I accepted gladly. Back-packers from all around the world were perched along the steps and sitting in the abundant tea shops that lined the hillside. Some were making jewelry, some were making music, but mostly they were talking—and drowning out the sounds of nature.

A baba (holy man) entered the tea shop I was in, sat at a distance, and watched me like a hawk. He was shirtless, wore a long orange cloth like a skirt, and had shoulder-length dark hair. He was silent and was served tea with just a wave of his hand—*What a mysterious man.* When the server returned to ask if I'd like more tea, I asked him about the baba with eyes like a bird.

"That's Silent Baba. He hasn't spoken a word in twelve years," he said.

"Silent Baba? Is he like... a sadhu?"

"Like, but not like."

"What does that mean?"

"He's more like a legendary healer here. He does ener-gy work."

Energy work? I thought of Vukosava back at the hotel, who had healed my neck and shoulders using en-ergy work.

"He doesn't speak... like, ever?"

"Not for the last twelve years."

The man left, and Silent Baba stood and walked to my table. He made a gesture, another sweeping motion with his hand as to ask, "May I sit here?"

I nodded, and he sat.

I looked into his eyes, tried to read what was happen-ing in his mind.

He looked back at me and smiled.

"Is it true that you haven't spoken in twelve years?" I asked.

He nodded.

"What made you want to do that?" I asked. Then I realized he couldn't answer. *Or could he?*

He looked around and threw his hands up. He mimed an answer that appeared to be, "In a world so full of noise, why would I want to add to it?" Of course, this was a guess, but it felt like that could have been his answer.

The people here seemed steeped in their spiritual evolution, like the many tea bags that rested in mugs of hot water at cafes named after yogi catchphrases. "Peace Café, Joyful Café, Hope Café, Open Heart Café, Mandala Coffee Shop, Shiva Café, and the Bodhi Tree Café all boasted their best versions of the locally harvested black teas. It was hippie central, and ganga smoke filled the air. The conversations I overheard were about yoga, meditation, Ayahuasca, Reiki, energy work, and the importance of a vegan diet. I thought about the many women who had helped me along my path with their understanding of healing—the energy and lightworker warriors who had assisted me in cleansing my soul.

On the other hand, I couldn't help but feel that spirituality was for sale here and that Silent Baba noticed. But as Sri Mooji had said back in Rishikesh, *allow others the space to find their path.* Again, I thought of the women. The beautiful goddesses who opened their hearts and their homes to me. The ones who made the journey more interesting....

Silent Baba hissed at me and nodded toward the door. Tony stood in the doorway.

"Hey, Tony! Over here!" I said.

Silent Baba smiled a toothy grin.

"Tony, this is Silent Baba."

"Alright, mate! Nice to see you again!" Tony said.

"You two have already met?" I asked.

"Yeah. When Zoey and I came out of the mountains at dawn, you were smoking a chillum with some other mate," he said to Silent Baba. "Weren't you both covered in ash?"

Silent Baba nodded.

"Right. So, Melissa, we have a room. It's at the very top of the hill. There might be something else open there if you'd like to check it out?"

"Sounds good," I said. "I'd love some rest. *But wait. How did this baba know that Tony was there for me? Huh. It seems like superpowers can be found in silence.*

The big day finally arrived—it was time to make our way to the Dalai Lama's Temple complex. At the entrance, some people were standing at a table. They greeted Tony, Petar, Zoey, and me, and before we were allowed to enter, they looked inside our bags for security reasons.

The temple and surrounding gardens were spectacular. The scents of pine and citrus wafted through the air. Tibetan flags hung above us, zigzagging from the building on the right across to the one on the left. I thought of Opal's house in San Francisco. The structures to which the flags were attached housed hundreds of monks. *Had I heard that right? Hundreds of monks live here?*

We found a lovely open space to sit on the lawn. A monk carrying a large teapot and cups approached us, bowed, and offered us chai. We accepted. Tony left for a few minutes and returned with a small silver radio.

"I wanted to hear this in English, and this Israeli man just appeared and handed me the radio on his way out. What luck, right?" he said.

Was it luck? Or did he manifest that?

The radio played a static-infused English translation of the Dalai Lama's speech in the towering temple beyond.

I wanted a closer look at what was inside, so I left our group and walked up the steps to the entrance. Before going through the large doors, I had to pass through a metal detector and received a physical pat-down. It makes sense—sadly, many peace leaders have been killed over the years. They need protection. I passed through security and entered the temple. I took two steps inside and stopped because that was as far as I could move physically. There before me, hundreds of monks were sitting in rows, in a meditative lotus position. They were all wearing traditional red-orange robes and had shaved heads, except for a small patch in the back. Equally spaced and eerily still, they looked like potted seeds waiting to sprout. The rows began on the floor at the edge of the raised stage and continued to the entrance where I stood. On the stage sat the Dalai Lama and three other men I didn't recognize. The Dalai Lama spoke; the others translated, and the monks listened. I stood there until I felt awkward—like an intruder in a sacred ceremony. It felt as if it was intended for those who had dedicated their lives to this path. I hadn't devoted my life to a spiritual practice—yet. It seemed I was still collecting the pieces of what that would look like for me.

I returned to the garden—to the radio. Whereas the temple was filled with monks, the expansive gardens were filled with people from all over the world, here for the Dalai Lama's teachings. The Dalai Lama said that for the outer world to have peace, the individual must have inner peace—that to achieve a happy life, we must look from a broader perspective. We need to face our convictions and our belief systems; we must challenge ourselves to do so. He advocated for the cultivation of human values like forgiveness, tolerance, and self-discipline, which I wanted to embody.

The hot sun beat down on my brow; I covered my face with a scarf. I took my shoes off, lay back in the grass, and listened to the crackling translation.

The Dalai Lama encouraged harmony among religious traditions and said that all world religions have the potential to create positivity. He said it's essential they respect one another and see the value in their respective traditions. He said that human beings experience several aspects of the truth. He stressed the importance of education—and said that the current education system is no longer adequate as it's mainly oriented to acquiring things with material value. He asked that we look at our education systems carefully and find a way to teach inner values.

I admired His Holiness's wisdom and commitment. As a preschool teacher, I know that education plays an essential role in everyone's lives and in building better societies for all. We stayed for a couple of hours, listening, drinking chai, and resting in the garden before agreeing it was time to go. Tony and Zoey had decided to travel to Thailand. Petar received news that his grandmother's health was failing, so he was returning to Switzerland. I wanted to visit the wizard in Germany, to share what I'd discovered and work with him more, so I traveled with Petar, as Charles' hotel was close to Switzerland.

Chapter Five

Downsizing Miracles

It was mid-May when I arrived at the hotel. I fell back into my role as the Housemeister. During the next several months, Charles and I had many conversations about what I'd experienced on my journeys. We discussed where I was on my tour of discovery. *What might still be hiding in the shadows? Was there anything I was doing unconsciously to avoid seeing shadows playing in the background?*

I'd grown through my authority and control themes. I'd developed a better understanding of the over-responsibility I'd taken on in my family—like having tried to change the dissolving relationship between my parents before excusing myself altogether. Working through those issues led me to experience a higher level of happiness, abundance, and freedom. But I still had work to do. There were remnants of those previous themes that needed integration, and the other two—food and sexuality—also needed my awareness.

I'd planned to leave and start that new journey of discovery, but before I could, I became very ill with a violent chest cold, coupled with a painful index finger. A splinter had lodged itself under my fingernail, and my finger was swelling steadily. For several days, I lay in my yurt, wheezing and breathing shallowly. I applied a eucalyptus salve to my neck daily, and the room smelled pungent.

Several empty tea mugs were scattered around. I lay on my back, facing the transparent dome, and watched as the wind made the tree branches dance.

I heard a gentle knock at the door.

"Come in," I said, gasping for air. The gasping turned to violent coughing.

Charles entered the yurt.

He sat down beside me on the bed. I sat up and tried to steady myself as the coughing continued. He placed one hand on my back and the other on my heart and closed his eyes. After a couple of minutes, he removed his hands, lifted my sore finger, and pulled on it twice. I winced.

He smiled at me as he set my hand down.

"So? I'm off to the Sahara now—and you?" he asked.

"Well, first, I'd like to feel better. Then I'll go to America for a visit."

He nodded. "So so so," he said, and walked to the door.

"What's my homework this time?"

"Nothing. The door is now open; it will be coming to you now."

"OK... Hey, why don't you ever talk about magic? I mean, I want to learn. Why don't you tell me how to do it?"

"The gifts are lost through communication. Talking about it brings one back into ego. So? So so so...."

I was perplexed—yet again—by Charles' cryptic speech. But I was so tired; I fell asleep. I woke up eighteen hours later, the following day. When I woke up, I was healed. I mean entirely. The swelling and pain in my finger were gone. It was like my crazy chest cold had never happened. *No way. Can he work miracles, too? How does he do this magic?* At that moment, what I thought was possible expanded, and my desire to understand these levels grew.

A few days later, I went through the house and hugged everyone on the team. Frank, the chef, asked if I'd return at the end of the year to help him with the Silvester Celebration, a huge, 200-guest, four-day-long event from December 29 to January 2. He promised it would be a lot of fun—so I said yes.

I retreated to my yurt to pack my bag. In essence, I realized that I was over-packed and over-prepared: I had band-aids, a stitch kit, antibiotics, and pharmaceuticals for a range of conditions. *How did I acquire so many things in such a short time?* I rummaged through the piles. I had tank tops, shorts, and skirts for hot weather, and long pants and bulky sweaters for cold weather. My toiletry bag had a life of its own. It overflowed with glitters, razors, mini-lotions, and soaps. Then there was the mystery sack that cradled the random, various bits and bobs that made things more interesting. My favorites were a set each of the flag and LED poi and a kit to make bracelets to gift to other beings along the way, to remember and be remembered. I had Burning Man goggles, my four-foot-high "Free Hugs" banner, stickers, and other sundry items.

I'd accumulated so much stuff while volunteering and living in Germany, and I realized now just how little I'd needed.

The repacking dance was slow. I heard the mantra I'd always chanted to develop my belief that backpacking around the world was possible: *I always have what I need and when I need it.* My experiences had reflected, over and over, that this was true. There had been moments when I'd left things behind that I'd later felt I'd needed. Whenever that feeling had arisen, what I'd required had always appeared. There were so many of these moments, I couldn't imagine them as coincidences but instead intentional manifestations coupled with divine interventions. I saw how much weight I was carrying.

I had filled my sixty-liter backpack; there wasn't much room left. I looked at my bag. It could be lighter, and the more I was able to let go, the more space I made for magic. I wanted freedom from attachment to material things and understood how little I needed to survive—and thrive. The lower I'd sunk into myself, the more illumination, contact, and support I'd gained.

It's been incredible! I'm eager to learn new levels of this kind of understanding and connection. I have to let go again.

I unpacked the backpack and looked at the piles around me: *I'm going to take another leap into trust, cut the baggage down, and let the magic flow.* Piece by piece, I reduced the clothes from seven of each item to three. The large compression bag now closed on its own. *That was easy.*

Then came the medicine bag. This was difficult to let go of, as my loving mother (who's a doctor) had filled it to the brim because of her fears that I would be somewhere, catch something, and not have the treatment I needed to survive. I'd carried this load for three years and had only used one antibiotic packet for myself while in Morocco. Then I remembered Sarah. She was a Canadian girl of about eighteen who traveled super light. When we met, I'd seen her hobbling down a path at the Rainbow Gathering in Palenque, carrying a small backpack and leading a dog. She had a strange limp and a bandage around her leg, so I had approached her.

"Hey, are you alright?"

She sat down slowly and told me a story about how some people had stolen her dog, Luna. "The people who had her wanted money—like a ransom," she said. "We don't have any money. With the help of some locals, I tracked them down. I found Luna in a building and kicked through the glass window to get her out. That's how I cut my leg." She turned to her dog and patted her on the head.

My heart went out to both of them. "Can I see the injury?" I said. I might have something that'll help you."

She nodded and unwrapped the dirty bandage, exposing her calf. The cuts were dirty, deep, and already infected. "Stay here for a sec, yeah? I'll go get my medicine bag and some water."

I returned, washed, and re-dressed her wound.

"How's your pain level?" I asked.

"Yeah, it hurts, mostly when I walk. And we walk a lot."

I had several bottles of painkillers leftover from my knee surgeries and some antibiotics for infection and offered them. Sarah knew which ones would work for her. As we parted, I silently thanked my mom. That wasn't the only time my medicine stash had been helpful for another traveler. Yet, I had to let it go. I kept two packs of antibiotics and placed the rest in a small box to leave at the hotel. I'd have to explain this later to Mom when she asked to see what needed replacing. I took the risk.

I emptied the bag of games and glitter and kept the "Free Hugs" sign and the flag and LED sets of poi. My bag was now half the size, two-thirds of the weight, and I felt lighter. It was time to catch the train to the airport and return to America.

Year Four - Optional Questions for Self-Reflection: Acknowledgement

This one can be tricky. Acknowledge without judgment and embrace with awareness whatever thoughts appear in your mind. Listen objectively and remember not to antagonize or criticize the shadow. Negative self-talk may arise, but simply noticing and acknowledging this inner dialogue helps to calm it and move back into the light. Practice, practice. Write what you find in your journal.

Year 5

USA

Chapter One

Transformation Under Construction

The day I landed in L.A., I wanted to see my DJ buddy, Santiago, whom I'd missed on a previous trip. I'd first seen Santiago at Burning Man in 2004. He played a wicked set of breakbeat and drum and bass on the Lush camp stage.

I'd enjoyed Santiago's set more than any of the hundreds I'd heard over the ten days I was there. I hoped to see him play again. Two months after Burning Man, that wish had come true. I was bar tending at a nightclub in Santa Monica when in walked that awesome DJ from the desert party. No way! That's the guy! That's the DJ from Burning Man!

He played another great set that night in our club, and the club owner introduced us. Our friendship blossomed like spring flowers and has endured over all these years. Santiago was a gentleman; authentic, respectful, and kind. I admired him. His Columbian roots gave him a cultural flair, and he smiled at everyone who passed his way. He didn't take life seriously, enjoyed making people bounce on a dance floor, and was open-hearted and warm. I wanted to hug him again. It had been too long.

While waiting for my girlfriend Angelina to pick me up from the airport, I sent Santiago a message. He replied that he was in San Bernardino at the Beyond Wonderland Festival and was DJ'ing there that weekend. "How long are you in town for?" he texted. "If you wanna come, I'll get you a VIP bracelet. You can camp with us in the OG camp. Lots of old homies here. You should come."

Heck yes! I'm in!

Angelina's midnight-black Dodge Ram 1500 Hemi truck came to a screeching stop at the curb in front of me. She rolled down the window. "Quick! Get in!" she yelled. "I think the coppers aren't going to like me being here." Her eyes darted from mirror to mirror.

I laughed, threw my backpack in, and slammed the door. The tires squealed, and she sped away as if she'd just robbed a bank.

Angelina and I had met in 2003, when I first moved to Los Angeles. We worked together as bartenders in that nightclub in Santa Monica where the "OG" (original gangstas) crew was formed over time. She was small like me and also had the energy and enthusiasm of a classroom full of preschoolers. It took us some time to become close because the room just wasn't big enough for both of us. She didn't trust my openness and the fact that I didn't like to have secrets. She always told me I had a big mouth and didn't know when to keep it shut. I guess to some extent she was right. Once we became friends, though, we were inseparable. On many occasions, after the club closed, we would go to her house and talk until sunrise. That's where she'd tell me tales of her solo travel abroad to Italy and other places that had piqued my interest in traveling solo long before I started this journey. She lived close to Los Angeles International Airport and always insisted I call her first when I flew in, which I always did.

"What's up, girl? How have you been? Oh man, I have so much to tell you! Do you have plans already? I bet you do. You better make some time for me, girl. How long are you here for?" she asked, taking a pull from her vape pen.

"Yeah, hi!" I laughed. "Well, now that you mention it, I do have plans. But just for the first two days. Then I'll come straight to your house, OK?"

"I knew it! Where you goin'?"

"I want to rent a car and go see Santiago at the Nos Center. Think you can take me to get one?"

"Of course! When are you going? I wanna see you too!"

"Well—I'm staying for ten days, soooo I can come straight to your house in like two or three days? I wanna see you too!"

She agreed. In just a couple of hours, I had a car and headed to San Bernardino.

When I arrived at the festival, I told them who I was and that I'd be camping in the OG camp. They treated me like royalty. They snapped that VIP bracelet on my arm, gave me a pass for my car, and had me follow a souped-up golf cart right to the camp. After I parked, I saw Santiago and his wife, Kate. I jumped into his arms and hugged him tightly. He smiled and told me he loved me. I could feel it. I loved him, too. We turned to the camp, and I saw a drop-dead gorgeous man with light-brown skin and pitch-black hair. I turned to Kate and whispered, "Who's that?"

She looked over my shoulder. "Oh, him? That's Arif. He joined our group not long after you left and has worked on some of our projects. He's an engineer. Why? Do you like him?"

"Well, I don't know, but he sure is cute!"

"Come on. I'll introduce you."

We joined the others. Introductions were made, friendships were rekindled. Arif caught my eye. I watched him maneuver through the crowd as he made his way to me.

"Hey," he said. "We haven't met yet. I'm Arif."

"Hello, I'm Melissa."

"So, uh, you camping alone too?"

"Yeah. This trip was super spontaneous. I only have a hammock and a onesie pajama with me."

"Awesome. That's my tent over there. It has a lot of space. If you need to use it, you can. For whatever. It gets pretty cold here at night."

Well, that's forward. I wonder what he's really offering? I wonder what it is I want...

"Thanks, that's cool. I appreciate it."

Arif and I hung out during the festival and had a great time. The event's theme was 'Beyond Wonderland,' and there were around 60,000 people there. The stages towered above the crowd and offered light shows and pyrotechnics that I swear were alien-made. I'd never seen tech like that before. From a distance, we saw the pyramid-shaped main stage launch several lines of fire into the night sky—they lit up the entire venue. The giant pirate ship built on the frame of an Isuzu NQR is where we listened to Santiago play his wicked set of electronic breakbeat music that had me dancing for three hours straight. The ship once belonged to a designer from Space Island (a venue that housed a crew of set designers and DJs) but had been sold to the Beyond Wonderland group this year. The event was well-managed; there was lots of space (considering the large crowds), and visually, it was stunning. Three days later, though, I was exhausted and ready to go back to Los Angeles.

I visited Angelina for a couple of days, as promised. Then Arif and I spent the rest of the week together. He took me to meet his parents, and I invited him to join me in Dallas for a wedding where he could meet several of my family members. We spent our first few weeks together in bliss. After so many years of traveling and dating only myself, I thought, *Maybe I'm ready for partnership?* I wanted to spend more time with this interesting man. But I had a commitment to keep—so Arif and I parted ways, and I returned to Germany to help Frank with the Silvester Celebration.

The event was everything Frank had promised it would be. Satyaa and Pari, who led the Satsang and arranged the accompanying yoga and chanting mantra sessions, had for several years had a tradition of hosting the event at the hotel. The sessions were quite popular. The Satsang was similar to the meeting with Sri Mooji in Rishikesh, with discussions of "truth," but on a smaller scale, and with more music and opportunities for movement.

Traditionally, the word "Satsang" referred only to a gathering in the presence of a truly enlightened being, or satguru. In modern times, Satsang has evolved to mean any gathering in which spiritual reflection, discussion, meditation, or teaching occur. Satsang in a group can affect the ego profoundly, as entering into a shared space of support and unity encourages selfless emotions to arise. *Like the BioDanza, isn't it? And the Sahara....*

Satsang is believed to dissolve any sense of separation, allowing the inter-connectivity of all beings in the universe to become apparent. It's believed that extraordinary awakening can occur in the company of those committed to bringing out the best in one another. Satsang is an aid on the yogic path to moksha (liberation from suffering and the cycle of death and rebirth). It helps to remove the negative thoughts, material attachments, and mental obstacles that block this path. As such, Satsang helps keep people engaged in spiritually centered thoughts and helps them maintain focus on their spiritual path.

The days were filled with deep discussions on truth, mantra singing, and music made with a wide variety of instruments: flutes, bongos, bass guitars, accordions, and chimes, to name a few. Satyaa led Kundalini yoga classes that included singing and chanting. It was a different way to welcome in the New Year than I was used to. It was more... connecting, rejoicing, and loving. I liked it.

After the event, Frank invited me to Austria to experience snowboarding for the first time. *I'd had a daydream at Mom's house about flying down a mountain on a snowboard!* So, naturally, I said, "Yes!" Nestled on the side of the hill, Frank's rented A-frame, loft-style guest house with exposed wooden beams was cozy. I gazed out of the window at the lightly falling, powdery snow.

"Want to see my kitchen?" Frank asked in his thick German accent.

"Your kitchen?"

"Where I've been cooking... before the Jonathan Hotel."

"Oh yeah, cool! Yeah, let's see it."

"It's here," he said and grinned. "Take clothes. We go ski down the mountain today."

"What do you mean it's here?"

"Yes. Downstairs. Let's go!"

Frank had taken me to the lodge in Austria where he had first learned to cook for groups of people. It was similar to the Jonathan in that it offered the group atmospheres, but on a much smaller scale. It was peaceful and warm.

I ended up tumbling down the glacier's bunny hill on the snowboard while children as young as four flew past me on skis. It wasn't at all as graceful as it had been in the daydream I'd had—but it was fun. By the end of the day, I could get down that bunny hill without falling once. *Persistence paid off.*

A few days later, Frank and I returned to the hotel in Germany. I'd been in constant contact with Arif, and we'd discussed the possibility of traveling together—what that might look like, where we'd go, and what we'd do. Our next meeting was in China. The company he worked for sent him to install a Digital Domain Gunner (a Virtual Reality WWII simulation game) during the week of his birthday. I met him in Beijing. But the piece he was there to install was held up in customs, so there wouldn't be any work for him after all. So, we chose to explore this strange city.

We made our way to a store to buy snacks to keep in our hotel room. While we wandered the grocery store, a large aquarium-like stand at one end caught my attention. I approached it and saw several live creatures inside: Turtles, squid, shrimp. I walked closer. I saw a softball-sized frog sitting above the water on a tank filter. I peered into the frog's eyes. What I saw shocked me. I blacked out and hit the floor. I woke up crying and remembered: I'd seen the reflection of my eyes in the frog's eyes—it was as if he were me, and I were him.

Arif stood over me and shook my shoulders. He pulled me up from the floor, embarrassed. "Get up! What are you doing?" he said impatiently. "And stop crying like a baby."

"I... I saw myself in his eyes."

Uneasy and embarrassed, Arif walked away and continued shopping. I took another look at (and a photo of) the frog, which was now swimming toward me. I needed to remember this moment. No longer interested in food, I waited outside. Back at the hotel, Arif suggested we get massages. I agreed wholeheartedly. At the concierge, we asked where we could find the best massage. The man gave us the address and phone number of a therapist, hailed a taxi and explained (in Chinese) to the driver where to take us.

In the therapy office, we realized that this would be no ordinary massage. Our therapists were both blind. The woman at the reception pointed this out when she took us to our respective rooms, which were separated by a curtain. I have to admit, I'm a bit of a massage connoisseur and have tried different styles in almost every country I've visited. But this proved to be a unique experience. My therapist was incredibly responsive, and the fact that I didn't speak Chinese and he didn't speak English was no problem. He listened to my body. Through the curtain, I heard Arif asking for more pressure, which his therapist somehow understood. When the man applied that new force, Arif screamed out in... was it... pain? Pleasure? I wasn't sure. Neither was his therapist—he called an English-speaking friend and put him on speakerphone to ask if Arif was OK.

"Yes. I want it to cause pain. The more pressure, the better. Tell him to keep going and dig deeper!"

More screams belted through the curtain, and both of our therapists laughed. It was absurd. It seemed that Arif didn't want the man to listen to the requests his body made—his idea of a successful massage was pressure and pain. I thanked my therapist for giving my body exactly what it needed.

Back at the hotel, we relaxed before going out for the evening to a party Arif had found online by using a unique VPN to gain access. *Does the government restrict the internet in Beijing? What's that about?*

I was ready to go before he was and told him I wanted to have a cigarette while he finished primping and whatnot. Outside, a man joined me in the smoking area, and we struck up a conversation about why we were in Beijing and how we were each enjoying the city. After the cigarette, I waited for Arif, but when he didn't appear, I went up to the room. I found him ready to go—with his suitcases packed. "Everything OK?" I asked.

"Yep. Everything is just fine. You go on enjoying yourself with that man down there. I'm making plans to go back to LA."

Do what? "OK, do you still want to go to that thing you found online?"

"Well, I did, but I can see that you've already found something else to do."

What? "You can't be serious. I was waiting for you, having a smoke. That man came outside, and we talked while I waited for you. What's your problem?"

He stomped around the room. His big, dramatic movements added to the size of his story.

"Can't we just go to the party?" I asked.

He agreed, and we went to the party. But his attitude persisted throughout the evening and into the next two days. I was ready to get the hell out. I prayed to make it through the week without exploding. I failed. On the second to last day, I'd had enough. I snapped. I threw my boot off toward the wall while screaming at him.

He was instantly calm. "Just look at yourself. I see you. What's your problem?" he said.

"Are you kidding me? What's my problem? Is this what you wanted with all that hating on me and acting like an asshole? You wanted to see me lose my cool and explode so you could point the finger at me? You are the reason I've become aggressive! How can you not see that?" I was grateful the week was over. I wanted to get back to Germany and was eager to catch my flight out the next day.

When I returned to the hotel, I spoke to Charles and explained what I'd experienced in Beijing. He pointed out two things that assisted me greatly in growing from the situation. First, Arif's bad attitude is often just a way to get attention, and many people who experience harmonious love can't believe it. It throws their system into shock. This is especially true if they carry within them a pattern of unworthiness or unlovability. They do things (mostly unconsciously) to sabotage this, to keep their "unlovable" story alive. Second, the outburst of anger I'd had may have been due to him not meeting my expectations. I wanted to have fun together, without drama. The honeymoon was over; the unpleasant parts of our personalities were showing.

Arif and I didn't speak for a few days, but we were in contact and ended up meeting a few months later—this time in Rio de Janeiro. We both worked at the Olympic Games—he was the engineer for the NBA Virtual Reality Game his company was offering, and I worked as his assistant. And again, the same scenario played out. After twenty days in a confined space, I realized we were provoking reactions in one another that were too much to handle. I no longer felt light and happy in his presence, and I think he felt the same—too much drama. I wished we could have a well-balanced partnership; there were so many things I adored about him. But the repetitive games wore me thin. I insisted he look at this pattern with me—but got a definite "No." He wasn't willing to see that he had a role in our play. Instead, he insisted it was all me, that my "spiritual practice and teachers" were fake dogma and bullshit. He said I needed a reality check. I felt that looking at our issues together was the way through, that the way to keep growing was to see and speak our truths. We were at an impasse.

Any spark of hope I'd had of us growing together was extinguished. I decided to end our relationship. I suggested we could remain friends if he wanted but said I was not willing to play these games, that I could hear and respect his "No."

Being in a relationship is a great way to evolve in inner work, as interactions with others allow us to see ourselves clearly. Still, Arif and I could really trigger each other—it turned sour fast, and all the plans we'd made of renovating an RV and traveling the States together disappeared.

The whole experience with him was helpful, though—it showed me that I did want a partnership, but one with a foundation built on the willingness of both people to "see" ourselves.

I still had the pull to build that RV, though! I researched and found a few great options—one, in particular, I'll share with you in the next chapter.

Before I left Germany, I asked the wizard what he saw for me—and if I had any homework.

"When you're reaching the end of your series of themes, your crooked front tooth will begin to turn," he said. I laughed, hugged him, and left to make my way back to the States.

Chapter Two

Saṃsāra. The Game Changer

Saṃsāra and I met online when I was still in Germany. I searched for her on the usual sites for months but came across only typical "out of my league" types. But then I found "the one." She ended up testing my faith, my temper, and my perseverance. Most of all, she tested my willingness to stop at nothing to follow my dreams. I knew we were meant for one another right from the start, even before I met her in person.

We didn't meet until a couple of months later, after the summer was over and fall had begun to creep in. Fall has majestic ways of making everything look so different in a short period. After flying from Germany with a brief stopover in Atlanta, I stepped out of the airport terminal in Florida. I felt like I was breathing in the heat from a steam shower. My future with Saṃsāra began here—in the dirty south, surrounded by white sand beaches, friends and family, and trash cans. Lots and lots of trash cans.

Over three months, I fell in love with a machine. Saṃsāra is an early 90's Ford E250 Conversion van. Saṃsāra is a Sanskrit word that means "wandering" or "world," and it has the connotation of cyclic, circuitous change. Saṃsāra is sometimes referred to with terms like transmigration, karmic cycle, reincarnation, or "a cycle of aimless drifting, wandering, or mundane existence," which was synonymous with where I was in my life.

Saṃsāra's exterior and her fading grey lines showed her age. There was a sad, tear-soaked darkness about her that permeated every corner. The neglect and disregard she'd been subjected to made her all the more appealing. She was what I needed; I was what she needed.

We needed to purge together, to expel and recreate. This is one of the main reasons we met. We started to see each other every day in Mom's driveway from 10:00 a.m. to 5:00 p.m. It took some time for me to search around, expose her sensitive spots, get to the core of who she was. *Who would we become together? How would we serve each other?*

I'm sure that by now, you've come to understand that I have a semi-permanent case of wanderlust and a desire to grow. When I got back to the States, I chose to remodel and live out of a conversion van to satiate those needs. But I wasn't prepared for what I'd gotten myself into.

Designing and building a nineteen foot by six foot, comfortable, affordable, and efficient space was both challenging and rewarding. Before I started building, I spent time in my hammock daydreaming. I imagined where we'd go, what we'd do together. I saw us driving to all sorts of places: catching sun on beautiful beaches, playing games like Farkle or Rummy at my grandma's house; spending long, slow days at hot springs or in forests; parking in shady spots while I went hiking in the mountains. I imagined visiting festivals and taking friends old and new on short trips into wild and not-so-wild spaces. I saw myself traveling in her, reading, writing, volunteering, and, of course, daydreaming.

Rebuilding Saṃsāra was a crucial test of my patience. *Didn't that wizard say something about me not being* familiar with slowness and receiving? To complete what I set out to do, I had to surrender and allow—difficult for me. Whereas I wanted to go out and do everything alone, instead, I consciously allowed others to help me. I had no idea what I was doing, so I was forced to move slowly. It was a good opportunity to put all of my recent lessons into practice.

One day, my best friend Paul pulled into Mom's driveway in his Chevy Silverado.

"Whatcha doin', Shiny?" he said.

"Shiny" was a nickname Paul had given me when I'd returned for a visit after three years of traveling. When I asked him why that name, he said, "Because you're all shiny now."

"Looking at the mess I've gotten myself into," I said.

"Yeah. It's going to need some work for sure. I'll be right back."

As quick as he'd come, he was gone. I sat on the lawn, head in my hands. I looked at Saṃsāra. *How is this all going to come together?* I'd bought her for $3,000, but she'd need a considerable investment of time and cash before we'd be able to go anywhere. *How will this work out?* I lay in the grass and looked up at the powder-blue sky. *I have faith. It has to work. I want it bad enough. I have just what I need and right when I need it.* I imagined it would all work out effortlessly and then released the desirable thoughts—just as Paul pulled back into the driveway.

He'd arrived with his trailer. He jumped from the truck and went to work. He swung the heavy rear door of the trailer open and pulled out an aluminum table. "You're going to need some things to tackle this beast of a project," he said, unfolding the legs of the table and setting it close to the van. "I think I have enough here to get you started."

With lightning speed, he filled the table with tools. He'd brought a jigsaw, a power extension cord, sandpaper, a power drill with bits, carpenter pencils, a tape measure, utility knives with fresh blades, power and ground wires, and safety goggles and gloves.

"Wow! Thank you! What would I do without you?" I said.

"You'd be fine, I'm sure. I think you should start by ripping that gross carpet out and see what's under there. I have a job to do, but I'll come back later and help you. Take the seats out first. See you in a bit."

He was off—that was just like Paul. I'd met him in middle school, and we became instant best friends. We'd been inseparable in high school, and over the years, we'd been on many adventures. After graduation, he'd gone into construction work and became a talented carpenter. I think his love for fixing things and passion for creating beauty fueled his work. He could build and fix just about anything—from re-roofing the local shopping mall, laying the foundations for a new building, or something as simple as fixing a friend's toilet or broken door. No job was too big or too small for him. He loved challenges and would always say, "Yeah, we can fix that." He always found a way. Paul had a daughter with a woman he'd met in Washington, but sadly, no matter how hard he'd tried, his child's mother wasn't interested in him be a part of their lives. That was the one thing he couldn't fix, and it broke our hearts.

I looked at the table of supplies he'd left. Right, unbolt and remove the four captain-style chairs. The van looked and felt more spacious with the chairs out, and I decided that only two of the four would go back in. I hacked away at the carpet with the utility knife. Paul showed up minutes later and helped me tear it all out. It was worse than I'd thought—the subfloor was rotten. Insects were burrowing underneath.

"Ewwww! Gross! It all has to go, doesn't it?" I said.

"Totally has to go."

"Damn. OK, well, I guess I'll work on getting all the rotten stuff out first. You think I should try to keep some of the wall pieces as a template?"

"Wouldn't hurt. I've gotta get on, but I'll come by again and check on you in a couple of days." Just like that, he was off again. After removing the flooring from the first half of the van, I looked toward the back half. There was a huge air conditioning unit on the roof with stains around the edges. I removed it and found that the wood between the fiberglass sheets was rotten, and water had crept into the back cabinets. Shit. What am I supposed to do about that? I put a tarp over the top of the van, secured it, and went inside the house. I collapsed onto the couch in tears.

"Is everything OK? Mom asked.

"It's such a mess! It needs so much work. I don't know how to do half of it," I sobbed.

"Maybe get rid of it? I saw a Mercedes camper for $30,000 near my work. Maybe we should go have a look at that?"

"$30,000, Mom? I've put three grand into this van. I don't have enough money for that Mercedes."

"I could help you get it if you like it," she said.

I thought about her offer. It was kind of her to want to help me out, but she'd already done so much for me. I couldn't accept it. I needed to persevere, continue what I'd started. I liked the idea of building the RV—I knew I'd learn a lot in the process and kind of wanted the lessons.

Plus. I wanted it to fit me—something I knew a cookie-cutter Mercedes couldn't do.

"Thanks, Mom, but I'll make this work. It just might take more time than I imagined. Are you OK with me making a mess in your driveway for a few weeks?"

"Of course. Let me know if you need help with anything."

"Tomorrow, I'm tearing out the kitchen if you want to help with that?"

"OK. Did Paul bring all those tools out there?"

"He did! I'm so lucky to have such a great friend—and a great Mom. Thanks for letting me do this here. I love you."

"Love you, too."

The following day, Mom and I got right to it. We removed each panel that held the stove, mini-fridge, and sink and kept the pieces to trace and rebuild if needed. That evening, Paul showed up and helped me with the ceiling. We took a break from applying epoxy over the new wood I had picked up from the local lumber supply store and the fiberglass—until we noticed smoke billowing out of the van.

"What's that? Is it on fire?" I asked.

Paul jumped to his feet and ran to the bus. "It's the epoxy rags!" he said.

He grabbed a pair of gloves and tossed the wadded-up towels onto the driveway.

"Ahhhh, I remember Charles saying something about that at the hotel. They have to be laid flat in a ventilated area, or they explode."

"Yeah. Whuuuupppsss," he said.

When the smoke cleared, we got back to work. When I'd purchased the van (while I was overseas in Germany), I'd had no idea that what I'd chosen had to be gutted. While I worked, I tried to see if anything was salvageable. However, it became apparent that almost everything had to be tossed out—two-thirds of Saṃsāra's interior was wet. A couple of weeks later, Saṃsāra was empty, minus her propane system. I stood in the driveway and stared at the valves and knobs. I have no idea what I'm doing.

Mom popped her head out the front door.

"Everything OK?" she asked.

"Well, yes and no. I think these propane valves need fixing, but I don't know anything about this, and I'm scared to mess with them. I don't want to blow myself up in your front yard."

"Why don't I call someone? Like a professional RV person?"

"I can't afford a professional RV person, Mom. They charge like $80 an hour."

"I'll pay for it. Better that than an explosion."

She closed the door and disappeared into the house. I climbed under the van to inspect the propane tank. *What have I gotten myself into? Is my faith being tested? Or was this just a stupid move?*

I crawled out and grabbed my computer. I googled RV propane systems and watched videos in the hopes that I could learn what to do. A couple of hours later, a mobile RV specialist pulled into the driveway.

"Hello. You need some help with your propane system?" the young man said.

Moooom. I said I couldn't afford this!

"Hey there. Did my mom call you?"

"A woman called and said she needed help. Don't I know you?"

Did I know him? I wasn't sure.

"Don't you have a brother? And didn't you used to live on Birch Street?" he asked.

"I do. I did, yeah."

"I've been to your house. It was a long time ago, but you threw some great parties there. I went to a couple of your Kung-Fu BBQ parties. Your door was always open, I heard, and lots of people came by. I'm not surprised you don't remember me."

That was true. My door was always open, and many people went in and out of that house during the two years I'd rented it. On Sundays, I'd hosted Kung-Fu BBQ parties where I'd play old Kung-Fu movies on the television and feed anyone who came by. I'd been making a lot of money as a cocktail server at the time and wanted to share. That was the best way I knew how.

"What's your name?" I asked.

"Brian. I knew your brother. He brought me over a couple of times."

"Ah, cool! Well, nice to see you again! My mom called you. I bought this bus, and it needs so much work. As you can see, I've stripped it down to the metal and wanted to build it back up, but I think the propane system needs checking before I do all that, and I'm scared to touch it."

"Let's have a look at it. I'll just grab a couple of things from my truck."

Brian was incredible. Not only did he teach me everything I needed to know about the propane system in less than twenty minutes, but he also checked the water lines to the shower, toilet, and sink and suggested I upgrade them.

"Yeah, you have a monster of a project on your hands. Congrats for taking it on—that's pretty impressive. You're going to need a new valve here and some better insulation around the hot water holding tank. The stuff there now is all rotten. I have some of the water lines, and when you're ready to install them, I can come back and help you."

"Thanks so much. I don't have a lot of money—this project is costing more than I thought. Is there anything I can do in exchange for your help? I'm a great painter if you need any painting done."

"Actually, I do. I'm painting my living room. My parents could use some help at their house. We can figure something out. I'll get the valve for you and come back when I have it, and we can go from there, cool?"

"Sounds good, thanks!"

Brian had been an RV specialist for over two decades, and after he left, I thanked Mom for calling him. He was humble, kind, and an incredible RV tech. Over the next few weeks, he'd pop in periodically, check on my progress and help out here and there. My faith was restored.

The Samsāra therapy and "treatments" (that's what I call them, though I'm no doctor) lasted five months. When I didn't know how to proceed, I caught myself getting angry. Each time that happened, I took a break. I'd throw a tool, then walk away and climb into my hammock. *I have to stay focused. I want this to work.* I'd practice the deep breathing exercises I'd learned and bring myself back to a calm state of mind. Then I'd imagine all the fun Samsāra and I would have once we were rolling. It seemed to help.

Once the trash cans were gone and I'd cleared the debris from the driveway, I invited some friends to come and play with Samsāra. New guests approached with respect and admiration for who she was becoming. They decorated her with small gifts in one way or another. She seemed to like the extra attention. Mom had hand-painted lotus flowers in the bathroom, a Cheshire cat on a cabinet (with a quote that read "You may have noticed I'm not all there myself"), and a forest with hummingbirds on Samsāra's engine cover, which was nestled between the two captain's chairs. These little details gave Saṃsāra a unique identity and expressed who we were. The "Astroturf" grass that grew across the driver and passenger floorboards was attractive—and stimulated my bare feet. The LED lights I installed lit up Samsara's darkest corners. Friends donated materials, time, love and put energy into Samsāra's creation. It was wonderful to allow others to give to us so freely (finally). *Is this what it feels like to receive? To work together in harmony with others? I think I like it.*

As we prepared Saṃsāra, I was excited to explore this mobile, minimal way of living. I was eager to find new ways of being of service. I wanted to remain open for surprises along the way, but kept the daydreams of desert retreats, sunset dinners, and forest hikes in mind. *What are my intentions this time? I want to feel free to be as I am—in flow and in nature.*

A few days before we set out on our first adventure, I invited everyone who worked on Saṃsāra on a camping trip. We tested all her parts, ate delicious BBQ, played together, and rested in the nature of North Florida. My RV guru, Brian, mentioned that I didn't have any safety measures in place during the weekend trip.

"Like what?" I said.

"Well, you don't have a carbon monoxide detector or smoke alarm. Have you installed anything to protect your batteries?"

"Well, um... no." I laughed.

"If you want, I'll help you install those. I'd recommend having them."

I heard a familiar voice in my mind: *You know how to do that—you don't need any help.*

"I'd love your help," I said. "Thank you." *I have made progress with the 'I have to do everything alone' theme, after all!*

We installed the safety features. It was time to go. I turned to Chico, my brave and smart eleven-year-old terrier. "Are you ready to go, boy?"

I already knew his answer. During the months of renovations, he had always been present, lying in the driver's seat, watching every move I made. Chico had come into my life in 2007, when I lived in Dallas. I was working at a low-income property as a program coordinator for the residents, and it was my job to bring the community together. Every week, I planned events for the children and families who lived there, kept the facilities in order, and secured donations of computers, literature, and healthy snacks to share with the struggling community. One day, on Thanksgiving, as I prepared to serve meals to 250 residents, some of the children came to me.

"Miss Melissa! Miss Melissa!" a ten-year-old girl named Botswana squealed. "We need your help! There's a scared little dog outside, and people are throwing rocks at him! Come quick!"

I followed the children outside and saw this tiny, terrified, disheveled little dog, trembling against a tree.

"Look! His collar is too tight!" Botswana said. "We need scissors!"

I looked closer, and indeed; his collar was so tight around his neck, I wasn't sure how he was still breathing. I went inside and grabbed a pair of scissors and gave them to Botswana, who seemed to have control of the situation.

"Will you take him home, Miss Melissa?" she asked. "We can't have pets here—and he needs help!"

"Well, right now I need to finish preparing all the food and have this party, but I'll tell you what. If he's still here when I'm done, I'll take him home. Promise." I replied.

Six hours later, the party was over, and I had forgotten all about the dog. I was loading supplies into my car when Botswana appeared. She had wrapped up the little dog in a toddler's t-shirt, and was carrying it in her arms. "Miss Melissa! Are you done now? Will you take Chico with you? You promised, remember?"

I looked at the two of them. Her big brown eyes showed concern and hope, and his little black eyes showed fear and worry.

"Chico, huh?" I said. "Why Chico?"

"Look at him. He looks like a Chico!"

He did look like a Chico. His wiry black hair and silver mohawk gave him a rough, yet cheeky look that was adorable. I pondered for a moment.

"You promised – remember?"

"I did. OK, I'll take him home."

And that was that. When I took Chico to the vet the following day, they told me that he was about a year old and in relatively good health. For the first week, all he did was sleep, but he became very overprotective of me after that. He wouldn't let anyone come within three feet of us without losing his mind. He'd growl and bark furiously until whatever he had perceived as a threat went away. This went on for five years. I always had to keep him on a tight leash. When I decided to go backpacking, my mom kept him at her place for five years, and he loved it there. Now that I was back, he couldn't wait to hit the road with me.

With Chico by my side and Saṃsāra almost ready to roll, I looked in the mirror and smiled. My crooked front tooth glared back at me. "I think it's time to straighten that tooth, huh, Chico?"

I ordered a set of home teeth-straightening aligners and finished the final details in Saṃsāra. A couple of weeks later, after my orders were in and the van was all packed up, we said goodbye to Mom and all our friends and set off for our adventure into the unknown.

Chapter Three

Life with Saṃsāra

Saṃsāra and I moved slowly west from Florida and stopped at a beach on the Gulf of Mexico. I opened her rear doors and lay in the daybed, watching the ocean waves roll in and out. Chico curled up in my lap and gazed into the midday sun. I reflected on what it had taken to get to this point. Patience, persistence, and the ability to surrender to the flow came to mind. *Thank you, friends and family, thank you, universe—for all the lessons and the support. I'm grateful.* We spent the night at the beach and, after a cup of tea and some oatmeal the next morning, we continued west.

The aligners for my teeth were proving to be a challenge. I had to consider everything I put into my mouth. Anytime I wanted to eat or drink anything other than water, I had to remove them. Then, once I was done eating or drinking, I had to brush and floss before putting them back into my mouth. This extensive process was bringing me into conscious contact with my food theme. At first, it wasn't very pleasant, but over time, I grew to respect it.

We stopped in New Orleans to meet with Harley's husband, Kendall.

In 2002, Harley had called me. She'd wanted to move from New Orleans to Atlanta, where I lived. "I have a three-bedroom house here, and it's just my cats and me. You can come and bring Munchkin if you want," I said.

"Can I bring my dog and my boyfriend?" she asked.

"Um. No boyfriend. Just Munchkin."

"You'll like Kendall. I won't come without him."

"Oh, alright. See you all soon then."

I liked Kendall immediately. His love for Harley was genuine. He was a great chef, was easy to talk to, and easy to be around. I could see why she chose him—and eventually married him.

When Kendall and I met up in Louisiana, I saw that the pain of Harley's passing still lingered in him, as it did in me. *Her death had cut him just as deep.*

He took us on a small river speed boat through the bayou. I enjoyed the trip, but Chico hated it. We arrived at their family's camping cabin on the water and ate way too many crawfish. After dinner, I mentioned that we intended to visit the Redwoods Harley had wanted to see before going to the spirit world.

"I thought you'd say that. I brought some of Harley with me," he said. He reached into his pocket and pulled out a small silver capsule. "I kept some of her for you."

The look in his eyes as he handed me her ashes broke my heart.

He still loves her. I still love her, too.

"Thanks, I said," and held the capsule to my heart. "I'm sorry I wasn't at the celebration of life party. Watching her suffer for so long was a catalyst for me, and after she left, I left."

"I know. It's all good. It was a crazy night. She visited me in my dreams."

We spent the evening catching up and trying to laugh, but mostly we processed the grief of losing Harley. Even after five years, the sadness remained in both of us. I hoped that one day we'd be at peace.

The next stop was Dallas. I wanted to see Grandma. We pulled up to her house and found her standing out front as if she knew we'd arrive just then.

"Hello, Missy. Is that your new home?" she asked.

"Hey, Grandma! It is! Wanna have a look?"

"Why, of course. It's big! You build that all by yourself?"

"No. A bunch of people helped build her. I didn't know what I was doing half the time."

She laughed as she climbed inside.

"Well, it's really nice! You guys did a great job! Where are you planning on goin'?"

"We're headed to the Redwood Forest in California. Do you remember my friend Harley who died? She wanted to see that forest but didn't make it. We stopped in Louisiana, and her husband gave me some of her ashes. I'm taking them there."

"That's very nice, Missy. I'm sure she'll appreciate that."

I didn't know if she would or not. I still felt some level of guilt for not getting her there when she was alive and thought that this trip might help bring healing for that. I wanted her to know that I still honored her request and would do what I could. Even if it meant just taking her ashes. The thoughts made my stomach tighten. My chest ached.

"Would you like to play cards?" I asked.

"Sure, we can play Rummy."

I stayed with Grandma for a few days and helped her around the house. Before I felt that it was time to push on, I cut the grass, painted her Redskin room (a room dedicated to her favorite football team—the Washington Redskins), and she taught me how to make some of her favorite recipes.

Our next stop was the primitive Faywood Hot Springs on the edge of the Gila National Forest near Silver City, New Mexico. Mineral hot springs are naturally detoxifying, help improve circulation, and relieve stress—I wanted it all. I pulled Saṃsāra into a shady spot so Chico would be comfortable. It was a perfectly cool and overcast day, so I didn't have any reservations about leaving him in the bus with the double cross-breeze windows open for a couple of hours.

The geothermal resort had a natural, rustic feel and offered both clothing-required and clothing-optional pools to soak in. I paid the twenty-dollar fee and entered the clothing required section. The three pools in that area produced unusual, yellowish-colored water. It didn't have the sulfur smell I'd expected, which was nice. Peacocks roamed freely, and there were only two other guests, which made the visit peaceful and serene.

I soaked for an hour and thought again about what it took to get there. I thought about all the people who had contributed to the success of this adventure. The list was long. *Thank you so much for being so helpful. All of you.* I realized that human beings need each other— they really need each other. We're a social species that relies on cooperation to survive and thrive. I was happy to have opened myself up to that. I felt blessed to have such wonderful people in my life. After the soak, I sat in a lounge chair and fell into a daydream that took me through a desert and some canyons. When I opened my eyes, I knew where we'd be going next.

We camped that night in the desert, and the following day, we headed seven hours north to one of the world's seven natural wonders—the Grand Canyon. I'd heard that, on average, three people die each year from falling over the rim, so I kept my distance. On the other hand, Chico coasted the edges of the massive cliffs fearlessly while I kept a tight grip on his harness leash. After a few hours of hiking, we camped for free just outside the park's boundaries. It was a beautiful, quiet place. I set up my hammock and fell into a daydream. This time I saw Las Vegas. *Really? Vegas? Why would we go there?* We stayed another night before packing up and making the four-hour and twenty-minute drive to the Las Vegas Strip.

I put Chico in his backpack, and we entered Circus Circus. We wandered around the brightly lit, loud casino floor and stopped at a slot machine. "Wanna play, Chico?" We sat down, and I slipped a five-dollar bill into the slot. I've never been a gambler and prefer to hold on to the little that I usually have, but I was also open to the possibility that Chico was lucky. He touched the spin pad, and the dials on the machine whirled and clicked. The first wheel stopped, then the second and third. An alarm sounded—Chico had won! Our five dollars became a hundred dollars. I pressed the cash out button and took the ticket to the cashier. Chico and I fueled up on breakfast and used the rest to fuel up the bus. *We always have what we need, when we need it.* We left Las Vegas, opting for the quiet of nature, and camped in the desert on our way to LA.

Los Angeles was just too much. We only spent a couple of days near the beach visiting a few friends before I started to feel overwhelmed. We were still craving nature—time to contemplate and breathe in stillness. We drove into the mountains, found Cold Brook Campground, and Ron, the campsite host, greeted us. I asked about the fees and the best possible spot for Chico and me, as we had come for relaxation, reflection, and decompression. Ron was super helpful and recommended the ideal site for us to camp. He told us about a great hike up to a waterfall and mentioned that a bear was roaming the area.

I prepared the van, hung my hammock next to a babbling brook a few feet away, and settled in for the evening, listening to the splashing of the nearby waterfall. Everything was great—until the next day when a group of twenty family members arrived to have a loud BBQ at the campsite to my left. I tried to rest in the hammock, earplugs and all, but with the gang of kids splashing a couple of feet away in the brook, the peaceful solitude I craved was gone.

I was preparing Saṃsāra to roll when the bear Ron had mentioned waltzed right into our camp. I closed the doors, grabbed my camera, and filmed him. He stood on his hind legs and peered into Saṃsāra's window! The family at the next campsite got into their cars and watched the bear circling Saṃsāra. After he lost interest, he strolled across the path behind us and sat down. As I pulled away, I saw the kids' throwing apples at the bear, which he seemed to enjoy catching and eating.

I drove eight miles up the hill to Crystal Lake Campground. It wasn't long before Ron showed up, asking, "Everything OK?" The man who had been camped on my right told him I'd left angry, that the family party was being disrespectful (which wasn't true), encroaching on the campsite I'd reserved (which was true).

Ron's concern was genuine. I appreciated his dedication to ensuring that guests at his site felt welcome and comfortable.

"All is well," I said. "I just needed quiet time, and it wasn't happening there. This campground's bigger, fewer people... it's tranquil. Thanks for checking on us."

After he left, Chico and I went to bed.

The next day after lunch, Chico and I took a midday nap, zipped up in the hammock. I was sound asleep when Chico started barking frantically in a tone I've never heard from him. I sat up quickly and came face to face with that bear. It peered into our hammock and startled Chico, but his barking scared the bear more than it scared us. I grabbed my Canon DSLR and filmed it as it ran away and attempted to climb a tree. When the bear realized Chico wasn't chasing it, it walked away.

We spent a few hours at this new campsite but missed the waterfall sounds of the Coldbrook Campground and decided to give it another go. As I drove down the mountain, Saṃsāra's brakes started to overheat. We pulled into the campground in a cloud of stinky smoke.

Ron greeted us. "Downshifting to either second or first gear will help with that problem," he said.

"Thanks, Ron," I said. "I wasn't aware of that. I've always driven manual cars that weigh a lot less than this van."

We rolled into the campsite, hoping for the same beautiful spot as before, but it was occupied. Undeterred, we went back to Ron to seek advice. As gracious as always, he recommended another, even better space. He took Chico and me on a walk and showed us out-of-the-way "secret hiding spots" to post up that were secluded yet close enough to reach in a few minutes' hike.

Ron shared his love for animals with me as he produced a bag of cat food for two young strays who lived in the forest. "I feed and pray for them every evening," he said pouring the food into the empty bowls. A few moments of silence passed before we walked quietly to the brook. I watched him carefully move rocks that campers had stacked up. "I move the stones back to ensure the free flow of water. For me, the ecosystem is essential, and maintaining it is a priority. I take my campground host job seriously."

I respected Ron. The site was beautiful, the people were kept in check, and Ron ensured everything was maintained and in proper working order.

I wanted to know more about this forest angel, so I asked him to join me for dinner. After a lengthy conversation, I'd made a new friend. Ron taught me how to respect and care for nature even more than I do now, how to become a campsite host (www.volunteer.gov), and what it meant to be kind to all creatures. He's been the only person yet to guess what the Chinese tattoo on my arm says—which told me that he's also an excellent observer of character.

Chico and I stayed for a few more days and drank in the tranquility. I was dangerously close to running out of money and decided to try a campsite hosting gig as Ron had. I went to the website he suggested, found an opening at a camp in Ojai, and applied. The next day I had a response and an invitation to interview. *Great! Chico and I can meet interesting people, care for nature, and make a few dollars. This should be fun!*

Chapter Four

Twist of Fate

The interview with Beth, the supervisor at the Ojai campground, went well, and she offered me the host position. I'd join a team of three who were already posted up at the campsite and got right into the routine. My job was to greet campers, accept payments, and keep the bathrooms and sites clean. I loved the people I worked with, and everything was going fine until about a week later, a woman appeared. She threw daggers in my direction and asked Beth, "Who's that?"

"She's our new hire—a great fit. She works hard, very friendly." Beth replied.

I could feel that this woman didn't like my face for whatever reason. "Who is that woman?" I asked Beth.

"Brenda, the operations manager. Don't worry about her. Just stay out of her way. She'll be gone tomorrow."

That evening, the staff gathered for a BBQ, and the entire time, Brenda blasted me with dirty looks. Toward the end of the evening, I confronted her. "Do you have a problem with me?" I asked. "We've never met, so I don't understand why you keep looking at me with disgust. Have I done something to offend you?"

Brenda folded her arms across her chest and leaned back in her chair. "I have good news and bad news for you," she said smugly. "The bad news is that your position here is no longer available. The good news is we'll be sending you to our crown jewel campground in Big Sur."

Something told me this wasn't good news. *She has ill intent; I can feel it.* But as it was closer to the Redwood Forest, I agreed to go.

"You'll leave tomorrow morning. Get your things ready tonight if you like."

A half-mile-long collapse of shoreline had ensured that Big Sur would be shut off from most of the world for several months. Chunks of the infamous and highly traveled Highway 1 had crumbled into the ocean and now, the only way in was over a treacherous and scary one-lane mountain road. For ninety terrifying minutes we crept slowly along the narrow, windy path with deadly drop-offs. Suddenly, the ocean came into view. We stopped and sat for several minutes, in awe of its magnificence.

The campsite was pristine in its natural beauty during the day and splendid in its silence in the evenings. There were a couple of highly evolved raccoons with opposable thumbs that robbed unsuspecting campers during the night—Wow. Just wow. They were fun to watch as they stalked their unprepared victims. They worked as a unit. One raccoon would scout the grounds first. Then it would report back to a large tree at the southeast corner of the campground…that's where the rest of the gang hung out. There were nine members of this bandit family. They'd head out to ransack and loot their (usually, but not always) sleeping targets. I sat on top of Saṃsāra and watched this for the first week—and then started warning campers to lock up anything before dark they didn't want the bandits to steal. "Close your car windows and hide the children and dogs," I told them. OK, that last part isn't true, but you get my point. Those rascals could destroy a campsite in under two minutes and disappear with their bounty—leaving only their dirty little footprints behind. Some campers took my advice and ended up having a campsite breakfast in the morning; others disregarded it and got robbed to varying degrees. I was happy watching those masked scoundrels do their dastardly deeds. It was truly majestic to witness nature retake Big Sur so quickly once human traffic was limited.

Working at that campground as a camp host for those weeks was a great experience. I met travelers who taught me things and allowed me to explore their rigs and traveling ways. One nomad, in particular, caught my attention with his converted senior-citizen bus. He had gutted and rebuilt a 24-foot-long, 8-foot-wide bus into a beautiful rolling home. It had everything—a kitchen, compost toilet, dinette table for four, and a bed that could sleep six. It was wide and spacious, and I imagined that I'd choose something closer to that size if I ever built another bus.

The campground was bustling, even with the Pacific Coast Highway closure. Every day, somewhere between seventy and two hundred guests braved the detour and camped in one of the thirty-five pitches. There were two more campgrounds located not far to the north and south, but only ours was situated on the cliffs at the ocean. The other campgrounds were similar in size but had four to six staff members maintaining them. One day, I headed to one of the campgrounds and talked to the admin team. "Is it customary to have only one person working such a busy campground?" I asked a woman named Clare.

"Usually, two to four people are working at your site," she said. "I'm not sure why you're there alone. How many trash and firewood runs do you do a day?" Clare asked.

"I make two trips a day during the week, four on weekend days."

"Wow, that's a lot of weight. You OK over there?"

"Actually, no. My body isn't made for this. It's really starting to hurt. I need help."

"You should send a message to Brenda, the operations manager. She should send you help. That's crazy, you're there by yourself. It's way too much work for one person."

It had been three weeks of back-breaking work: hauling away trash, bringing in firewood— physically, I couldn't handle anymore. I sent Brenda an email asking for help.

"I'll do what I can," she said.

The following week, I sent another message. "Hi Brenda," I wrote, "…I can't continue without help—the amount of weight I'm expected to haul in and out of the campground is too much. Can you send one of the ten nearby staff members from the other parks to help me out?"

"I'll do my best," she wrote back.

My body was tired and not getting better. Another week went by. Then the inevitable happened—I fell down a short flight of stairs. I twisted my neck, back, hips, and knees—everything was skewed in abnormal directions. I drove to the campsite where Brenda was. "I've fallen," I said. "I need a doctor."

"Were you drunk?" Brenda asked.

"I don't drink alcohol. I think my body finally gave out. I need a doctor."

Brenda sent me on a two-hour drive north. When I entered the clinic, they drug tested me and sent me away. I returned to the campsite. Brenda had moved her camper into my spot. "Park on the street," she said.

"Park on the street? I need power for the refrigerator in my bus. Why can't I stay onsite?"

"There isn't a place open for you."

"I need to see a doctor. My body's not right. When can I see a doctor? I do have health insurance with the company, don't I?"

"After your drug screen comes back. If it's clean."

"I can tell you right now it's clean. I don't drink alcohol or do drugs. I need help. I needed help several weeks ago, but felt that you ignored me. I tried to tell you over and over that...."

At that moment, I realized what Brenda had done. For whatever reason, she didn't want me working with the company, so she'd put me at this site alone, hoping I'd quit.

But I loved it there and wanted to stay. I just needed help. *I should have left when I'd noticed she had it in for me. Now what?*

I walked to the street where my bus was parked and slept sitting up—my body wouldn't lie flat without intense pain. I couldn't continue to camp on the side of the road because my fridge would drain my battery in little more than a day. So, the following day, I left. I was close to the Redwood Forest and thought: *Now must be the time to look for a special place to spread Harley's ashes.*

We headed north toward San Francisco. At the Redwoods, we stopped. Saṃsāra stopped. Time stopped. Deep breaths. Lots and lots of deep breaths. We spread Harley's ashes among the giant trees she'd longed to see. Chico and I created an altar for her. On it, we placed a framed picture of Harley and me, taken when I took her skydiving in Atlanta one year on her birthday. I included a letter to her, saying how much I loved her and valued all we'd shared over the years. We also left a GeoCaching "Travel Bug" for another wanderer to find and take somewhere else.

Later, in the new year of 2018, a team of Geocachers called the "DNA Kids" collected that travel bug. They logged their find into the geocaching.com website with a lovely note on how they'd found the altar and were happy to carry Harley's bug to their next destination for another explorer to find and transport some place new. Reading this notice made my heart sing; I hoped she'd be able to control its direction from beyond this world.

After the Redwood Forest, I felt it was time to end the trip. I was still in pain from the fall at work, and long story short, I felt that the company I'd been working for had done me wrong. After a couple of months of getting nowhere with treatment, temporary disability, and unemployment insurance, I'd officially run out of money—and I'd run out of patience. I was developing distrust around working with people. I knew I would have to take my health and well-being into my own hands. *Would I have to sell Saṃsāra?* I didn't want to. I had to. I had to heal my wounded body and spirit—yet again—and needed the money.

Saṃsāra, Chico, and I sat in a private campground north of San Francisco and attempted to heal and bring some gifts to the renovation project of the land that was taking place there. The campground was a majestic forest retreat blessed with abundant mountain spring water. The place was beautiful. The volunteer team I was a part of took care of the sites, painted cabins, developed the camping and volunteer areas, and kept the grounds clean while guests were there. Several friends from Southern California visited, and we stumbled upon a hidden swimming hole called "Socrates Falls" that reminded me of my old wizard, Charles. Some of those friends brought gifts, ranging from laser-cut stencils for making signage, a light-up plexiglass sign of the camp's logo, and donations of time and money to help with upgrades and expenses.

However, the owner did not seem to appreciate fully the gifts we brought. Something was still being provoked in me. There was something I needed to see; something I couldn't yet understand. *What's next?* I couldn't imagine going on any farther in this way but couldn't see what was meant for Chico and me. I'd spent most of the last few years making up and receiving daydreams while lying in my hammock, only to watch them appear in my reality a short time later. This had always worked with ease. But in the last couple of months, things had changed. It seemed like every time I'd paint a picture on the whiteboard of my mind of what might be, some invisible hand would wipe it clean. *Wait a minute. This is MY imagination. Whose hand is that erasing my creations?*

This confusion went on for a while until I quit trying altogether. It appeared I wasn't being allowed to create in this way anymore. *What the heck?* Finally, one day, I decided to let go and surrender. Instead of daydreaming about my desires, I decided to ask the universe for guidance. *Would you mind bringing me what is meant to be next? My old way of doing things isn't working.*

After a couple of days, I received a message... an invitation to Europe. My wizard-magician, Charles, said, "It seems that the quality you want to bring to the campground you're at is not appreciated, is it? You know, we love that level of quality here." I was no longer surprised by Charles' magical 'knowing' and divine timing. I now understood that he was able to pick it all up by remote viewing. I knew I'd say yes. Before I replied, though, I threw an image of the hotel on the whiteboard in my imagination. Guess what? It stuck—it was the first thing that had held in months.

I replied to his message: "Yes, Charles, I'll come." I told him about the whiteboard experience. "What the heck is that about?"

"It seems you're in the space between stories now. The old (ego-driven) story has fallen away, but the new (heart-driven) story has not taken hold. Don't worry; it's on the way. You should be out of the vacuum space soon."

I thanked him. "Seems I'm meant to return. I'll make the arrangements," I said, "but it will take a little time as I have a few things to do first."

That was the day I decided to sell Saṃsāra. I wrote an ad and placed it on Craigslist, and within twenty-four hours, the buyer appeared like magic. Two young gypsy women were starting a tour of their own, and Saṃsāra was just what they needed. After meeting them, I couldn't have agreed more. Saṃsāra and the gypsies were perfect. I shed a couple of tears and smiled as I handed over Saṃsāra's keys. The women promised to care for her and respect her as I had, and we parted ways.

Next, I decided to stop using the aligners for my teeth. Not because they were a constant challenge, but because they didn't seem to be working properly. I had reached the end of the series of sets, and although my tooth had definitely turned, it was far from straight. I contacted the company, sent them photos, and was surprised when they offered me a full refund.

Only thirty-six hours later, Chico and I were homeless again and on the move. It was time to move forward, to move beyond, to create something new. I had no idea what that would look like. But first, I had to get to Florida and get my body right. My good friend Charles Dinkel drove to San Francisco to pick up me, Chico, and all of our things. He took us back to Los Angeles and let us stay with him while we figured things out. The physical therapists in California were doing an excellent job of helping me strengthen what they said were weak muscles. But the worker's comp doctors were trying to tell me that there was nothing wrong other than some old injury, even though I'd never injured my neck or back. My knees, yes, but that wasn't where I was feeling the pain any longer. It was mainly in my back; it needed serious attention. I was getting nowhere with these doctors, and I'd run out of options. I decided to fast one day and massage my body with coconut oil. I needed to hear what it had to say. I spent a few hours alone at Charles's house and drank water while talking to my body. I caressed my toes one by one, my heels, behind my knees, my lower back, arms, neck, chest, and hair. I did it all—twice for good measure. It was terrific. I've never given myself a full-body massage like that before. It took the pain from a ten down to a tolerable six and kept it there long enough for me to fly back to Florida to my mom's.

Chapter Five

Rolfing

I arrived at Mom's and felt OK for a couple of days—until the low back pain struck again. The discomfort went from that steady six back up to a restless ten. Three nights passed without sleep. I started to lose my marbles.

"Honey, I think we should go to the ER," Mom said.

The MRI taken that day showed 12mm x 11mm x 6mm fragments of a herniated disc to the L5-S1 and damage to the L4-L5 disc, the last two disks at the bottom of the spine. The doctor came in, and his first words were, "Well, it isn't your imagination."

That's good to know—because imagining this pain would be wrong on so many levels.

The doctor suggested a spinal fusion due to the size of the herniation and the damage to my disks. I wasn't fond of the idea of anyone fusing any part of my spine under any circumstances.

"Is there another option?" I asked.

"Well, we can start you on a rigorous regime of steroids to reduce the inflammation, but you'll have to be very careful with your back from here on out."

"Yeah, I'll try those, thank you."

Five days later, the inflammation was under control, and I could lie flat and sleep a bit better. The next step was to realign the twist I felt in my body. A friend advised me to see a Rolfing healer that lived in the area and said she'd been a game-changer for him after an accident.

Her name was Nanette. She was around six feet tall, and despite her dominant physical presence, she had a gentleness about her that was calming and reassuring. We arranged a session and met at her home. When I arrived, she led me to a giant graph of squares on the wall in her therapy room. It was a grid of sorts, and as I stood there, she observed me from across the room. "Turn to the right," she said. And then "now please, to the front again, OK, left now. And please, show me your back." I obliged, and when she was satisfied with her observations, she led me over to sit on a heated massage table.

She showed me a book with "before" and "after" pictures of clients who had received a series of ten Rolfing sessions. The photos had been taken at each successive session. It was impossible not to notice the difference. The first and last photos of each client spoke volumes—the posture differences were dramatic. She explained that manipulating the fascia all over my body would improve my overall well-being.

"I fell down some stairs," I told her. "Only three stairs, but the way I fell twisted my whole body. My hip, neck, and back are contorted, my L5/S1 disk is herniated and hurts like crazy. I have a hard time sleeping. It's better now but not great."

"Yes, I can see that your hip is twisted up and to the right. The left side sits lower and behind. Don't worry. We'll get it right."

I lay down on the warm bed, and she positioned some heated booties on my always-frozen feet. She placed rolled-up towels under my knees and a pillow under my head. The room smelled faintly of lavender, and I relaxed as she moved around the table.

The session lasted a bit over an hour and was pretty intense. Imagine 2000 pounds of pressure, focused on a point no larger than the eraser end of a pencil. Now imagine that eraser being pulled along your skin at a snail's pace. Perhaps slower. For the most part, it wasn't as bad as it may sound, and I might be exaggerating a bit on the amount of pressure used. But there were a couple of points that triggered an intense (but internalized) scream from me.

At the end of the first session, I felt an inch taller. My chest felt more open, and my shoulders slumped forward less. It was a nice feeling. The stinging, stabbing, simultaneously dull pain had settled a bit, and that night I slept through the night for the first time in weeks. It was heaven.

I went back twice in the following two weeks. After the first three sessions, the pain level I'd been experiencing dropped significantly. Not only that, my breath reached a place low in my lungs that felt unfamiliar. I'd been breathing shallowly for years, and my posture wasn't helping. Now my body felt more "open." The pain in my back held steady at a level three, and my sleep was regular again. Oddly, I felt more confident, perhaps because I held my head higher as she reshaped the way my neck supported it. I watched my body, and a couple of weeks after the third treatment, I noticed it wanting to fold in on itself again. I began practicing stretches to keep myself in the new, pain-free, open posture.

Session eight was tough. When Nanette put her pinky finger up my nostril, the buried memory of my nose being broken crackled through my mind. Suddenly, I felt pain— but not in my face. I felt it in my heart. It was an electric sadness, and it cut deep. "Please," I said. "That's enough."

She removed her finger. I curled up in a fetal position and watched it all play out in my mind's eye. The color of the tent we were all in. The ghost stories that were being told. I saw my eleven-year-old self, telling a scary tale until everything went black. *What happened? Why am I so dizzy?*

I stumbled out of the tent, across the expansive lawn, into the house. I collapsed on my bed and heard the others explaining to Mom what had happened.

"That's it!" Mom said. "Your friends need to go home. You guys? To your rooms for twenty minutes!"

Twenty minutes later, Mom came in to check on me. Her scream was sudden, fierce. "Your nose is broken! Who broke her nose?"

One of my brothers cowered in a corner.

Did you punch your sister in the face and break her nose?" Mom screamed.

He had. She knew it by the way he was acting.

"That's it—all of you. Get in the car. We have to go to the emergency room. Now!"

The film played on. As a doctor sprayed numbing liquid up my nostrils, I floated above the chair. I swallowed the spray—the only thing numbed was my throat. He placed two thumbs on the side of my nose that had shifted toward my ear and threw all of his weight down. A loud craaaccckkkk echoed through the room. Mom fainted and fell out of her chair. The doctor ran to her, closed the door to the hallway, and lifted her feet onto a chair. I'm not sure why—perhaps to assist with her blood flow? She was out cold. He returned to me and continued to smash my nose back into place. The sudden memory of that event released a lot of emotion—I sobbed.

When the mind movie was over, I rolled off of Nanette's heated bed, gathered my things, and silently left the room. Each step was labored. I arrived home and lay down to rest at 3:00 p.m. and woke up again at 7:00 a.m. *What just happened?*

By the tenth session, everything had changed. Nanette had corrected the fall's twists, and I had zero back pain. My chest was open, my pelvis was properly seated, and my shoulders now sat as they should. Emotionally, I was feeling confident and relaxed. I felt balanced. This woman and the Rolfing technique impressed me. It was another profound lesson about the human body and how it works. After the sessions, I was healed, renewed, and aware of my body posture. It was time to fly. I left Chico at my mom's and flew to Germany.

When I arrived at the hotel in Germany, Charles invited me to join another tour into the silence of the desert. The theme for this journey was "Creators of the New Time." I was already curious about what would be created this time around. Perhaps I could look at that mistrust pattern that had arisen due to my interactions with Brenda, the campground operations manager. *Letting those misgivings take hold won't serve me.* I'd also just begun an online conversation with a man named Jeremy, to whom I'd been attracted to over the years. Each time he had approached me, I'd run away. I found myself becoming attached to seeing him again—if I did, I decided, I wouldn't run away.

It was September 28, 2018. We prepared the truck to go to Tunisia. On our last evening in Germany, ten days after I'd left him in Florida, I dreamed about my best friend, Paul. The dream told me that his body was very sick. I sent him a text the next day, telling him about the vision. I texted, "How are you feeling?"

He replied, "I've been feeling under the weather for sure. Hope to feel better soon. I have tons of work to do. I noticed I looked a bit green this morning." He attached a

picture of a brand-new, electric blue Harley soft tail motorbike, calling it the "PT Soft Tail."

"Oh dang! That's a nice bike! Do you need doctor
mom?" I asked.

Whenever a family friend had a medical issue, we
always consulted my mom first because she's a doctor. As
Paul had been part of our family for almost three decades,
she was used to seeing him for random things—one time,
for example, he had what's called a "treble hook" stuck
in his foot! Over the three days it took me to travel from
Germany to Tunisia, Paul didn't answer. So, I just let it be.

Year Five - Optional Questions for Self-Reflection: Integration

Here is where you love what you find into submission. You are allowed to hug it and love it. You can tell yourself, "I love the loser inside of me. I love the part that is afraid, that feels unlovable. I love discovering these fragmented parts of myself and bringing the light of my consciousness into them. Journal what you feel. What you sense from the experience.

Worldwide

Chapter One

Forty Days in the Desert

As usual, Charles gave all the excursion participants questions to be answered and returned to him before we'd enter the void. Below are some of the questions that I received:

1. What has called me into the desert?
2. What does the Sahara symbolize for me?
3. Where I am in my life now: positives, painful things, sadness, questions about where I want to go in my life (orientation questions).
4. Painful experiences in my life that had the most impact and may still be ruling in the life experience. (Belief patterns, persuaded by something, some idea.)
5. Extraordinary experiences in my life with pleasure and happiness: What is it in my life that I like that I am creating?
6. What are my unique talents and skills?
7. What am I unskilled at, or where am I limited?
8. What is ready to be released?
9. That is what my life is burning for, and is my pleasure, and what I love to create. If your mind says you are totally crazy, then it's a good sign.
10. How is my trust in the universe doing at the moment?
11. The new woman I wish to be when I return from the desert is?

12. What do I hope to receive from the team?
13. What is left that I want to share (after all these questions)?
14. Are there any questions missing? Something I wished was asked here?
15. How did I receive the questions? How was it for me to be with these questions?

The following forty days in the Sahara were such a wild ride that they warrant their own story. Every day I kept a morning and evening diary of the inner and outer events as they unfolded—the miracles, the mysteries, and the mayhem. Fifty thousand words of what it felt like to meet and greet the shadows that appeared. I hope to share them with you in the not-too-distant future.

At the end of that journey, I ended up with a severe case of food poisoning and a text message from Mom that said: "Honey, you need to come home as soon as you can."

I texted back. "Is something wrong with Chico? Is he OK?"

"Chico's fine. It's Paul. He's not well."

I spent the following hour booking travel arrangements from the edge of the Sahara. The tour was over, and I flew home from Tunisia.

Chapter Two

Back to the Beginning

When I arrived at the airport, Mom drove up with Chico to greet me. Naturally, my little pup lost it when he saw me, which always makes me laugh. As we drove away, although she was semi-smiling, Mom looked genuinely worried.

"OK, so what's going on, Mom?"

Tears formed in her eyes. "Honey, Paul is very sick. He came to see me a couple of weeks ago asking for some pain medicine so he could go to work. I knew he wasn't well, but didn't say anything. I told him he needed to go to the Emergency Room, but he wanted to work. A few days later, he called and asked if I could bring him some pain medicine. So, I went to his house. He was in horrible shape—pacing the house and grabbing his stomach. I gave him a sedative that evening so he could get some rest. I told him he had to go to Emergency, that I'd take him. He said he was fine and fell asleep, so I left. He called again the next day. That's when I called you. Melissa, I think he has cancer and that it's really advanced."

In my heart, I'd known something was wrong...but cancer? My heart dropped; my stomach jumped into my throat. First Harley, now Paul? My other best friend? Something was different this time, though. I'd felt helpless with Harley, but I didn't feel this way with Paul. I'd found the answers I'd been looking for during six years of travel. I was confident he'd survive.

When we got to Mom's, I dropped off my bags, hooked up the battery in my Toyota, and drove straight to Paul's house. As confident as I'd felt, that changed the second I saw him. He lay in his bed in a puddle of sweat. He clutched his stomach. Tossed. Turned. Screamed out in pain. My heart ripped in two. I sat beside him and placed my hand on his belly. Instantly, I felt the heat of his misery. It was intense. I tried to hold back tears, keep my head high, stay positive—but Mom was right. Paul was walking a fragile line between life and death. My heart ached for him.

I retreated downstairs and contacted some of my tribe in California. I asked them to send me the highest quality CBD cannabis medicines they could, right away. I contacted trusted friends in Austria to get their advice. They shared a protocol they'd been using successfully to treat various cancers. This protocol consisted of sulfur crystals (MSM), iodine, vitamin C, and dandelion tea. They also suggested I buy pH test strips and plenty of alkaline water, as cancer cells thrive in an acidic body. Two days later, all the goods arrived. I insisted we start the protocol right away and told Paul that even if his doctors recommended chemotherapy, the protocol was safe to use in conjunction with that. After my experience with Harley, I was against radiation; however, I knew Paul might need some to save his life.

For the following seven days, we used the suggested protocol. We also performed body talk massages where we used the CBD oil to massage Paul's abdomen and paused to listen to what his body was saying. He had so much heat radiating from his stomach and a burning feeling low in his belly that cooled when we gently massaged it with the oils.

We visited several doctors for tests, including a PET Scan, Brain MRI, Heart ECHO, and a Bone Marrow Biopsy. Usually, these can take some time to complete, but Paul's primary doctor knew that Paul was in trouble and fast-tracked the testing appointments. All of them were done within two weeks.

When the results came back, we learned that Paul had Stage 4 Non-Hodgkin Lymphoma cancer and a tumor growing in his spleen. The doctor recommended a high dose of chemo right away. After eight treatments, he said, Paul should be fine. Still, I felt that if Paul were open to doing the energetic work and examining why he has this cancer to begin with, he'd be able to pull through with less radiation therapy.

"Do you know what you're holding in your body?" I asked, while holding his hand as he lay stretched out in his recliner chair.

"Yes," he said. "Grudges." He looked away.

"That's exactly the metaphysical meaning behind the condition of your spleen. Are you ready to look closer at these grudges, even if they cause you a bit more discomfort and agony than you're already feeling?" I smoothed his wrinkling forehead.

"First of all, those grudges are done as far as I'm concerned. Why would I want to cause any more pain than I'm already in? That's crazy!" He winced as he tried to pull himself into a seated position.

"You know, when I was with Harley, when she was sick, I felt helpless. Her death was a catalyst for my journeying. I wanted answers to why these things even happen. I admit I don't know everything, but I learned some things about energy, diet, patterns, and illness. I'd like to use some of these lessons to help you if you're interested." I helped him out of the chair.

"No."

Paul stood and walked to the sliding glass door of his living room. He stared into the garden. This was the second time I had to accept another person's "No." It took every bit of my energy not to push but instead simply to be present and love him.

A month after Paul had been diagnosed and after his second chemo treatment, our local tribe held a benefit to raise some money and awareness for him... and show how loved and supported he was. Two hundred people showed up, and we raised a few thousand dollars to pay his bills so he could relax, focus on healing, and stop obsessing about needing to work. We put blasts out on Facebook, asking friends to send prayers and share the information.

Two months into treatment, Paul's doctors were calling him a "miracle case." His response to the treatment was unlike any they'd ever seen; he was healing at an unprecedented rate. The news made my heart sing. Paul was a warrior who wanted to live, and he had a vast tribe supporting his recovery in so many ways. People gifted prayers, money, home-cooked meals, alternative medicines, and healing massages.

Paul was loved and wanted here on planet Earth, and his system was responding. When he reached the point where the constant pain he'd been experiencing was gone, I asked again if he'd like to look closer at his shadows.

"No," he said.

This time, I didn't accept it. Instead, while I cleaned his house, I played guided meditations (that addressed the themes I saw playing in his system). He escaped the first couple of times—making excuses to go to the store, but I persisted. One day, he sat through a twenty-minute guided meditation. When it was over, he opened his eyes and said, "Wow."

I smiled. "I have more if you feel ready now?" I said.

"Yes."

His answer made my heart sing. I played another one for us on the theme of surrender. Afterward, he slept in his recliner chair, a smile on his face. I left to take care of some things and made a playlist of suggested future meditations for him if he decided to continue.

We met every day for four months. Paul was relaxed, moved with ease, and drove his motorcycle again. I decided it was time now for my regenerative work to continue and made plans to go to Guatemala.

"I'm happy to see you feeling better. You look good." I said.

"I feel pretty good. Think I'm ready to get back to work."

"Yeah. I know you love to work. I'm not sure if you're out of the woods yet—the body can fall ill again if the necessary inner work stops."

"Yeah… right? I like those meditations."

I handed him a gift box.

"What's in here?" he said with a smile. He lifted the lid.

"It's a USB drive. Music and meditations. There's some more CBD oil so you can keep using massage to communicate with your body. It'll talk to you if you slow down and listen. But you already know that."

I hugged him close. "I love you, Paul. I'm going to Central America now to recharge."

Lake Atitlan in Guatemala was not as I'd remembered it when I'd started my trip seven years ago. The water seemed darker, and the streets lacked the vibrancy of young travelers' energy. *Had it changed that much? Or had I changed? Perhaps both...* I walked the path that ran parallel to the lake in San Pedro. Each step left a plume of dust that puffed in slow motion into the air around my feet. I paused and closed my eyes. *I need a quiet, comfortable place to stay. It needs to have a hammock, good food, and a lakeside view.* I imagined lying in a hammock, peering into the ripples of the lake. I reached for an imaginary fresh fruit smoothie and took a long, slow pull. Then I opened my eyes and started walking. A street dog joined me and took the lead. It padded along in front of me for a few minutes before it stopped, waited for me to notice it, and then turned into a gated entrance.

I followed. Through the gate was a long, narrow courtyard with a view of the lake. To my right was an open kitchen. Two women smiled at me as they prepared corn tortillas. The scents of stewing tomatoes, sesame, and cinnamon hung in the air of the open terrace. The dog lay in the center of the courtyard; I swear he winked at me. To our left was a single-story structure. *Ahhhh, I see what you did there, dog.* There were eight hotel rooms, and a hammock hung on the patio of each one. I winked at the dog. *Thanks, buddy.* I booked four days at the hotel, ordered a smoothie, and climbed into the hammock.

Being in Guatemala, where my journey had started, put me in a state of reflection that lasted three days. On the fourth day, I left the hammock. I invited the dog, who had decided to hang around with me, to join me on a wander. When I posted on Facebook that I was headed to Guatemala, a friend suggested I meet a man named Josh, who lived at the lake and was considered part of our extended online family. After a quick introduction on Facebook, we met for lunch at a local restaurant in San Pedro.

When I saw Josh, I sensed that this meeting could spell trouble. He was half Guatemalan, half American, and one hundred percent fine. His arms were sleeved in tattoos, and dark glasses shaded his eyes. *Uh oh.*

"Hey there. This place looks cool. Is the food any good?" I asked.

He slid half of his body from the barstool, so he was half-sitting, half-standing. He turned toward me.

Awkward silence.

"Uh. Yeah, I don't know. I've never eaten here. I usually come for drinks." He looked at the floor shyly.

I looked at the lakeside seating. "Let's grab a menu and go over there, yeah?" When we were seated, I told him about when I had first come to the lake and how I'd loved it. He told me how it had been in my absence.

"Not too many tourists come here anymore," he said. "There isn't a lot of work, and last year it flooded. Some buildings are still underwater."

I closed my eyes and went back seven years. Memories of a lively, fresh hippy town with street performers, artists, poets, musicians, and crafters danced through my mind's eye. A warm, soothing sensation, prickled with electricity, flooded my body.

"How long are you here for?" he asked.

"A month, I think."

"Cool. Well, if you want to see some of my favorite places, I'll take you around."

"Sounds good. Thanks."

Josh knew of some small, private rooms with a shared kitchen for rent at five dollars a day and took me to see them. The double duplex-style structure was gated and consisted of four rooms, one on each corner of a square courtyard. Bamboo fencing surrounded by low bushes and flowers enclosed each private space. Two hammocks hung in half sun, half shade, and a litter of kittens stumbled around on wobbly legs under one of the four round tables in the garden.

"I love it. How can I reserve a room?"

"I'll take you to the owner. It's on the way back to your other place."

After reserving the room for a week, I went back to my hotel and packed my backpack. As I turned to close the door, I felt a wet nose touch my leg. *Oh, hey, buddy.* My furry friend nudged me. He looked toward the hammock, looked back at me, and winked. *Great idea, my friend.* I set my bag down and lay in that hammock one last time, then wrote my intention for this new journey in my journal. *I'm here to ground myself. I'm here to define how I want to be the creator in my life—what I want to contribute to this world. I'm here to learn, grow and expand. I'm here to see how far I've already come.*

I spent the first week at my new digs in ritual. I did rooftop yoga, sat in stillness, practiced Qi-Gong and breathing exercises. I worked on getting my 40-day Sahara diary journal out of its leather- bound book and into my computer. I played with the kittens. I daydreamed daily. Josh popped in and out on occasion and took me hiking and swimming, which brought my heart rate up—in more ways than one. *I think I like this guy... maybe now I'm ready for partnership?*

A couple of weeks in, Josh and I grew closer and started to open up and share with one another. He told me about how women kept coming and going from his life—how he'd meet a traveler, fall for her, and she would leave. *Uh oh. Was I going to be another part of this pattern for him?* I shared how I was seeking inner peace and attempting to figure myself out while traveling the world.

During the third week, Josh invited me to take a little vacation with him from the lake over to Monterrico Beach for a few days. As we waited to buy tickets at the bus station, I looked at the posters on the walls. I had a strange premonition: *I wouldn't be returning to the lake with him. He'd be going to Semuc Champey without me, although I didn't know when.* I pointed to a poster of Semuc Champey and smiled at him. He hardly noticed as he bought our tickets and transfers, and we were on our way.

During the second bus ride of that trip, I saw a young woman with blond hair sitting a couple of seats in front of us. *She has something to do with it.*

The beach was sizzling hot. The courtyard of our hotel had a pool in the center, and after we dropped our bags off, I changed into my swimsuit and dove into the crisp, cool pool water. That's when the woman from the bus rocked up and went into the room on the opposite side of the pool from us. *Yep, he'll be leaving with her. Why can I see this and not know what's next for me?*

The sun began to set, and I took my poi and headphones to the beach. I listened to classical music and played as the sky changed from red to orange. I wanted to know what would be next and asked the universe for direction as the sun disappeared from the horizon. I found Josh resting on the red floor cushions on the open terrace and sat down next to him with my computer. Then the answer came: "You'll be going back into the Sahara, leaving soon." *Really? Come on. I was just there in October, and I like it here right now; thank you very much.*

I turned to Josh. "This is going to sound weird, but I'm being called back to the Sahara."

"What? When are you going?"

"I think I need to book my flight to leave Guatemala City in three days."

That's when our clash began. He spun right back into what I saw as a process of "avoiding loneliness" and "abandonment shadows." Clearly, I was a part of provoking these themes in him. He canceled our hotel reservation immediately and asked for a refund for the last two days of our stay. Then he joined the blond woman for beers.

I felt genuinely sad. I'd known it would happen, but I didn't realize it would happen right in front of me—a difficult pill to swallow. I tried to step out of the way, but it wasn't easy. We'd grown so close, shared so many private, intimate moments. I wanted to process our separation, talk about the beautiful things we'd shared, wish each other luck on our journeys. I realized later that my suffering was coming from my unmet expectations. Instead of surrendering, I fought for those expectations. For the next forty-eight hours, we struggled. It wasn't pretty. I packed my bag, said my goodbyes to Josh and the new girl, and made my way to the airport.

While I'd done quite a bit of inner work, I still needed to do work in the area of relationship and partnership. *Maybe a chance to explore this theme is waiting for me in the Sahara?*

Back in Florida, I checked in on Paul. He was returning to the way of living that (I thought) contributed to his failing health. "How have you been while I was away?" I asked.

Paul admitted he'd stopped the protocol and the chemo after two treatments, he'd stopped the massages and meditation, and he was trying to get back to work. As he spoke, a sharp pain hit him in the belly. He winced and placed a hand over his abdomen.

"Paul, you have tools and understanding now," I said and put my hand over his.

"You can choose to listen to what life is trying to tell you and live, or you can continue in your old way—which might kill you. I'm ready to be wrong, but I feel there's something to this work. I'm headed into the Sahara for forty days. All I wanted to do was lay in a hammock in Guatemala, but I was called to the Sahara."

"Right. Guess I should get ready for another appointment at the hospital. They've been wanting to see me...." He looked toward the door.

"I'm here for a couple more days. Let me know if you need my help, OK?" I hugged him tightly, told him I loved him, and was off to Mom's house to pack (yet again) for the Sahara Desert.

Chapter Three

You Asked. You Shall Receive

We prepared the truck in Germany for another tour into the desert. A tall young man crossed the garden with a huge backpack. One of the participants—kinda cute. Charles sat at a table in the garden with three others and reviewed a checklist. I put the tools away.

We'd do another forty days in the desert. *What has called me there? What's waiting for me?*

Pain.

We took our normal route down through Italy and crossed the Mediterranean on the large ferry. As usual, I slept most of the way. We arrived in Tunis, but this time, I wasn't excited to be there. I had a feeling that this trip was going to hurt, and I just wasn't eager to get into it. On previous trips, I'd been crushed and pulled apart repeatedly, only to be built up again. The tearing down and building up reminded me of physical therapy. But this wasn't therapy for the body. It was therapy for the soul.

Never underestimate the power of the unconscious human mind. I struggled on.

When I doodled in the sand with a stick during my last trip into the desert, the same picture kept showing up—a man and a woman who had vibrations between their heads, hearts, and lower chakras. They were in a full-body "Yes" to each other. On this trip, the sand drawings began to appear again. *Am I here to make way for a partnership? My heart longed for such a union. Am I ready?*

I noticed that each tour was different—we never took the same path twice. Charles was quite good at detecting what the group needed and when, and he adjusted accordingly. We'd walk between five and twelve kilometers (when we did walk) each day, and we'd experience four days of solitude—but never in the same places. I'd off-load emotion and purge pain, processing it mostly alone. *Would it ever end?*

Our group met for evening meals and occasional discussions, but I kept to myself as much as possible. The days were so heavy, by the evening, all I wanted to do was eat quietly and retreat to my tent for rest.

Thirty days into the trip, our group of eight became four. For the final two weeks, it would be the two older gentlemen, me, and that tall European guy I'd seen in the garden in Germany named Simon. We parked the team truck on top of a high dune that gave us a 360-degree view of the expansive desert. There were waves and waves of sand for miles in every direction that also seemed never to end. It was hot. I crawled under the truck for some much-needed shade and found Simon resting there. That's

270

where it all started. We talked about what we'd seen during our month-long journey into ourselves. Slowly but surely, we took off our "masks" and really looked at each other. Even the clothes we wore didn't protect us from the sincerity with which we saw ourselves and one another. We were unconditionally vocal with each other over the next few days, sharing our hopes, fears, expectations, and dreams. We shared intimate parts of ourselves without ever touching.

I loved Simon's ability to tell the microscopic truth—to share what was in his heart, fearlessly. It encouraged me to open up and share. We were alive to our feelings and spoke our truths. *This is good. I can feel the connection between us—that full-body "Yes" that I'd been dreaming of.* It was another week before we left Tunisia, and during that time, Simon and I had become very close. I liked him, and he liked me, too. After the trip, I invited him to work with us at the hotel in Germany. Together, we built structures in the garden—and built each other up. We kept discussing what was on our hearts. The profound self-honesty became our anchor in the tour of self-discovery we experienced together.

After a year of working together at the hotel, Simon and I took a two-month-long road trip across America. That was when I fell in love with him. I loved the ease with which we traveled, the grace that flowed between us, the curiosity and humor that was always present. We traveled ten thousand miles on an unpredictable road in a small Toyota sports car. Together, we could handle anything.

It's been a little more than two years, and not everything between Simon and I has remained as perfect as it was back in the desert, at the hotel in Germany, or during that road trip. Living in a relationship isn't always easy. We recognize that life in the outside world is hostile

271

to love. The commitments one makes, the worries, fears, stress, pressure, desires, goals, self-realizations—all of these are present in the hustle and bustle of everyday life. But we know that relationship requires us to learn to deal with the shadows that emerge from the union, and we are both up for the challenge of dancing with those shadows. There's the difficulty of being apart—and the difficulty of being together: the fear and the joy of looking into the future. The sharing and the keeping to oneself. Getting to know oneself, holding space for the other person's development, and always creating something new. The dance is playful and fun. We've used the lessons we've learned and integrated them into our union. We do yoga, breathing exercises, and meditation together. We call each other out—gently. We listen when the other speaks. We vibrate together in all ways, and it's beautiful to behold.

Chapter Four

The Gift

It was late August when I first heard the call: "You need to go to America." Simon and I had just left Germany for Belgium. A month later, in late September, I heard it again. "You need to go to America. Florida. Soon."

"I don't know that I can commit to staying here very long," I told Simon.

"What's going on—inside?" he said, placing his hands gently on my hips and pulling me into him.

I love this guy.

"I keep hearing this call that I'm needed in the States. In Florida. December 21 seems to be important, but I don't know why. Every week, it gets louder. I need to book a plane ticket." I buried my face in his chest. *We have a place here—he has a job. I'm going alone.*

He lifted my face to look into my eyes. "I wonder what it could be?"

"Yeah, me too. I thought it had something to do with this book, but that can be done from anywhere. I mean, it would be cool to be there when I release it for preorder, but I don't have to be there. It's something else…."

"Just come back to me. Do what is calling you—but come back, OK?"

I really love this guy.

It was late October 2020. COVID-19 was in full effect. Travel was limited, industries were either on pause or closed. The earth was healing—I could hear more birds singing. I was curious about this auspicious date that kept appearing. *Did it have anything to do with the planets?* I turned to the internet. December 21 is the winter solstice; it signifies a "return to the light." This year's solstice was unique—a grand conjunction of Jupiter and Saturn. These planets had started moving toward one another in October, creating a V-shaped pattern, and on December 21, they would shine as one bright star. Astronomers said it would be a once-in-a-lifetime event—it wouldn't happen again until 2080. Astrologists believed it was a time of great transition—of ascension to a new fifth dimension. They suggested that the portals opened wider, so to speak, that the energies exchanged between the heavens and the earth were intensified. Interesting... By the end of October, the call was coming in daily, so I booked a flight to Florida for mid-December.

I sent a message to Paul.

"Hey, how's it going? I'm coming to the States soon," I said.

"That's great, Shiny. I'd love to see you. I'm alright. I still haven't gotten back to work like I'd like to, but yeah, things are OK. I can't do what I used to. Don't really like that."

"Not fun at all. Let me know what you want to do when I get there? See you soon!"

A couple of weeks later, I landed in Florida. It was December 13, and as usual, I drove straight to Paul's house. His front door was wide open, and I didn't bother to knock. I skipped down the hallway into his living room and found him stretched out on a recliner chair.

"Hey! What's going on? You, OK? You don't look bad, but... you don't look so good, either. What's up?" I asked.

He rocked himself into a seated position.

"Well, muscles don't grow when you don't do shit."

"What do you mean 'don't do shit'?"

"Don't do shit. Like, doing nothing."

"What about your appointments with the doctors? The meditations? The massages? Aren't you doing those?"

"Nope."

"Like... you just stopped everything?"

"Yep."

"When?"

"I guess it was January."

"This whole year? You haven't done anything?"

"Not a damn thing."

I felt my cheeks flush. I was confused. *Why would my warrior friend, who loved life more than anyone I know, just... give up?* I looked around the room. He had given up. A stack of unopened mail had been pitched on the table. Dishes were piled high in the kitchen, and dirty laundry spilled out of his bedroom through a doorway. I looked toward the window at his orchards. They were dead.

"Yeah, the place is a mess. I've been meaning to clean it up," he said.

"Want some help?"

"Sure, that'd be great."

Paul always let me clean his house. I'd done it for years and always enjoyed it. It was a time for us to re-entangle our energies. To catch up on things we'd missed during our time apart. To bring order to chaos.

"I feel this pull to cleanse and meditate," I said. "I think it'll be for three days. Mom's friend gave me some expiring hotel points, so I got a room by the beach. I feel like I'm preparing for something, but I'm not sure what. Anyway, I'm going into it," I said.

After we finished cleaning, I said, "Is there something else I can do to support you before I go?"

"I don't know."

"I'll come by in the morning on my way out and ask again. Cool?"

"Sure. See you in the morning. Thanks for the help. Place looks great Shiny."

Something was about to happen. I could feel it in my chest. What is it? In less than a week, I planned to have the book I was writing available for preorder. I'd decided that December 21st should be the date. It kept coming up anyhow. *Am I preparing for that?*

I stopped by Paul's in the morning and found him glued to the recliner.

"Hey, good morning. I'm headed off into the stillness. I just wanted to check on you before I go. Did you think of anything you need?"

"Not really. I don't know."

"Hmmm. OK. Well, I'll be back in three days and will come by, OK?"

"OK, Shiny."

"I love you."

"Love you, too."

The three days of stillness were good. I brought spring water, spirulina tablets, fresh fruit, and a couple of hand-fuls of mixed nuts to use during my mini fast and cleanse. I lay on the couch and listened to guided meditations, and concentrated on my breath. I cultivated presence and talked to my body. Every morning I swam in the pool, practiced the Wim Hof method of breathing, and challenged myself to swim farther and farther without coming up for air. On the fourth day, I felt grounded, centered, and renewed. I was ready to return to the world. I drove to

Paul's house, but his truck wasn't there. That's cool. He's not in that chair. I wonder what he's doing....

In the evening, I passed by again, and his truck still wasn't there. Now that's odd... I better send him a message. It was December 19. "Where you at, P?" I texted.

"I was sittin' by a lake house super early this morning, a place I always wanted to have. This girl pulled up behind me in a black Mercedes and asked what I was doing. I told her, "Nothing, just looking at the lake house." She got in my truck, and we started talking. She asked me what my name was and then showed me she had it tattooed on her chest." He laughed.

"What? No way..."

"Yeah. I'll send you a pic....."

Sure enough. There it was. His name spelled out across her chest.

"I was workin' that manifestation muscle. It seems it's still on point," he said.

"That's awesome, P. You sound good."

The next day, I called Paul again. "What are you doing? Where you at?"

"I'm at my mom's house. Cleaning a ceiling fan. Shit's gross," he said.

"Let me know when you're back on this side of town, yeah? I'd love to see you."

He was quiet for a moment. "Yeah, I'll holla atcha."

A day went by without a word.

On December 21, I missed a call from him and called him back. He didn't answer.

Later that day, he sent a text with a shiny heart emoji. "Riding with EMS to Pensacola."

Emergency Medical Services?

"You, OK?" I wrote back.

He didn't respond.

An hour later, my phone rang.

It was Paul's brother, Pat.

"Paul's missing," he said.

"What do you mean, missing?"

"Well, my mom said he went by ambulance to Pensacola, but nobody knows where he is."

"What? He wrote me this morning that he was going and called me. He said he'd call when he got to where he was going and let me know where that was... now he's missing?"

"Yeah. I'll keep calling around and find him. I just wanted to know if you knew anything...."

"Yeah... I mean, no... I don't know. Let me know what you find out, OK?"

"Will do. Hope to talk to you soon."

I closed my computer and folded into myself.

The phone rang a few minutes later. Pat again. "I found him," he said. "He's in hospice in Pensacola. At Sacred Heart Ascension Hospital."

"I'm leaving right now. Send me the address, please?"

"Yeah, will do. I'm coming, too. I'll see you there."

During the hour-long drive to the hospital, I prayed. In my heart, I told Paul, "We're coming." Then something unexpected happened. He spoke to me.

"Take care of my daughter," he said. "Be there if she ever needs you, OK?"

Hold on, Paul. We're coming.

I pulled up to the hospital and saw Pat at the front door. He directed me to a parking lot, and I stopped my Toyota under a large oak tree. *Breathe.*

I joined Pat at the entrance.

"Something strange happened on the way here," he said.

"Oh? You too?"

"I swear Paul told me to look after his daughter. I haven't thought about that girl in years."

"No way. He said the same thing to me! I hadn't thought about her ever since... yeah, it's been a while."

We stood in the lobby at the hospital and looked at each other. We both understood what we were walking into.

On the fifth floor, we entered the hospice wing. A cool mist of lavender floated from an aroma diffuser that rested on the oval reception desk. The energy was calm and quiet. A nurse greeted us and took our identification. She walked us to Paul's room.

"Am I here to say goodbye to my friend?" I heard myself ask.

The nurse looked me in the eye. "He signed a DNR—a Do Not Resuscitate order. Yes, you're here to say goodbye to your friend."

As much as I didn't want to hear those words, I appreciated her honesty.

"Thank you."

"He's been exposed to pneumonia and tested positive for COVID-19, so we ask that you please don't go in and out of the room. We have some personal protective clothing for you—I'll help you," the nurse said. She handed us gowns and masks. "When you're ready to exit, ring the bell. I'll come to get you and help you take these things off properly."

We were covered head to toe and double-masked. She opened the door. I saw Paul's feet at the end of a bed that was tucked around a corner. I approached slowly, my heart beating in my chest.

Paul was unconscious. He had tubes and wires attached to his chest and arms. My heart shattered. I took Paul's hand in mine and wept. Pat held his other hand.

"It's OK to go, Paul," I said. "Don't be afraid. We're here. It's safe to go. Don't be afraid."

I felt his hand squeeze mine.

"Is he squeezing your hand too?" I asked.

Pat nodded.

I bowed my head to Paul's chest. His breath was long and labored. He took deep inhales and held them for a couple of seconds before forcefully releasing them. I could hear that his lungs were filling with fluid.

Pat fought back tears as he stood up. "I can't stay too long," he said. "I have a toddler at home and wouldn't feel good about bringing her COVID."

"I understand. I'd like to stay a little longer."

Pat rang the bell, and the nurse met him at the door.

I talked to Paul. I held his hand, told him how much I loved him.

"It's OK, Paul. It's OK to go. Don't be afraid." I said through tears.

I'd been in contact with Mom by text, who suggested that I limit my time in the room due to the contagious nature of Paul's condition. I stayed longer than recommended, but I wasn't afraid. I wanted to be sure Paul knew I was there, and I wanted to say the things in my heart. When I felt the time was right, I rang the bell, and the nurse escorted me out of the room.

The following morning, I prepared to return to the hospice. Again, during the drive, I heard Paul speak to me. "Will you please bring some music?"

I pulled into a shopping center and searched for a Bluetooth speaker when a call came from Pat.

"OK, this is going to sound kind of weird. This morning while I was in the shower, Paul asked me to bring him some music."

"No way. He asked me the same thing! I'm at a store close to the hospital buying a Bluetooth radio right now."

"Cool. I'll be up there in a bit. See you soon."

Mom met me at the hospital. We entered Paul's room together. Another friend, Lotte, was there, and we all sang to Paul. Then Mom and Lotte left me alone with him. I touched him. I caressed his toes and laid my head on his chest.

"I just wish I could see you one more time," I said. "I want to look into your eyes. I want to see you." I stood up, tuned the radio to his favorite local station, and returned to his bedside. As much as it hurt to see him this way, I felt an overwhelming sense of honor. I was grateful: I'd been called, I'd heard the call, and I'd listened.

I still want to see you....

I rang the bell for the nurse.

"I'll be there in just a minute," she said through the intercom.

I put my hand on Paul's chest. "I love you so much, Paul. So much. Thank you for being in my life. I just wish I could see you one more time."

Paul's eyes snapped open. He looked right at me. He sat up with great force, then swung his legs away from me and off of the bed.

"Paul! Hi! Nice to see you! Is there anything you want to say? Anything you need from me? Paul?"

He struggled to stand. And to breathe.

I held him by the shoulders and screamed for the nurse. "Help! I need help! He's trying to get up! I can't hold him!"

The door swung open. "I'm coming! Just a sec."

Mom stood in the hall outside the door. The nurse scrambled to get into her protective layers. Time seemed to stop.

I held onto Paul as he gasped for air. "Paul. Can you say anything? Paul?"

The nurse entered the room, medication in hand. "He can't speak. Every bit of his energy is being used to

281

breathe. His lungs are filling with fluid. It won't be long," the nurse whispered.

Together we lifted him back into bed, and she injected medicine into the IV portal in his arm. He whimpered. The broken pieces of my heart crashed to the floor as the nurse shuffled next to me. Within seconds, he was still. Lying on his back, the pauses between his breaths grew.

"He's leaving soon, isn't he?" I whispered to the nurse.

"Yes, I'm sorry."

Again, I felt a flood of gratitude. It surprised me. I guess some part of me expected to be devastated. Inconsolable. But I was grateful. *Are you avoiding something? Is this feeling covering up grief?* It wasn't. I was happy to be allowed to be with him. Honored. Grateful. For all of it. For every second we'd known one another. For every mishap, every adventure, every moment shared. For this moment, now. *I am grateful. Thank you. Thank you for everything. Thank you for allowing me to be here.*

That evening, Pat and I spoke on the phone, recalling funny and not-so-funny moments from our times with Paul.

"Hold on a sec, Mel. The phone is beeping."

I held my breath until I heard Pat's voice again.

"Paul just left his body. Say a prayer for me while I call my mom." He hung up.

I spent the next three days in a tent in nature. I needed time to process, to give myself to the silence. I slept. I listened to the birds. I slept some more. I gave thanks. On the fourth day, I was ready to emerge and do what was needed. I joined Pat to help with Paul's estate.

"Guess he got the last laugh. He got us to clean his house one more time," Pat said.

We laughed. We found things that told us more of Paul's story—like how he'd collected hundreds of handles and wall light sconces. We had no idea he was so fond of those things.

We threw two parties to honor and celebrate Paul's life. All his friends and family attended. It was beautiful, but I was tired. I'd spent weeks sorting through Paul's collections and planning the event. When the time came to speak to the crowd that had gathered, my throat froze. The words just wouldn't come. Instead, I talked about the treasure hunt we had planned for the guests.

For three days, I beat myself up for not saying what was in my heart. Destructive thoughts swirled in my brain: *You ruined that moment. That was your chance. You messed it up. But I can say it here...I can say it now...*

Paul was a hero to me. He taught me the meaning of unconditional love, selfless acts of kindness, and tolerance for (what I'd consider) ignorance. He was always open to anyone, even the many lost souls he let in and out of his house over the years. He wasn't judgmental. He was accepting of everything and everyone who came his way. He loved everyone equally.

He was kind, gentle, and enjoyed building things. He once told me that each year he pressed one million screws just to pay taxes. He was OK with it because it contributed to the whole. I admired his view and dedication to the community.

He loved women, boats, and sunset margaritas. Preferably all at the same time.

Paul was authentic. He was talented; he was brave. And today, we are here to celebrate his life. To honor the impacts he's made on every one of us. For the lessons. For the love. For the adventures. Here's to you, Paul. Thank you for sharing your time, love, and tools with us.

After the events to celebrate Paul, I was called—yet again. This time, I went to Texas to see my grandmother. I sensed that this would be my last chance to see her, and I wanted one more play date. I wanted to tell her how much I loved and appreciated her. As the sun set, we sat at her favorite table on the patio, where she could smoke cigarettes, and played Farkle, the dice game she loved. Grandma had onset dementia and couldn't remember how the game was played, but I just let her roll until she was done, asked how many points she had, and wrote down whatever number she gave me. I told her stories about my adventures around the world, and she listened with delight. I told her I loved her, thanked her for all the wonderful things she shared with me, and said goodbye.

A few weeks later, back in Belgium with Simon, I woke up from a dream in which I'd seen Grandma smiling. I turned my phone on and there was the message— Grandma had left her body that night. Again, all I could feel was gratitude.

Year Six - Optional Questions for Self-Reflection: Play with the Gifts

Unexpected gifts arise when you are liberated from the shadow. Maintain your practice. Revel in the fruits of your labor. Enjoy the gifts. The peace. The harmony. If another shadow appears, you have the tools to meet it, greet it, and love it into submission.

Works Cited / Recommended Reading

Angelou, Maya. *I Know Why the Caged Bird Sings.* New York: Random House, 2015. Print.

Bays, Brandon and Patricia Kendall. *Living the Journey.* New York: Atria Print, 2012. Print.

Bessel van der Kolk: *The Body Keeps the Score.* New York: Penguin Books, 2015. Print.

Boo, Katherine. *Behind the Beautiful Forevers: Life, Death, and Hope in a Mumbai Undercity.* New York: Random House Trade Paperbacks. 2012. Print.

Byham, William C. *Zapp! The Lightning of Empowerment.* New York: Ballantine Books, 1988. Print.

Coelho, Paulo. *The Pilgrimage.* San Francisco: HarperOne, 2008. Print.

Coyle, Daniel. *The Culture Code.* New York: Bantam Books, 2018. Print.

Dodge, Edward. *A History of the Goddess from the Ice Age to the Bible.* Walterville: Trine Day LLC, 2021. Print.

Eisenstein, Charles. *The More Beautiful World Our Hearts Know Is Possible*. Berkeley: North Atlantic Books, 2013. Print.

Engelhart, Matthew and Terces Engelhart. *The Abounding River Personal Logbook: An Unfamiliar View of Being Abundance*. Berkeley: North Atlantic Books, 2010. Print.

Ford, Debbie. *The Secret of the Shadow*. San Francisco: Harper, 2002. Print.

Harvey, Andrew and Seymour Bernstein. *The Hope: A Guide to Sacred Activism*. Carlsbad: Hay House, 2009. Print.

Hendricks, Gay and Kathlyn Hendricks: *Conscious Loving: The Journey to Co-Commitment*. New York: Bantam Books, 1992. Print.

Hicks, Esther and Jerry Hicks. *The Law of Attraction - The Basics of the Teachings of Abraham*. Carlsbad: Hay House, Inc. 2006. Kindle.

Jeffers, Susan Ph.D. *Feel the Fear and Do It Anyway*. New York: Hay House, 1987. Print.

Kahn, Lloyd. *Tiny Homes, Simple Shelters*. Bolinas: Shelter Publications, 2012. Print.

Maltz, Maxwell. *Psycho-Cybernetics*. New York: Simon & Schuster, 1960. Print.

Marshall B. Rosenberg and Deepak Chopra: *Nonviolent Communication: A Language of Life*. Encinitas: Puddledancer Press, September 2015. Print.

Millman, Dan. *The Journey of Socrates.* San Francisco: HarperOne, 2009. Print.

Obama, Michelle. *Becoming.* New York: Crown, 2018. Kindle.

Ozkan, Serdar. *The Missing Rose.* New York: Penguin Books, 2012. Print.

Paramahansa Yogananda. *Autobiography of a Yogi.* Los Angeles: Self-Realization Fellowship, 1998. Print.

Schucman, Helen. *A Course in Miracles.* New York: Foundation for Inner Peace, 1975. Print.

Singer, Michael Alan. *The Untethered Soul.* Oakland: New Harbinger Publications, Inc., 2007. Print.

Sogyal Rinpoche. *The Tibetan Book of Living and Dying.* San Francisco: Harper Collins, 1993. Print.

Urlauber, Jesus. *2020 The New Earth.* Norderstedt: Books on Demand, 2020. Print.

Wikipedia. "Biodanza." Last modified November 10, 2021. https://en.wikipedia.org/wiki/Biodanza

Wikipedia. "Earthship." Last modified September 20, 2021. https://en.wikipedia.org/wiki/Earthship

APPENDIX

Wanderlust Poem

I was desperately grasping, reaching out.
For some confused, undefined idea,
Forcing the once organic but now non-existent
Love that had lost its beauty.
Playing the victim, in the role of pain,
Questioning my worth, feeling insane.
WAKE UP! SHAKE THIS MADNESS NOW!
Making moves, abrupt, drastic change,
Broken-hearted but welcoming the strange.
It's time to evolve; it's time to transcend,
Forget all you have, all you know.
All that's familiar, it all has to go.
It's time now to move forward.
Without limits, without borders.
I'm not afraid, yet I'm fearful.
I'm not panicked, yet I'm anxious.
The detachment seems thorough and complete.
The release felt is a somewhat welcome treat.
The motions have begun, no turning back.
Time to push forward, time to seek,
Time to reclaim power - no time to be weak.
Watching my thoughts, clearing my mind,
Connecting with spirit, meeting again with the divine.
Now is the chosen time; I will make it mine.
The adventure begins with a trusted friend.

A goddess, no doubt, here to help a sister out.
Excitement, adrenaline, endorphins all on high,
The longer the road becomes, the less I will cry.
The less my mind will dive.
Thoughts of family pass through my soul,
Only now acceptance of the situation,
Will make way for this healing time to show.
Just let go.
Of hopes, of expectations, of illusions,
There's no room for false dreams here.
What's meant for the future will undoubtedly appear.
The love I have, it remains,
Lack of contact and communication,
Caused a deep sadness that can't be explained.
Release, let go of that closest to the heart.
Only then will the necessary experience start.
Clearing chakras, let the river flow,
One at a time, let it all go.
I am loving; I am kind, I am worthy,
of all that is divine.
Carpe Diem - You can seize the day,
Do take your time; the answers are on the way.
Continue to shine, to look within,
Be patient and let the process begin.
The search for abundance in all things,
That's the path I've chosen.
To mend my broken wings.
Beautiful souls, guides met along the way.
Assist in my healing, even if only for a day.
Stories shared; music made,
Days of doing nothing but lying in the shade.
I daydream along the way.
Follow your dreams; the goddess cards say,
Don't be fearful, don't be afraid.
There is magic deep within you.

That will lead the way.
Again, my thoughts drift to the intense love once had,
My heart begs for more; my mind tells me I'm mad.
Move on, Mel, like I have,
Those were the last words that he had said.
Now it's all logistical; the words exchanged,
Lack of depth, soul, and connection.
It's like a mechanical, robotic,
rusted reflection,
Of what used to be.
Let it go. Set yourself free.
So here I sit, contemplating,
questioning, observing, absorbing,
Learning about myself and my desires.
Family, community, intimate connectedness,
stands on one side.
Independence, spontaneity, and self-exploration
stands on the other.
That is my internal battle now.
Caught in this crossfire of ego.
And something divine.
Trying to find balance, comfort, peace,
Seems to be this challenge of mine.
Realizing that here and now, I've never
felt so conflicted, so alone, yet
so inspired to overcome.

About The Author

Melissa's courage and conviction tear open the envelope of preconceived notions about gender, self-imposed limitations, and the boundaries of love and adventure. As a former preschool instructor who understands the sacred child in all of us, Melissa is both playful and wise, compassionate and bold. These traits play out all over the world as she challenges herself and others, breaks some rules, and dances on the tightrope of possibility. Whether she is blazing across the Sahara Desert on a motorcycle, rallying a group of women in Tunisia to challenge their cultural boundaries, or risking her life to give free hugs in Turkey, Melissa's optimistic approach and winning spirit bring her help when she needs it, and love where she finds it.

Harley and Me

Hierve El Agua - Oaxaca, Mexico

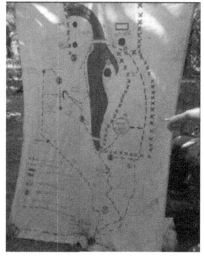

Rainbow Gathering - Camp Map

Earthship - Lake Atitlan, Guatemala

The Long Road Home

Charles Kunow (the Wizard) and
Me - Photo Credit: Axel Hebenstreit

On Board "Space" Sailing the Mediterranean Sea

Magazine Cover in Turkey

Free Hugs Sign

Nosen Bear Truck from Sahara Desert

Borrowed Motorcycle in India

Protection' in India - Wild Dogs

The Temple of the Dalai Lama - Dharamshala, India

Frog in China

Welcome to Rio de Janeiro - Olympics

Samsara Rebuild

All done! Samsara Is Ready

Chico and Me

Big Sur, California

Harley Memorial - Redwood Forest

The Sahara Desert

Ksar Ghilane, Tunisia

Paul and Me in the Hospital - Diagnosis of Cancer

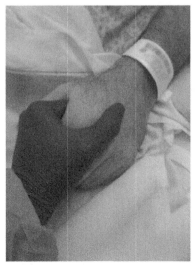

Holding Hands - Paul's Last Day

Grandma